My Date With MONSTERS™

PAUL TOBIN

ANDY MacDONALD

DJ CHAVIS

TAYLOR ESPOSITO

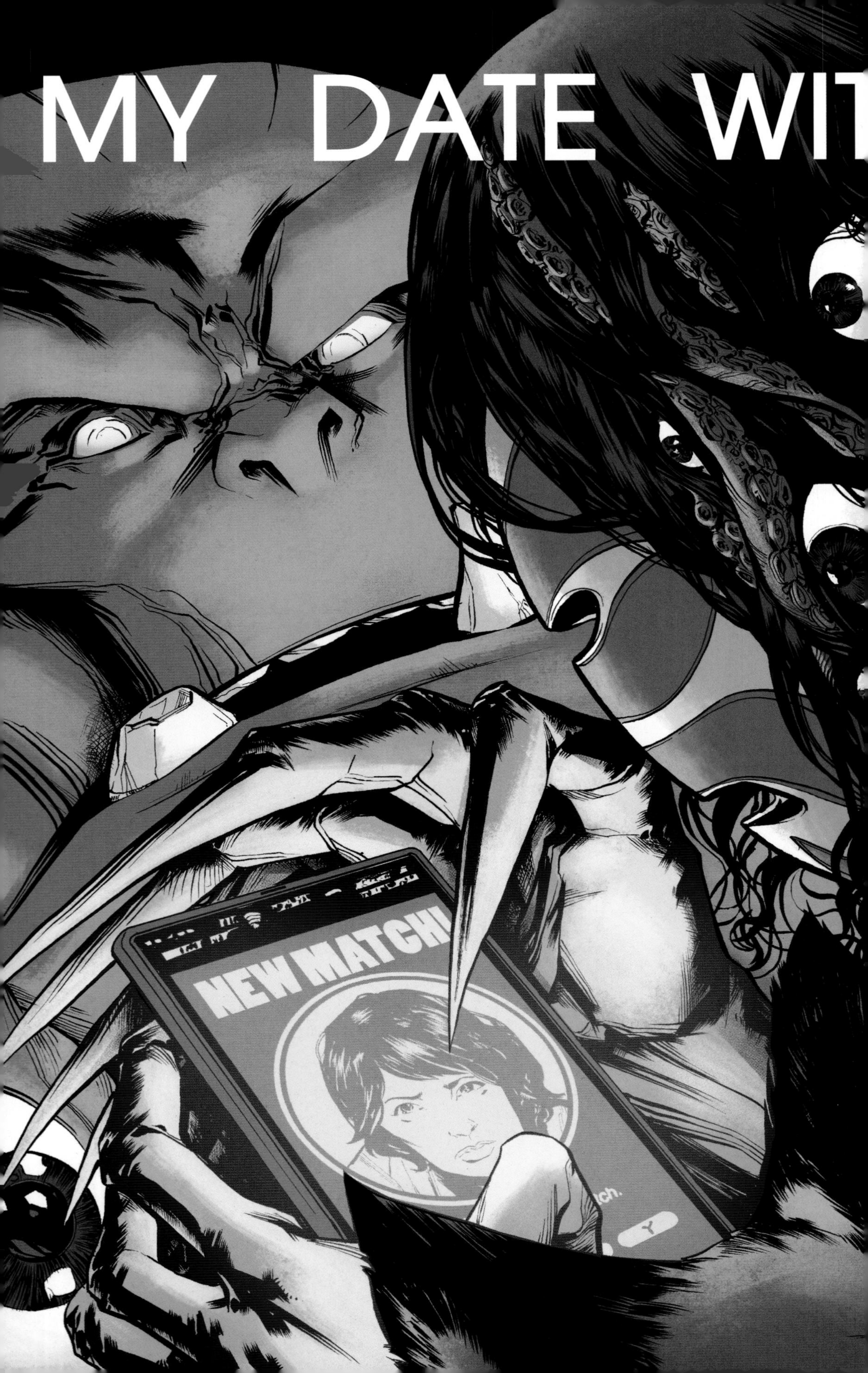
MY DATE WIT
NEW MATCH!

TH MONSTERS

PAUL TOBIN writer
ANDY MACDONALD artist

DJ CHAVIS colorist
TAYLOR ESPOSITO letterer

ANDY MACDONALD w/ **DJ CHAVIS** front & original covers
JAMES HARREN incentive cover
CLIFF RICHARDS ambassador cover
MIKE ROOTH Happy Hour cover
MATT DALTON w/ **SEBASTIAN CHENG, CHINH POTTER, MARIA FRANTZ, HAL LAREN** & **MAGGIE Z** variant covers

CHARLES PRITCHETT logo designer
CHARLES PRITCHETT issue #1 backmatter designer
COREY BREEN book designer
MIKE MARTS editor

created by **PAUL TOBIN** & **ANDY MACDONALD**

AFTERSHOCK™

MIKE MARTS - Editor-in-Chief • JOE PRUETT - Publisher/CCO • LEE KRAMER - President • JON KRAMER - Chief Executive Officer
STEVE ROTTERDAM - SVP, Sales & Marketing • DAN SHIRES - VP, Film & Television UK • CHRISTINA HARRINGTON - Managing Editor
MARC HAMMOND - Sr. Retail Sales Development Manager • RUTHANN THOMPSON - Communications Specialist
KATHERINE JAMISON - Marketing Manager • KELLY DIODATI - Ambassador Outreach Manager • BLAKE STOCKER - VP, Finance
AARON MARION - Publicist • LISA MOODY - Finance • RYAN CARROLL - Director, Comics/Film/TV Liaison • JAWAD QURESHI - Technology Advisor/Strategist
RACHEL PINNELAS - Social Community Manager • CHARLES PRITCHETT - Design & Production Manager • COREY BREEN - Collections Production
TEODORO LEO - Associate Editor • SARAH PRUETT & GIGI WILLIAMS - Publishing Assistants

AfterShock Logo Design by COMICRAFT
Publicity: contact AARON MARION (aaron@publichausagency.com) & RYAN CROY (ryan@publichausagency.com) at PUBLICHAUS
Special thanks to: ATOM! FREEMAN, IRA KURGAN, MARINE KSADZHIKYAN, KEITH MANZELLA, ANTHONY MILITANO, ANTONIA LIANOS, STEPHAN NILSON & ED ZAREMBA

PRINTED IN KOREA. First Printing: June 2022. 10 9 8 7 6 5 4 3 2 1

AFTERSHOCKCOMICS.COM Follow us on social media

INTRODUCTION

Man, this world is scary. I can remember the biggest fear of my early childhood was actual monsters. Why did my closet door keep creaking in the night? Monsters. What was in the woods after dark? Monsters. When I went swimming in that one Minnesota lake, what was beneath the surface? It was *monsters*, duh.

Luckily, I (mostly) grew out of those fears. Unluckily, I (entirely) found new fears: the world of dating. Talk about the unknown! But just as I'd been drawn to the mysteries of what left those weird hoof-prints in the forest, I was drawn to the smiles of certain of my classmates, and, also, (oof) those girls who worked at the A&W and delivered my order to my car, while wearing roller skates. (Well, *hello*, first fetish.)

These days I'm a Big Time Fearless Adult (←liar) and don't have any remaining fears except for my creaky body and looming tax deadlines, but I still love thinking about monsters of both kinds—the ones that eviscerate victims with bloody claws and the ones that ghost you after the first date. MY DATE WITH MONSTERS is a combo of those two fears, born from many friends' tales of dating (along with internet posts) about how BAD some people are at dating. Bringing your parents along on a first date? Monstrous. Showing up on a date wearing your unwashed gym clothes? Monstrous. Insisting on splitting the tab after eating the most expensive meal and drinking enough expensive cocktails to stun a mammoth? OBVIOUS monster.

As a writer, I wanted a way to merge these two fears together, and Risa Himura was born: a woman who *lives* in a world of monsters, who is *friends* with a monster, who has a daughter she has to *protect* from the monsters, and the only way to do it all is...to fall in love with someone who isn't a monster. But, man, that's a *CHORE*. Sometimes it's just easier to swing a sword than it is to swipe right.

Thanks to the gang at AfterShock (Mike! Christina! Teddy! Everyone!) And a HUGE thanks to Andy McDonald for making this world and the characters so real. Thanks to Taylor Esposito for the seriously sweet lettering and thanks to D.J. Chavis for blossoming the world with colors.

And, most of all, thanks to all the readers who've shared this strange journey with us. I hope we made it weird for you.

PAUL TOBIN
February 2022

1

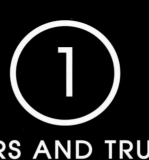

MONSTERS AND TRUE LOVE

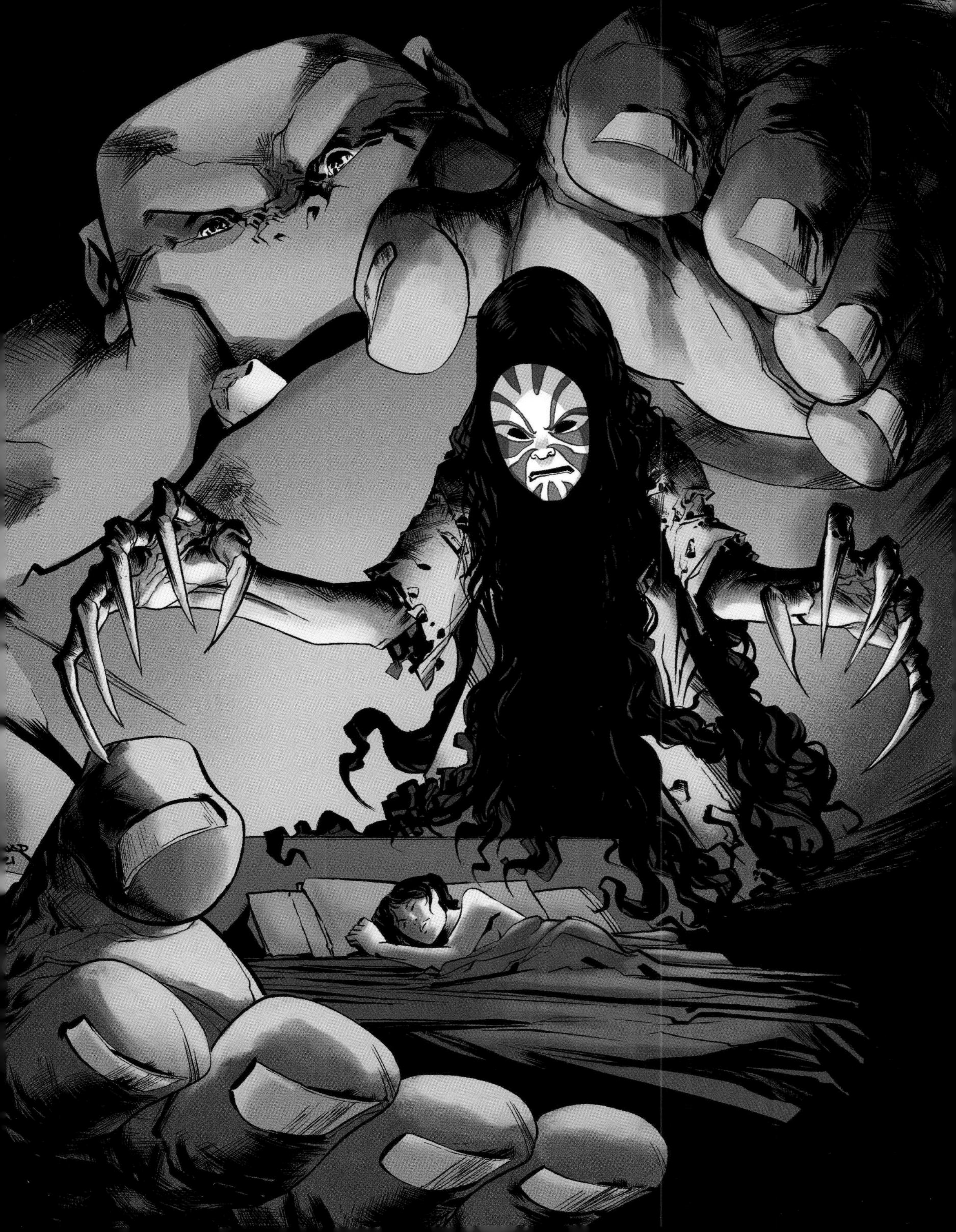

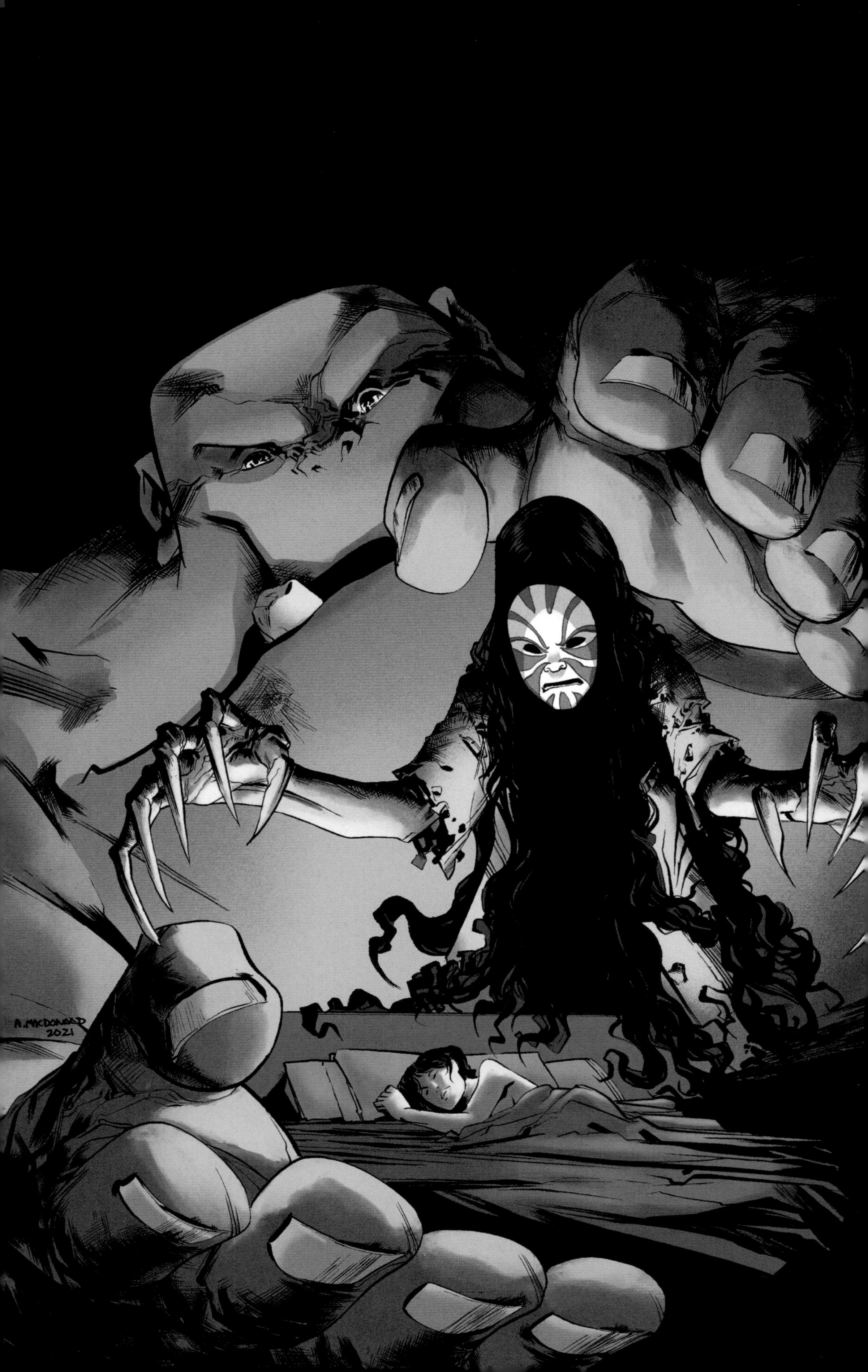

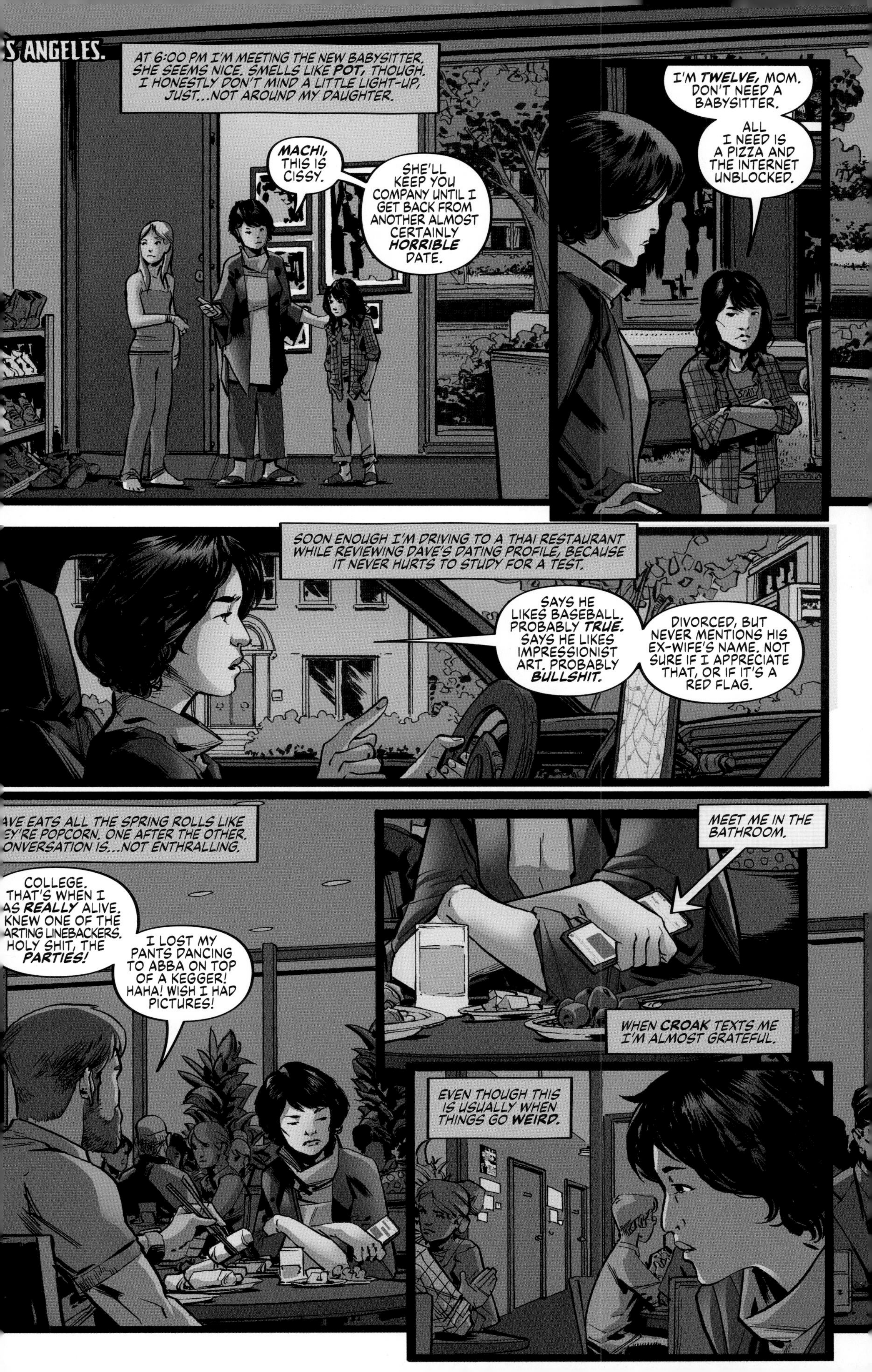
S ANGELES.
AT 6:00 PM I'M MEETING THE NEW BABYSITTER. SHE SEEMS NICE. SMELLS LIKE POT, THOUGH. I HONESTLY DON'T MIND A LITTLE LIGHT-UP, JUST...NOT AROUND MY DAUGHTER.
MACHI, THIS IS CISSY.
SHE'LL KEEP YOU COMPANY UNTIL I GET BACK FROM ANOTHER ALMOST CERTAINLY HORRIBLE DATE.
I'M TWELVE, MOM. DON'T NEED A BABYSITTER.
ALL I NEED IS A PIZZA AND THE INTERNET UNBLOCKED.
SOON ENOUGH I'M DRIVING TO A THAI RESTAURANT WHILE REVIEWING DAVE'S DATING PROFILE, BECAUSE IT NEVER HURTS TO STUDY FOR A TEST.
SAYS HE LIKES BASEBALL. PROBABLY TRUE. SAYS HE LIKES IMPRESSIONIST ART. PROBABLY BULLSHIT.
DIVORCED, BUT NEVER MENTIONS HIS EX-WIFE'S NAME. NOT SURE IF I APPRECIATE THAT, OR IF IT'S A RED FLAG.
AVE EATS ALL THE SPRING ROLLS LIKE EY'RE POPCORN. ONE AFTER THE OTHER. ONVERSATION IS...NOT ENTHRALLING.
COLLEGE. THAT'S WHEN I AS REALLY ALIVE. KNEW ONE OF THE ARTING LINEBACKERS. HOLY SHIT, THE PARTIES!
I LOST MY PANTS DANCING TO ABBA ON TOP OF A KEGGER! HAHA! WISH I HAD PICTURES!
MEET ME IN THE BATHROOM.
WHEN CROAK TEXTS ME I'M ALMOST GRATEFUL.
EVEN THOUGH THIS IS USUALLY WHEN THINGS GO WEIRD.

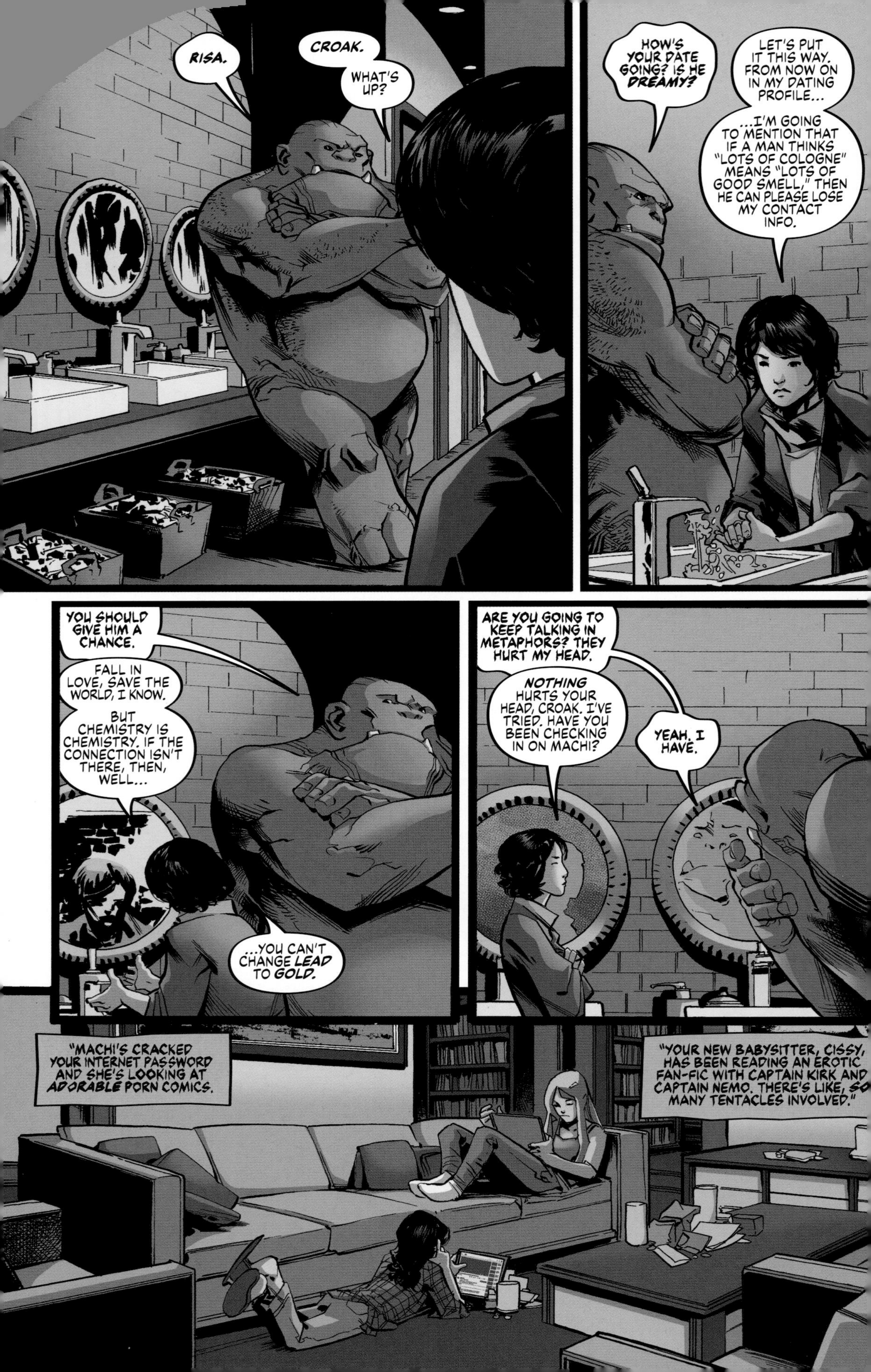
RISA.
CROAK.
WHAT'S UP?
HOW'S YOUR DATE GOING? IS HE DREAMY?
LET'S PUT IT THIS WAY. FROM NOW ON IN MY DATING PROFILE...
...I'M GOING TO MENTION THAT IF A MAN THINKS "LOTS OF COLOGNE" MEANS "LOTS OF GOOD SMELL," THEN HE CAN PLEASE LOSE MY CONTACT INFO.
YOU SHOULD GIVE HIM A CHANCE.
FALL IN LOVE, SAVE THE WORLD, I KNOW.
BUT CHEMISTRY IS CHEMISTRY. IF THE CONNECTION ISN'T THERE, THEN, WELL...
...YOU CAN'T CHANGE LEAD TO GOLD.
ARE YOU GOING TO KEEP TALKING IN METAPHORS? THEY HURT MY HEAD.
NOTHING HURTS YOUR HEAD, CROAK. I'VE TRIED. HAVE YOU BEEN CHECKING IN ON MACHI?
YEAH. I HAVE.
"MACHI'S CRACKED YOUR INTERNET PASSWORD AND SHE'S LOOKING AT ADORABLE PORN COMICS.
"YOUR NEW BABYSITTER, CISSY, HAS BEEN READING AN EROTIC FAN-FIC WITH CAPTAIN KIRK AND CAPTAIN NEMO. THERE'S LIKE, SO MANY TENTACLES INVOLVED."

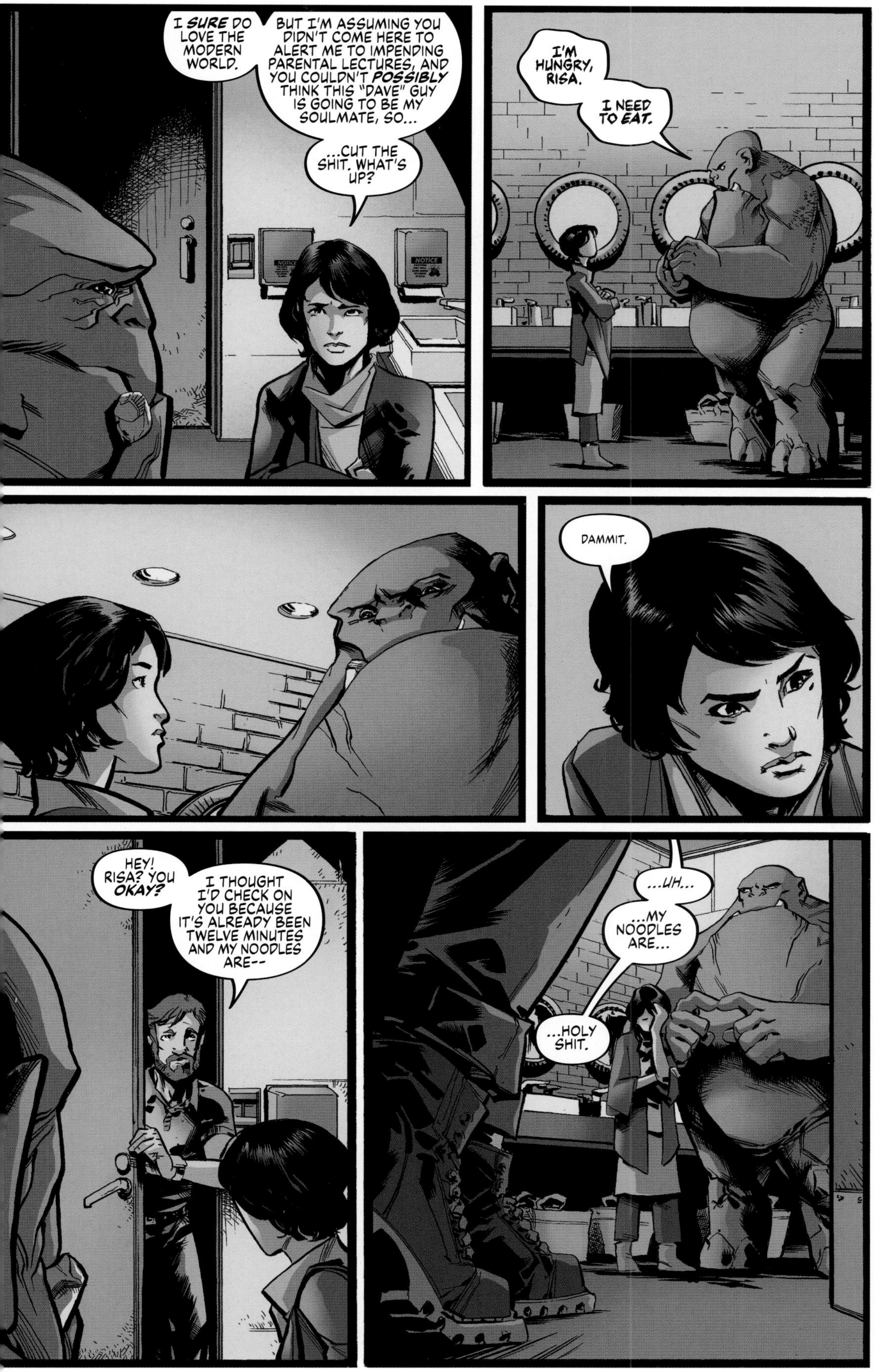
I *SURE* DO LOVE THE MODERN WORLD.
BUT I'M ASSUMING YOU DIDN'T COME HERE TO ALERT ME TO IMPENDING PARENTAL LECTURES, AND YOU COULDN'T *POSSIBLY* THINK THIS "DAVE" GUY IS GOING TO BE MY SOULMATE, SO...
...CUT THE SHIT. WHAT'S UP?
I'M HUNGRY, RISA.
I NEED TO *EAT.*
DAMMIT.
HEY! RISA? YOU *OKAY?*
I THOUGHT I'D CHECK ON YOU BECAUSE IT'S ALREADY BEEN TWELVE MINUTES AND MY NOODLES ARE--
...*UH*...
...MY NOODLES ARE...
...HOLY SHIT.

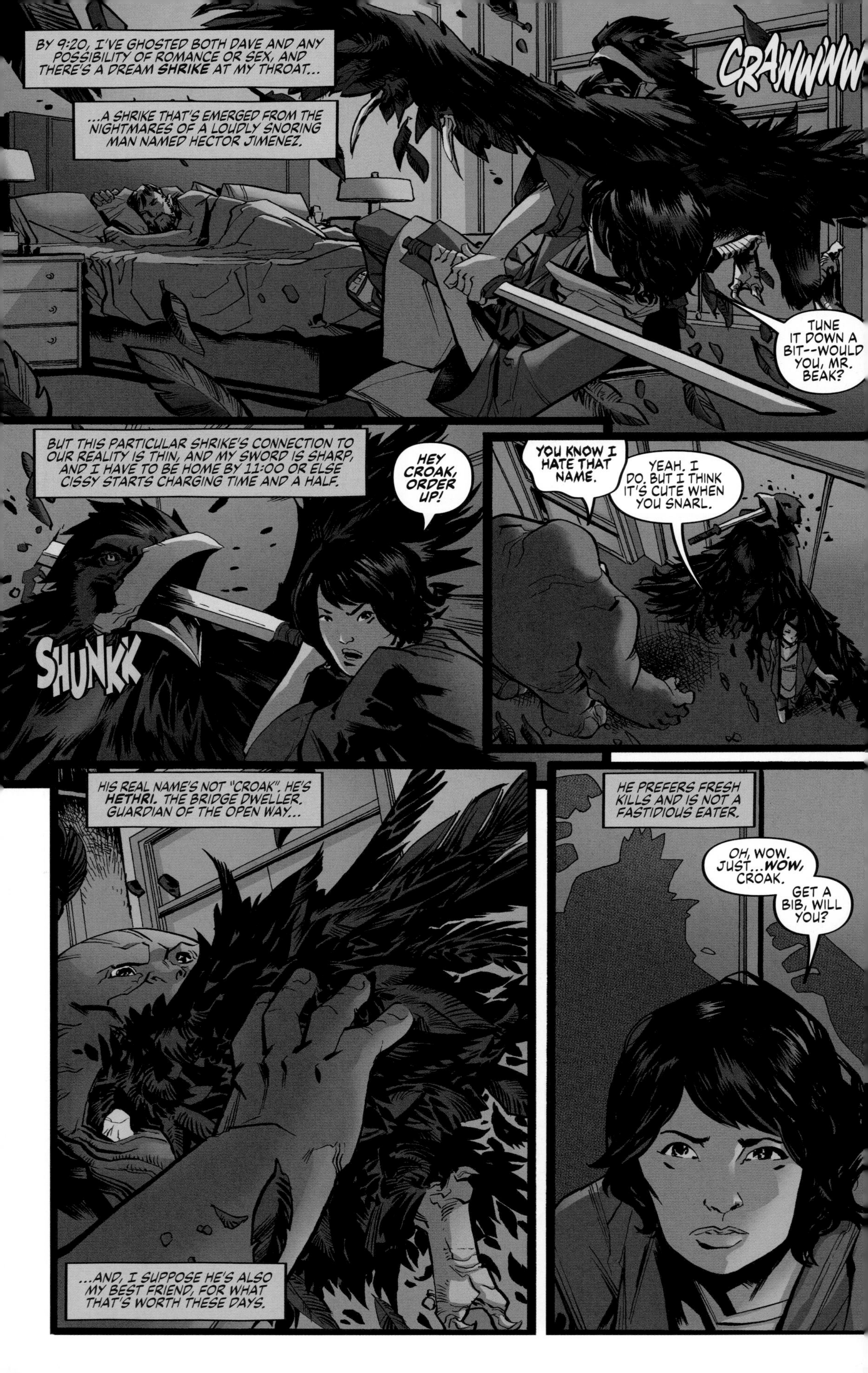
BY 9:20, I'VE GHOSTED BOTH DAVE AND ANY POSSIBILITY OF ROMANCE OR SEX, AND THERE'S A DREAM SHRIKE AT MY THROAT...
...A SHRIKE THAT'S EMERGED FROM THE NIGHTMARES OF A LOUDLY SNORING MAN NAMED HECTOR JIMENEZ.
CRANWWW
TUNE IT DOWN A BIT--WOULD YOU, MR. BEAK?
BUT THIS PARTICULAR SHRIKE'S CONNECTION TO OUR REALITY IS THIN, AND MY SWORD IS SHARP, AND I HAVE TO BE HOME BY 11:00 OR ELSE CISSY STARTS CHARGING TIME AND A HALF.
HEY CROAK, ORDER UP!
SHUNKK
YOU KNOW I HATE THAT NAME.
YEAH. I DO. BUT I THINK IT'S CUTE WHEN YOU SNARL.
HIS REAL NAME'S NOT "CROAK". HE'S HETHRI. THE BRIDGE DWELLER. GUARDIAN OF THE OPEN WAY...
...AND, I SUPPOSE HE'S ALSO MY BEST FRIEND, FOR WHAT THAT'S WORTH THESE DAYS.
HE PREFERS FRESH KILLS AND IS NOT A FASTIDIOUS EATER.
OH, WOW. JUST...WOW, CROAK.
GET A BIB, WILL YOU?

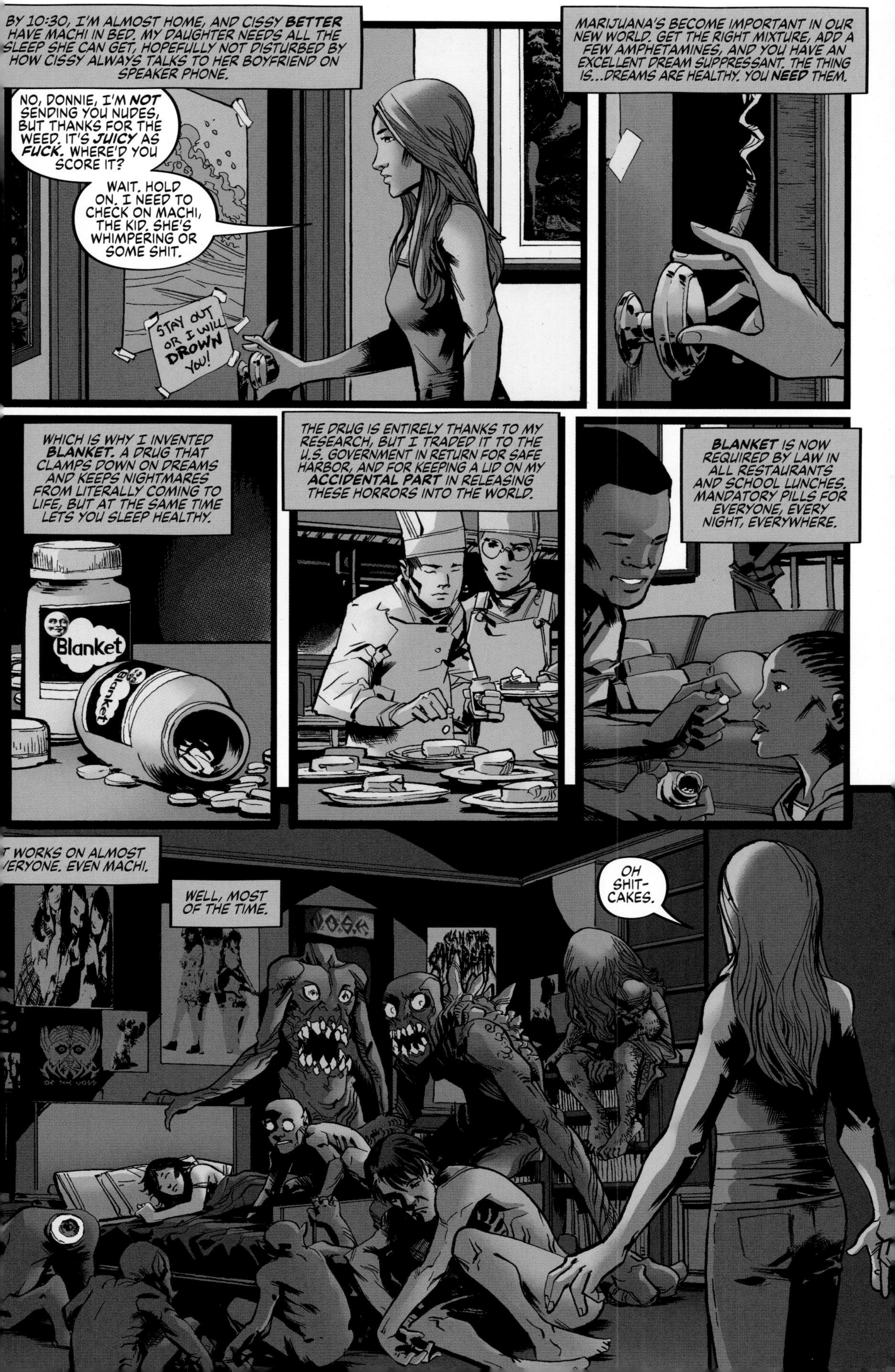
BY 10:30, I'M ALMOST HOME, AND CISSY BETTER HAVE MACHI IN BED. MY DAUGHTER NEEDS ALL THE SLEEP SHE CAN GET, HOPEFULLY NOT DISTURBED BY HOW CISSY ALWAYS TALKS TO HER BOYFRIEND ON SPEAKER PHONE.
NO, DONNIE, I'M NOT SENDING YOU NUDES, BUT THANKS FOR THE WEED. IT'S JUICY AS FUCK. WHERE'D YOU SCORE IT?
WAIT. HOLD ON. I NEED TO CHECK ON MACHI, THE KID. SHE'S WHIMPERING OR SOME SHIT.
STAY OUT OR I WILL DROWN YOU!
MARIJUANA'S BECOME IMPORTANT IN OUR NEW WORLD. GET THE RIGHT MIXTURE, ADD A FEW AMPHETAMINES, AND YOU HAVE AN EXCELLENT DREAM SUPPRESSANT. THE THING IS...DREAMS ARE HEALTHY. YOU NEED THEM.
WHICH IS WHY I INVENTED BLANKET. A DRUG THAT CLAMPS DOWN ON DREAMS AND KEEPS NIGHTMARES FROM LITERALLY COMING TO LIFE, BUT AT THE SAME TIME LETS YOU SLEEP HEALTHY.
Blanket
Blanket
THE DRUG IS ENTIRELY THANKS TO MY RESEARCH, BUT I TRADED IT TO THE U.S. GOVERNMENT IN RETURN FOR SAFE HARBOR, AND FOR KEEPING A LID ON MY ACCIDENTAL PART IN RELEASING THESE HORRORS INTO THE WORLD.
BLANKET IS NOW REQUIRED BY LAW IN ALL RESTAURANTS AND SCHOOL LUNCHES. MANDATORY PILLS FOR EVERYONE, EVERY NIGHT, EVERYWHERE.
T WORKS ON ALMOST VERYONE. EVEN MACHI.
WELL, MOST OF THE TIME.
OH SHIT-CAKES.

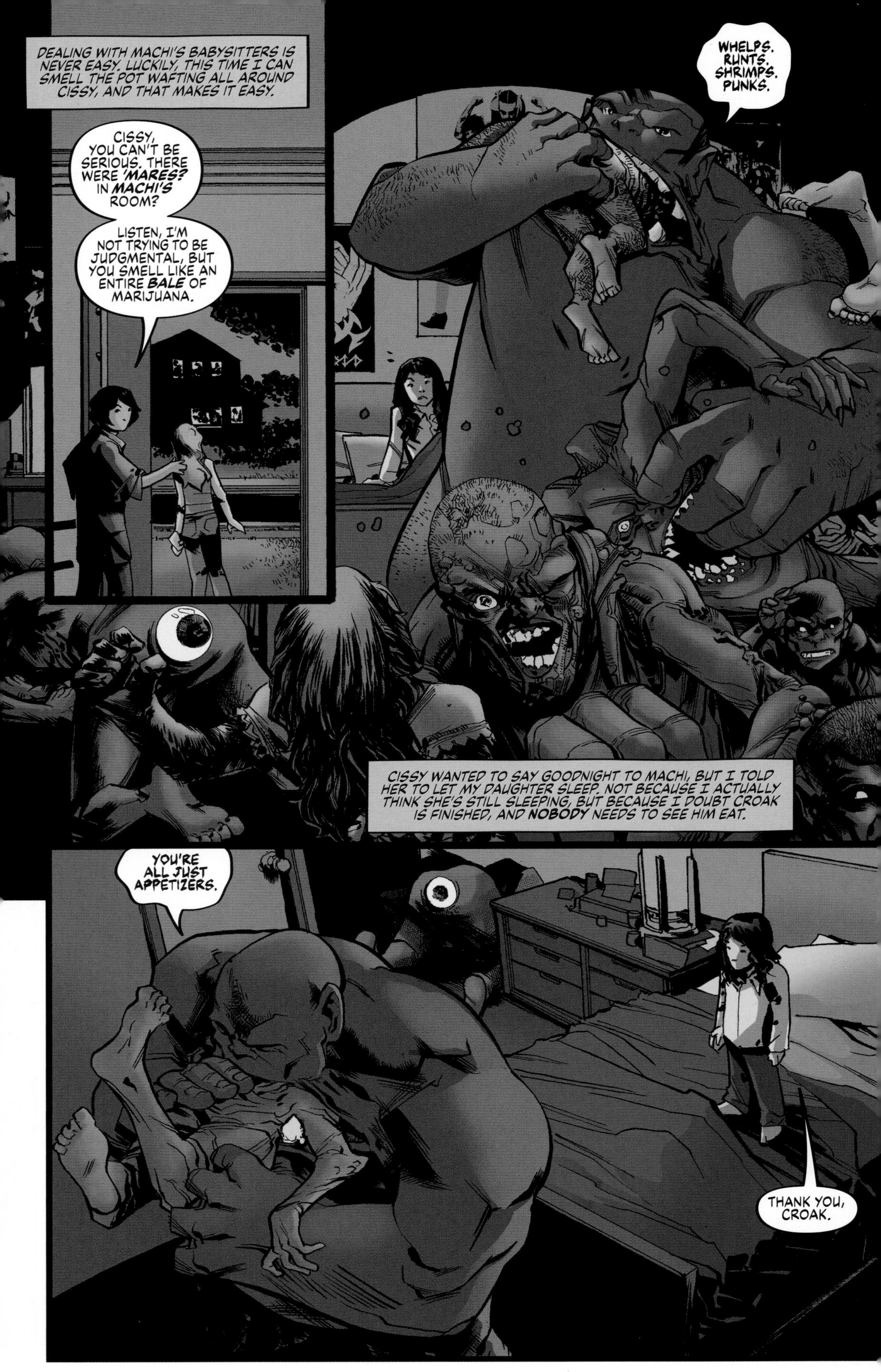
DEALING WITH MACHI'S BABYSITTERS IS NEVER EASY. LUCKILY, THIS TIME I CAN SMELL THE POT WAFTING ALL AROUND CISSY, AND THAT MAKES IT EASY.
CISSY, YOU CAN'T BE SERIOUS. THERE WERE 'MARES? IN MACHI'S ROOM?
LISTEN, I'M NOT TRYING TO BE JUDGMENTAL, BUT YOU SMELL LIKE AN ENTIRE BALE OF MARIJUANA.
WHELPS. RUNTS. SHRIMPS. PUNKS.
CISSY WANTED TO SAY GOODNIGHT TO MACHI, BUT I TOLD HER TO LET MY DAUGHTER SLEEP. NOT BECAUSE I ACTUALLY THINK SHE'S STILL SLEEPING, BUT BECAUSE I DOUBT CROAK IS FINISHED, AND NOBODY NEEDS TO SEE HIM EAT.
YOU'RE ALL JUST APPETIZERS.
THANK YOU, CROAK.

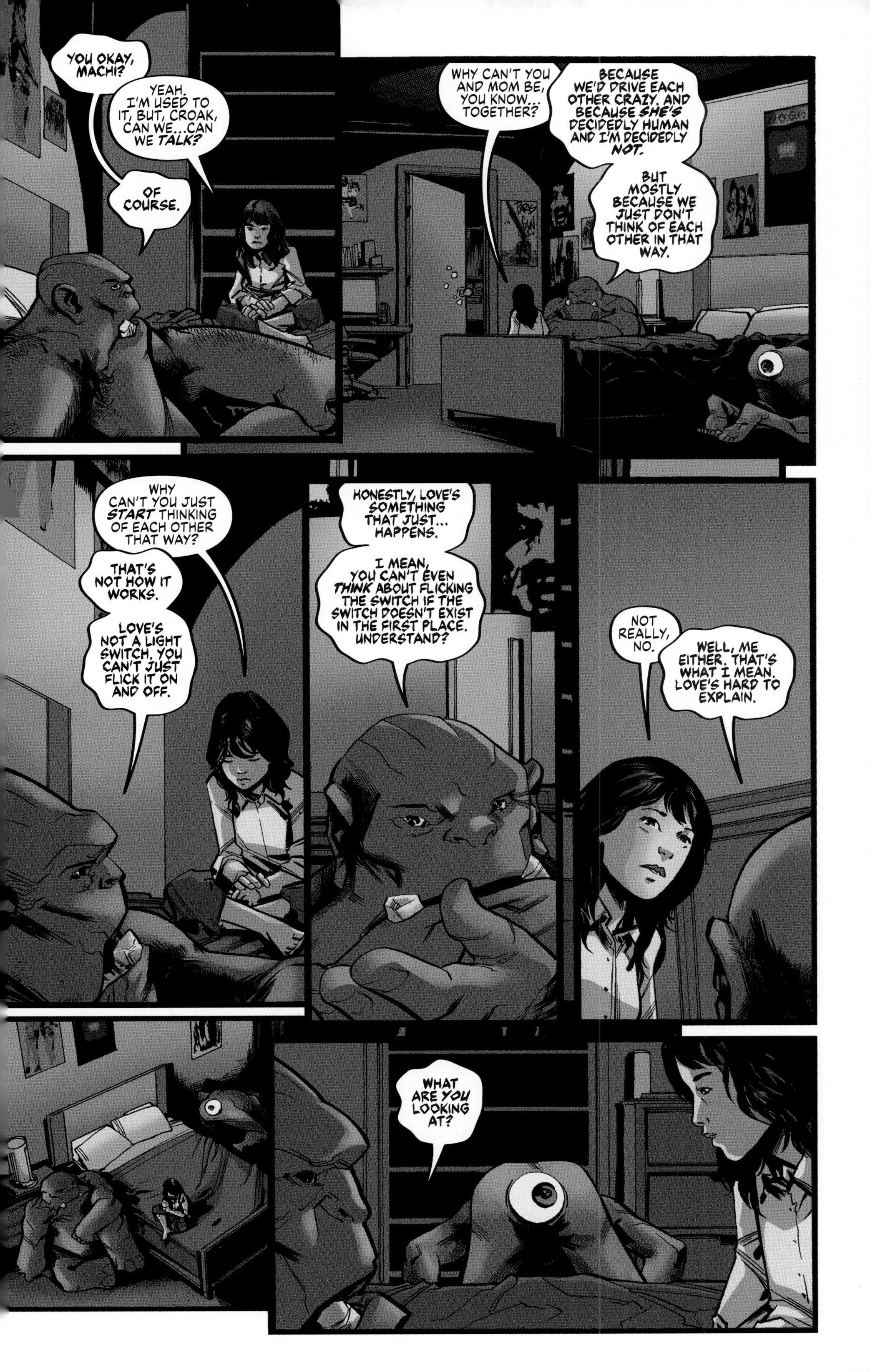

YOU OKAY, MACHI?
YEAH. I'M USED TO IT, BUT, CROAK, CAN WE...CAN WE TALK?
OF COURSE.
WHY CAN'T YOU AND MOM BE, YOU KNOW... TOGETHER?
BECAUSE WE'D DRIVE EACH OTHER CRAZY, AND BECAUSE SHE'S DECIDEDLY HUMAN AND I'M DECIDEDLY NOT.
BUT MOSTLY BECAUSE WE JUST DON'T THINK OF EACH OTHER IN THAT WAY.
WHY CAN'T YOU JUST START THINKING OF EACH OTHER THAT WAY?
THAT'S NOT HOW IT WORKS.
LOVE'S NOT A LIGHT SWITCH. YOU CAN'T JUST FLICK IT ON AND OFF.
HONESTLY, LOVE'S SOMETHING THAT JUST... HAPPENS.
I MEAN, YOU CAN'T EVEN THINK ABOUT FLICKING THE SWITCH IF THE SWITCH DOESN'T EXIST IN THE FIRST PLACE. UNDERSTAND?
NOT REALLY, NO.
WELL, ME EITHER. THAT'S WHAT I MEAN. LOVE'S HARD TO EXPLAIN.
WHAT ARE YOU LOOKING AT?

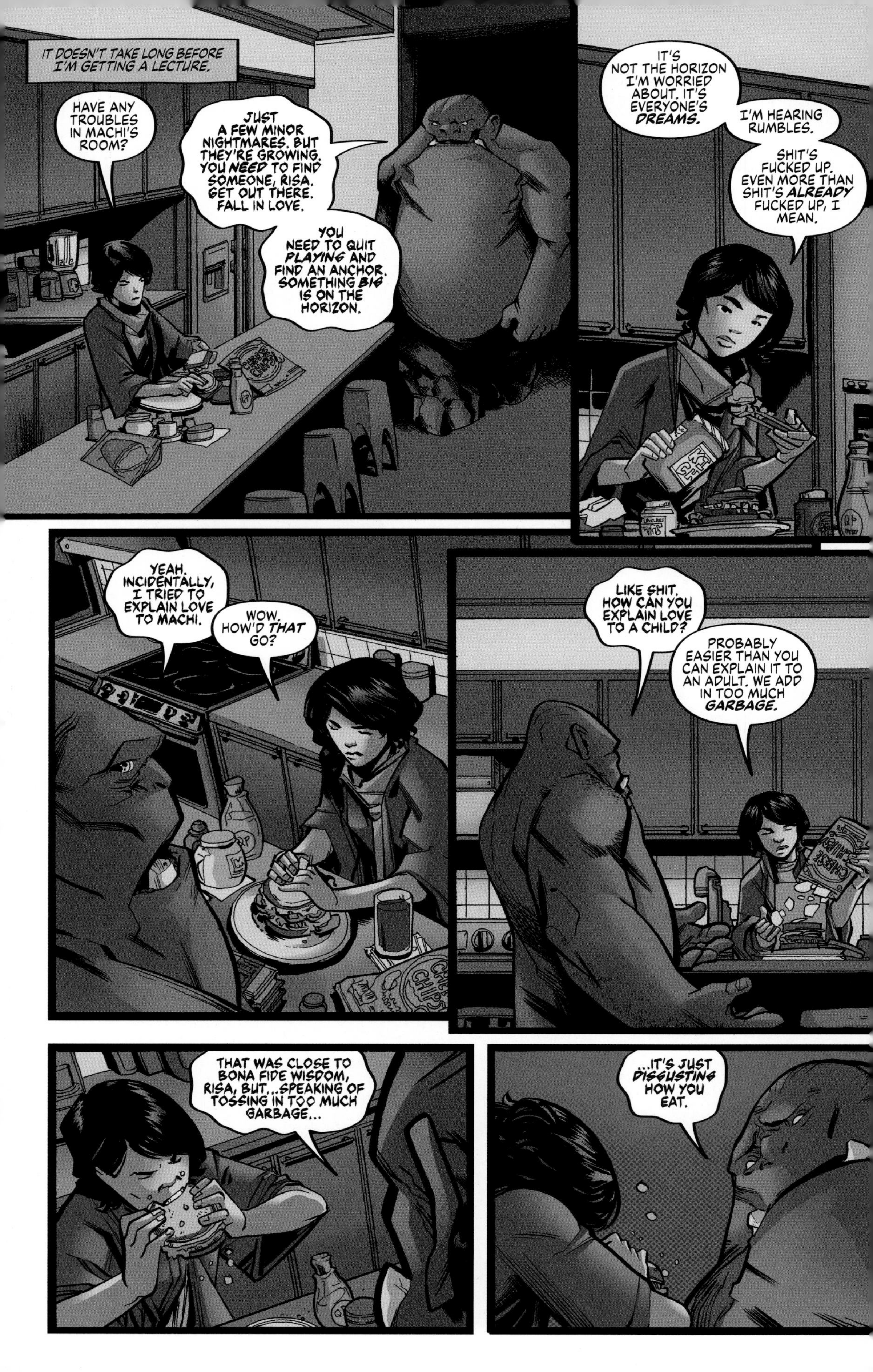
IT DOESN'T TAKE LONG BEFORE I'M GETTING A LECTURE.
HAVE ANY TROUBLES IN MACHI'S ROOM?
JUST A FEW MINOR NIGHTMARES. BUT THEY'RE GROWING. YOU NEED TO FIND SOMEONE, RISA. GET OUT THERE. FALL IN LOVE.
YOU NEED TO QUIT PLAYING AND FIND AN ANCHOR. SOMETHING BIG IS ON THE HORIZON.
IT'S NOT THE HORIZON I'M WORRIED ABOUT. IT'S EVERYONE'S DREAMS.
I'M HEARING RUMBLES.
SHIT'S FUCKED UP. EVEN MORE THAN SHIT'S ALREADY FUCKED UP, I MEAN.
YEAH. INCIDENTALLY, I TRIED TO EXPLAIN LOVE TO MACHI.
WOW. HOW'D THAT GO?
LIKE SHIT. HOW CAN YOU EXPLAIN LOVE TO A CHILD?
PROBABLY EASIER THAN YOU CAN EXPLAIN IT TO AN ADULT. WE ADD IN TOO MUCH GARBAGE.
THAT WAS CLOSE TO BONA FIDE WISDOM, RISA, BUT...SPEAKING OF TOSSING IN TOO MUCH GARBAGE...
...IT'S JUST DISGUSTING HOW YOU EAT.

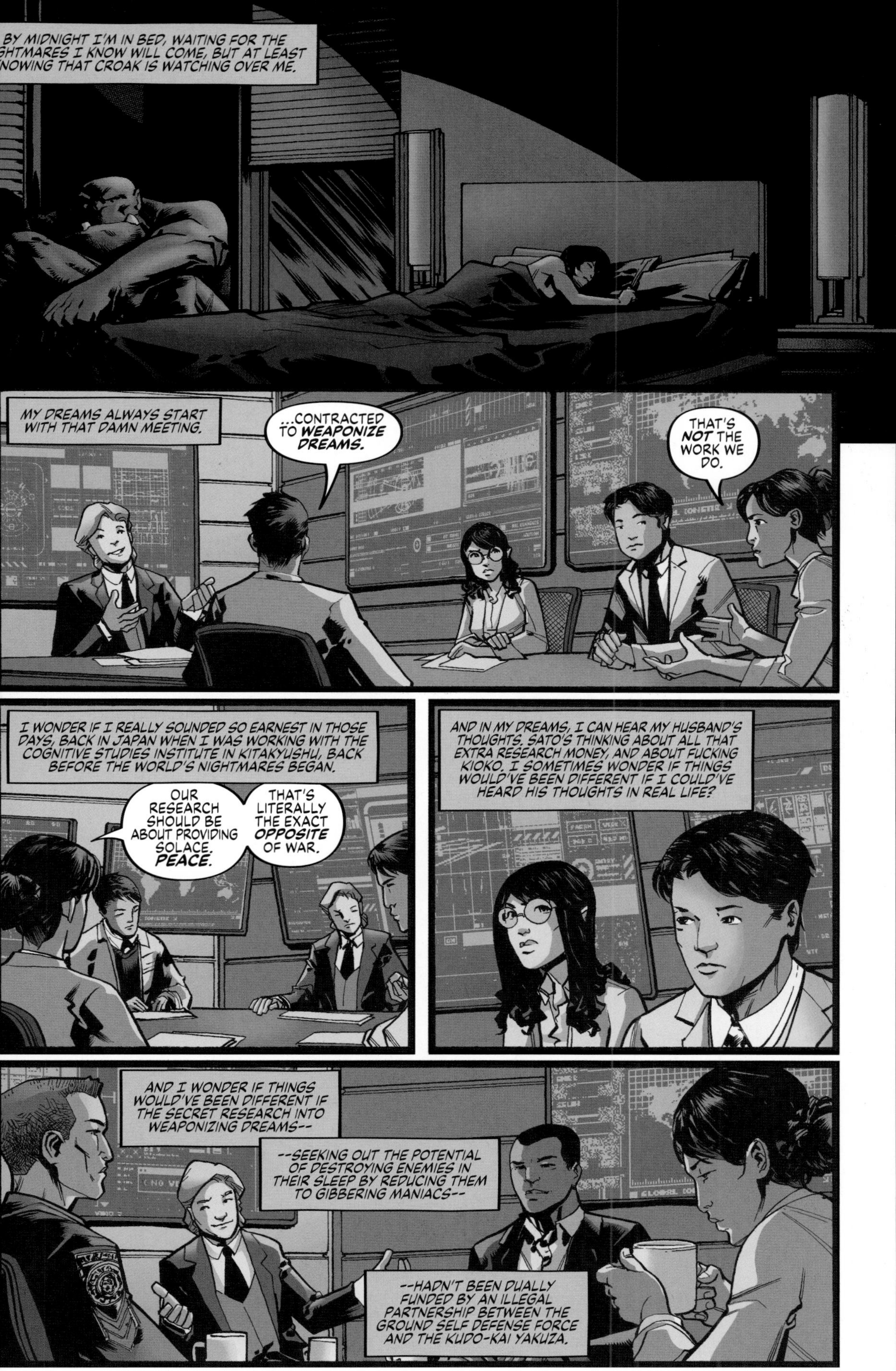
BY MIDNIGHT I'M IN BED, WAITING FOR THE NIGHTMARES I KNOW WILL COME, BUT AT LEAST KNOWING THAT CROAK IS WATCHING OVER ME.
MY DREAMS ALWAYS START WITH THAT DAMN MEETING.
...CONTRACTED TO *WEAPONIZE DREAMS.*
THAT'S *NOT* THE WORK WE DO.
I WONDER IF I REALLY SOUNDED SO EARNEST IN THOSE DAYS, BACK IN JAPAN WHEN I WAS WORKING WITH THE COGNITIVE STUDIES INSTITUTE IN KITAKYUSHU, BACK BEFORE THE WORLD'S NIGHTMARES BEGAN.
OUR RESEARCH SHOULD BE ABOUT PROVIDING SOLACE. ***PEACE***.
THAT'S LITERALLY THE EXACT *OPPOSITE* OF WAR.
AND IN MY DREAMS, I CAN HEAR MY HUSBAND'S THOUGHTS. SATO'S THINKING ABOUT ALL THAT EXTRA RESEARCH MONEY, AND ABOUT FUCKING KIOKO. I SOMETIMES WONDER IF THINGS WOULD'VE BEEN DIFFERENT IF I COULD'VE HEARD HIS THOUGHTS IN REAL LIFE?
AND I WONDER IF THINGS WOULD'VE BEEN DIFFERENT IF THE SECRET RESEARCH INTO WEAPONIZING DREAMS--
--SEEKING OUT THE POTENTIAL OF DESTROYING ENEMIES IN THEIR SLEEP BY REDUCING THEM TO GIBBERING MANIACS--
--HADN'T BEEN DUALLY FUNDED BY AN ILLEGAL PARTNERSHIP BETWEEN THE GROUND SELF DEFENSE FORCE AND THE KUDO-KAI YAKUZA.

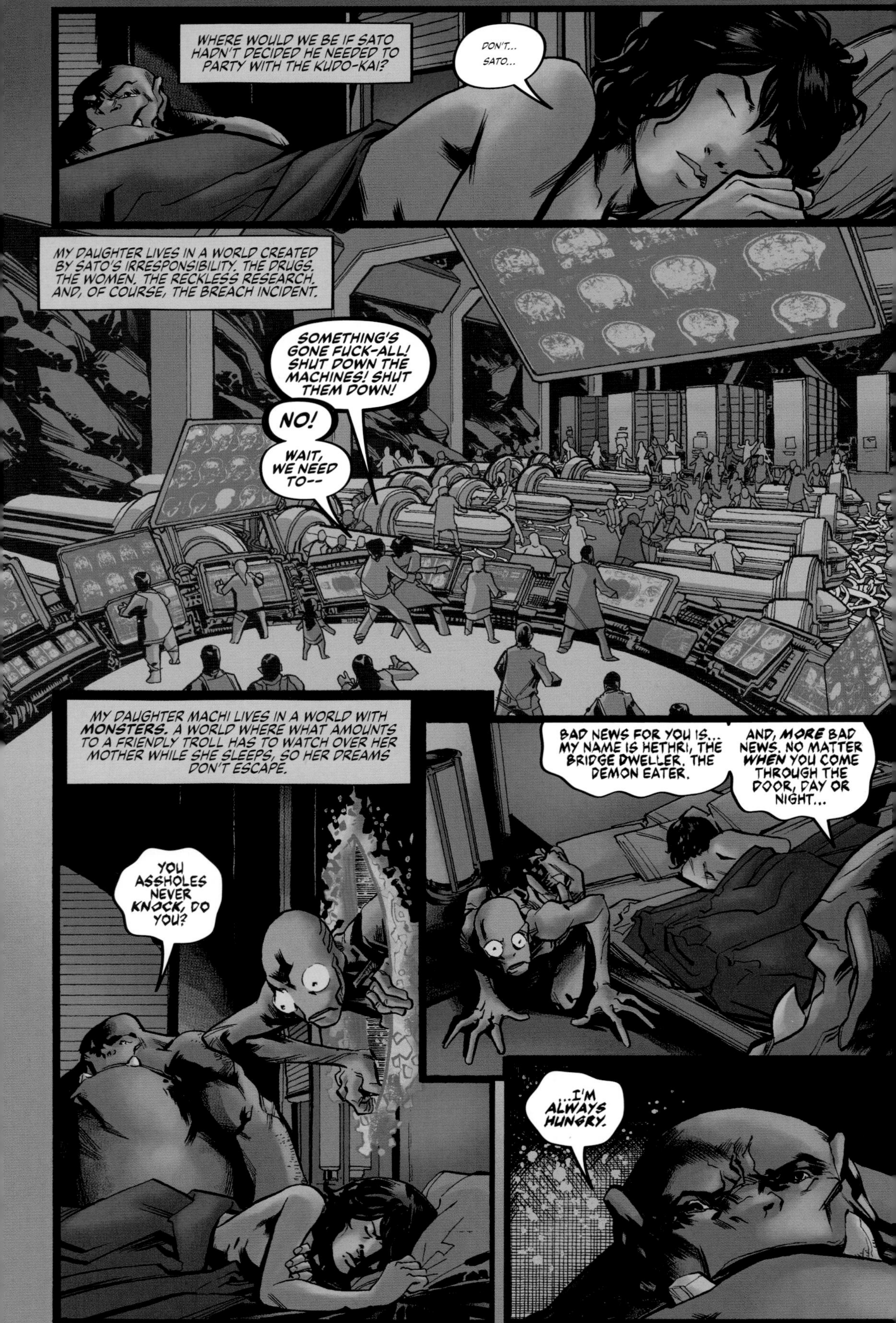
WHERE WOULD WE BE IF SATO HADN'T DECIDED HE NEEDED TO PARTY WITH THE KUDO-KAI?
DON'T... SATO...
MY DAUGHTER LIVES IN A WORLD CREATED BY SATO'S IRRESPONSIBILITY. THE DRUGS. THE WOMEN. THE RECKLESS RESEARCH. AND, OF COURSE, THE BREACH INCIDENT.
SOMETHING'S GONE FUCK-ALL! SHUT DOWN THE MACHINES! SHUT THEM DOWN!
NO!
WAIT, WE NEED TO--
MY DAUGHTER MACHI LIVES IN A WORLD WITH MONSTERS. A WORLD WHERE WHAT AMOUNTS TO A FRIENDLY TROLL HAS TO WATCH OVER HER MOTHER WHILE SHE SLEEPS, SO HER DREAMS DON'T ESCAPE.
YOU ASSHOLES NEVER KNOCK, DO YOU?
BAD NEWS FOR YOU IS... MY NAME IS HETHRI, THE BRIDGE DWELLER, THE DEMON EATER.
AND, MORE BAD NEWS. NO MATTER WHEN YOU COME THROUGH THE DOOR, DAY OR NIGHT...
...I'M ALWAYS HUNGRY.

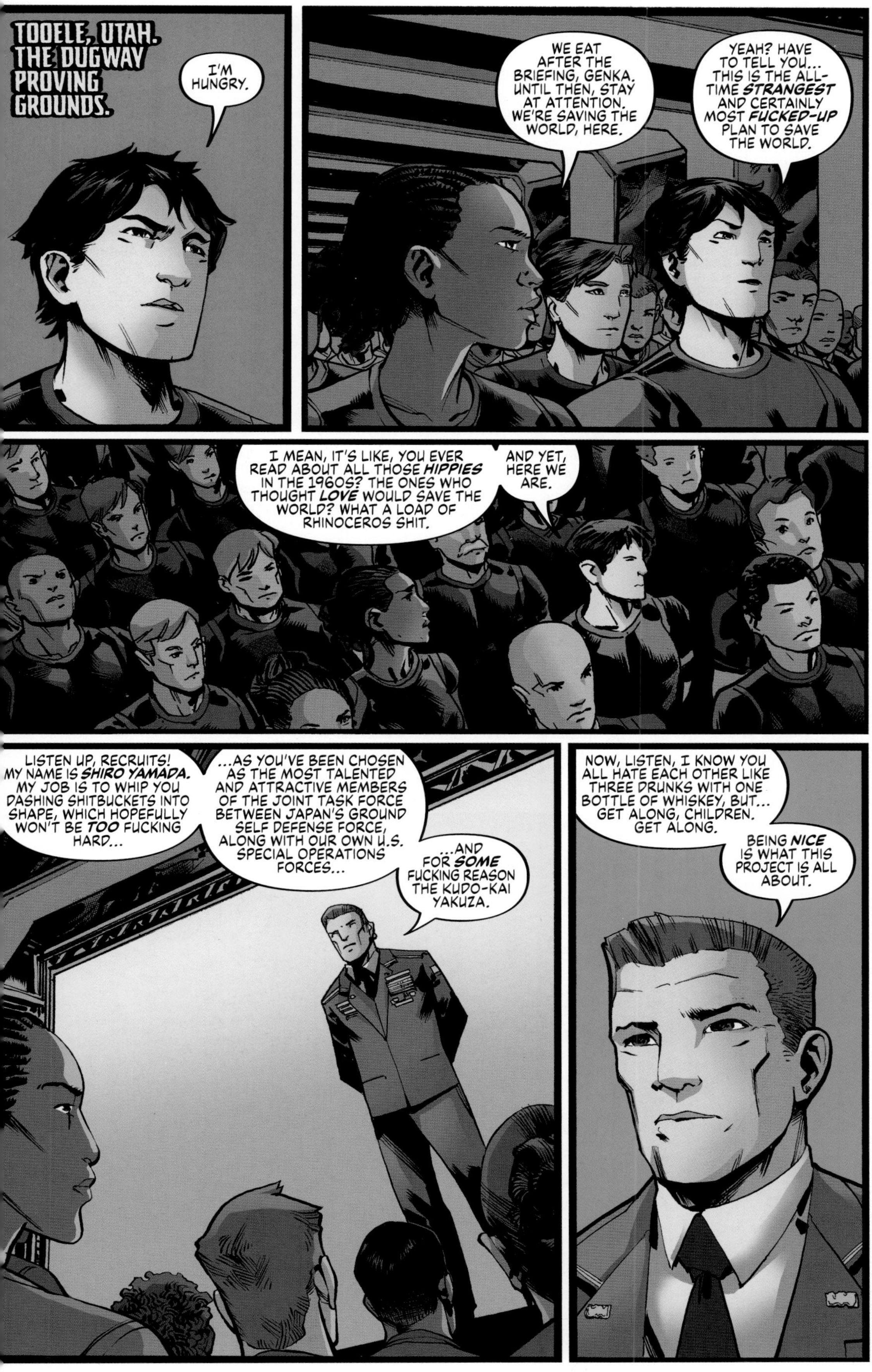
TOOELE, UTAH. THE DUGWAY PROVING GROUNDS.
I'M HUNGRY.
WE EAT AFTER THE BRIEFING, GENKA. UNTIL THEN, STAY AT ATTENTION. WE'RE SAVING THE WORLD, HERE.
YEAH? HAVE TO TELL YOU... THIS IS THE ALL-TIME STRANGEST AND CERTAINLY MOST FUCKED-UP PLAN TO SAVE THE WORLD.
I MEAN, IT'S LIKE, YOU EVER READ ABOUT ALL THOSE HIPPIES IN THE 1960S? THE ONES WHO THOUGHT LOVE WOULD SAVE THE WORLD? WHAT A LOAD OF RHINOCEROS SHIT.
AND YET, HERE WE ARE.
LISTEN UP, RECRUITS! MY NAME IS SHIRO YAMADA. MY JOB IS TO WHIP YOU DASHING SHITBUCKETS INTO SHAPE, WHICH HOPEFULLY WON'T BE TOO FUCKING HARD...
...AS YOU'VE BEEN CHOSEN AS THE MOST TALENTED AND ATTRACTIVE MEMBERS OF THE JOINT TASK FORCE BETWEEN JAPAN'S GROUND SELF DEFENSE FORCE, ALONG WITH OUR OWN U.S. SPECIAL OPERATIONS FORCES...
...AND FOR SOME FUCKING REASON THE KUDO-KAI YAKUZA.
NOW, LISTEN, I KNOW YOU ALL HATE EACH OTHER LIKE THREE DRUNKS WITH ONE BOTTLE OF WHISKEY, BUT... GET ALONG, CHILDREN. GET ALONG.
BEING NICE IS WHAT THIS PROJECT IS ALL ABOUT.

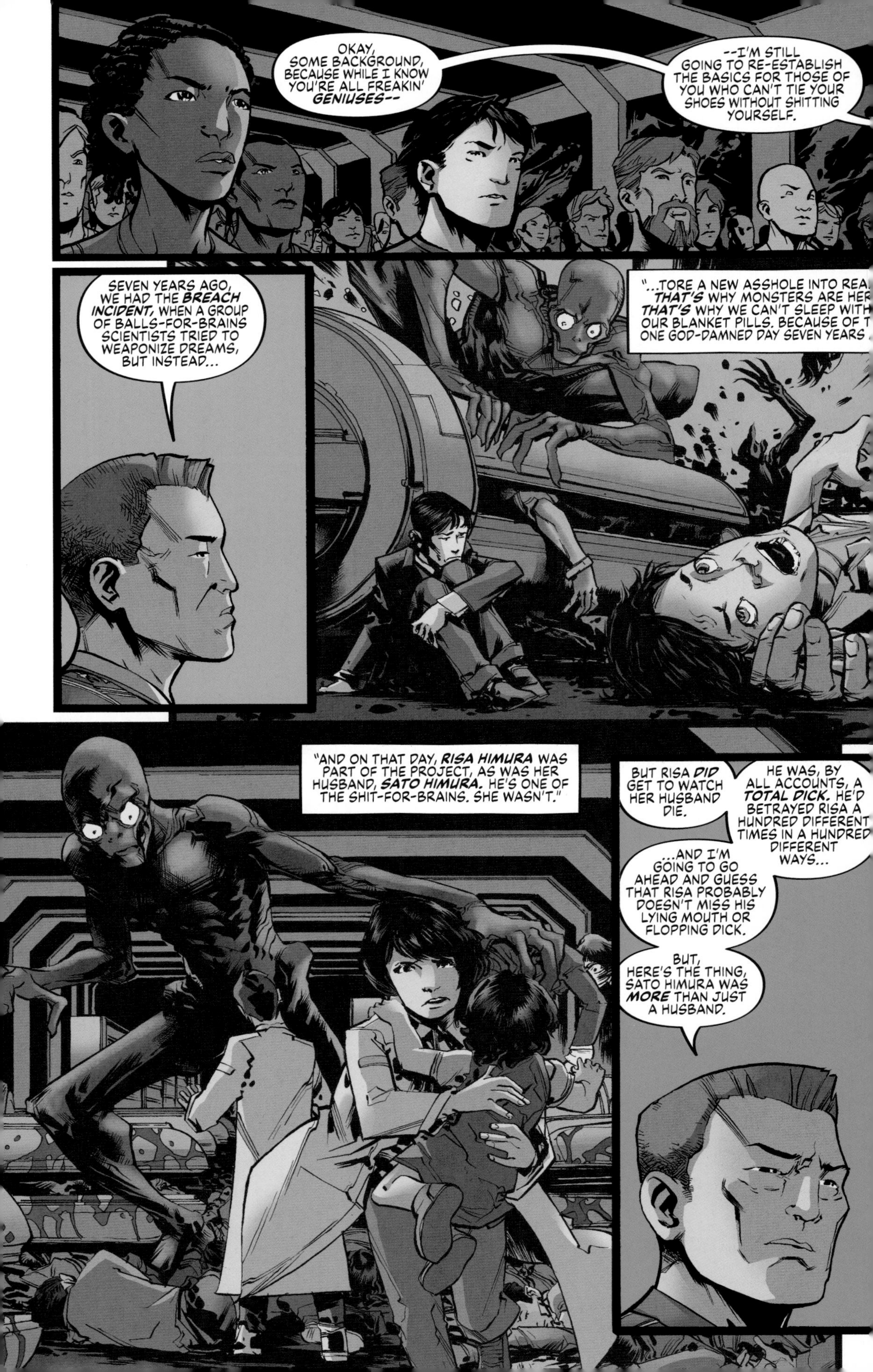
OKAY, SOME BACKGROUND, BECAUSE WHILE I KNOW YOU'RE ALL FREAKIN' ***GENIUSES--***
--I'M STILL GOING TO RE-ESTABLISH THE BASICS FOR THOSE OF YOU WHO CAN'T TIE YOUR SHOES WITHOUT SHITTING YOURSELF.
SEVEN YEARS AGO, WE HAD THE ***BREACH INCIDENT,*** WHEN A GROUP OF BALLS-FOR-BRAINS SCIENTISTS TRIED TO WEAPONIZE DREAMS, BUT INSTEAD...
"...TORE A NEW ASSHOLE INTO REA
THAT'S WHY MONSTERS ARE HER
THAT'S WHY WE CAN'T SLEEP WITH
OUR BLANKET PILLS. BECAUSE OF T
ONE GOD-DAMNED DAY SEVEN YEARS
"AND ON THAT DAY, ***RISA HIMURA*** WAS PART OF THE PROJECT, AS WAS HER HUSBAND, ***SATO HIMURA.*** HE'S ONE OF THE SHIT-FOR-BRAINS. SHE WASN'T."
BUT RISA ***DID*** GET TO WATCH HER HUSBAND DIE.
HE WAS, BY ALL ACCOUNTS, A ***TOTAL DICK.*** HE'D BETRAYED RISA A HUNDRED DIFFERENT TIMES IN A HUNDRED DIFFERENT WAYS...
...AND I'M GOING TO GO AHEAD AND GUESS THAT RISA PROBABLY DOESN'T MISS HIS LYING MOUTH OR FLOPPING DICK.
BUT, HERE'S THE THING, SATO HIMURA WAS ***MORE*** THAN JUST A HUSBAND.

"HE WAS A *FATHER.* AND WHEN HIS DAUGHTER MACHI WATCHED HIM DIE, THE NIGHTMARE OF WHAT SHE WAS SEEING HELPED CEMENT THE EXISTENCE OF NIGHTMARES IN THIS WORLD."

"EVER SINCE THEN, MACHI'S BECOME ONE OF SEVERAL FOCAL POINTS. THAT MEMORY SHE HAS, IT KEEPS THE BREACH *OPEN.* HER NIGHTMARES HELP USHER IN THE MONSTERS INTO OUR WORLD."

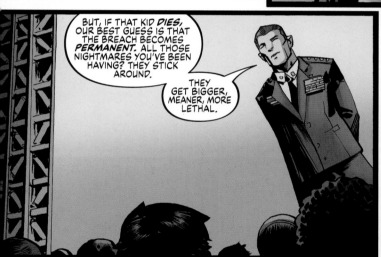

BUT, IF THAT KID *DIES,* OUR BEST GUESS IS THAT THE BREACH BECOMES *PERMANENT.* ALL THOSE NIGHTMARES YOU'VE BEEN HAVING? THEY STICK AROUND.

THEY GET BIGGER, MEANER, MORE LETHAL.

SO, ACCORDING TO OUR SCIENTISTS, THE *ONLY* WAY TO SOLVE THIS GODDAMN MESS IS TO BRING *PEACE* TO THAT KID, AND OTHERS LIKE HER.

"AND THE *ONLY* WAY THIS PARTICULAR KID HAS PEACE, IS IF SHE CAN *QUIT* REMEMBERING THE WAY HER DAD DIED, AND THE LOOK OF HORROR ON HER MOM'S FACE.

"AND THE ONLY WAY TO DO *THAT,* IS IF THERE'S A NEW LOVE IN HER MOM'S LIFE. WE'RE TALKING *TRUE* LOVE, SHITBUCKETS. AN *ANCHOR* FOR THAT KID. SHE NEEDS TO TRUST AGAIN, AND THEN...

"...POOF...

"...THE NIGHTMARES GO AWAY."

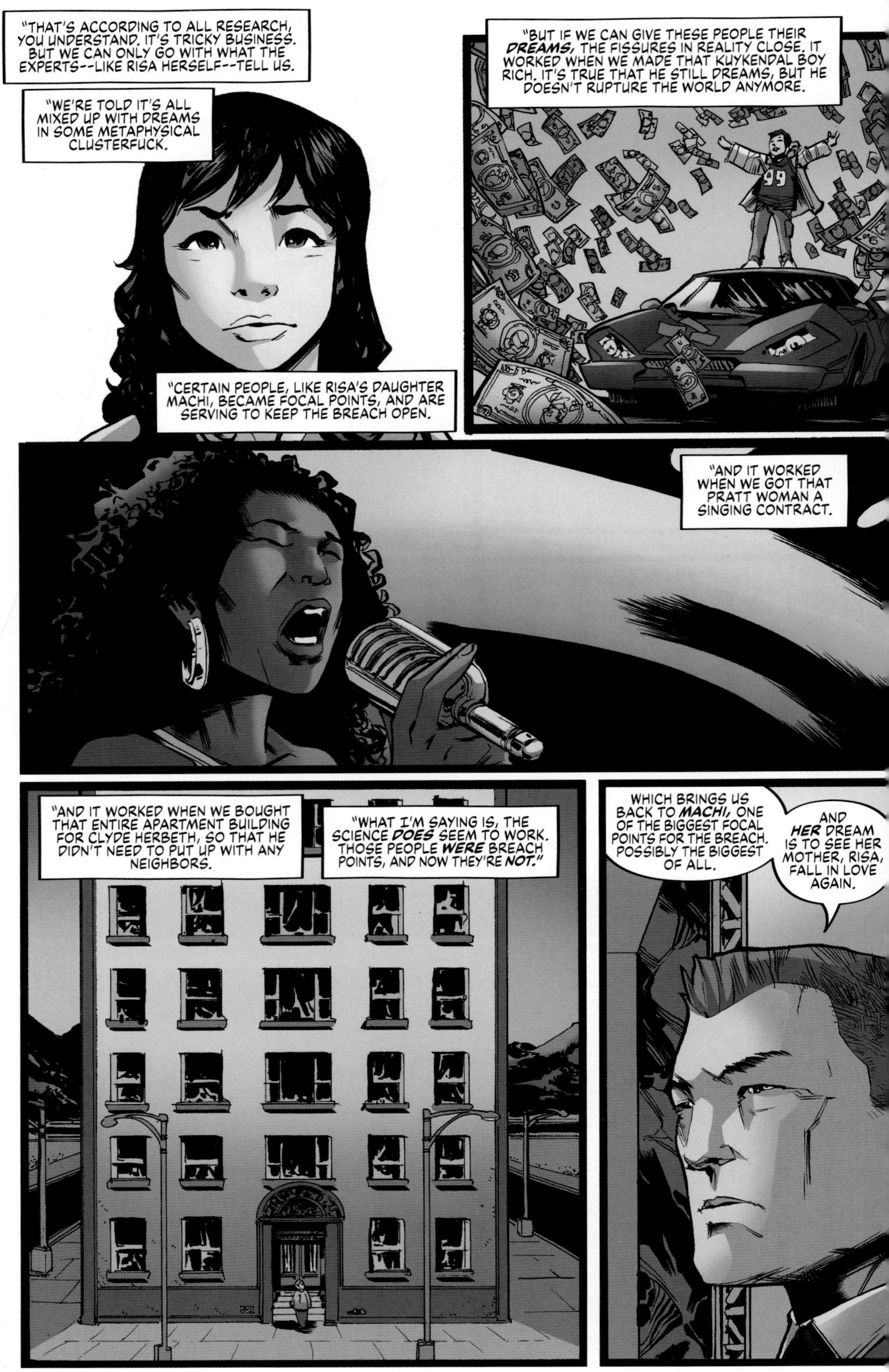
"THAT'S ACCORDING TO ALL RESEARCH, YOU UNDERSTAND. IT'S TRICKY BUSINESS. BUT WE CAN ONLY GO WITH WHAT THE EXPERTS--LIKE RISA HERSELF--TELL US.
"WE'RE TOLD IT'S ALL MIXED UP WITH DREAMS IN SOME METAPHYSICAL CLUSTERFUCK.
"CERTAIN PEOPLE, LIKE RISA'S DAUGHTER MACHI, BECAME FOCAL POINTS, AND ARE SERVING TO KEEP THE BREACH OPEN.
"BUT IF WE CAN GIVE THESE PEOPLE THEIR DREAMS, THE FISSURES IN REALITY CLOSE. IT WORKED WHEN WE MADE THAT KUYKENDAL BOY RICH. IT'S TRUE THAT HE STILL DREAMS, BUT HE DOESN'T RUPTURE THE WORLD ANYMORE.
99
"AND IT WORKED WHEN WE GOT THAT PRATT WOMAN A SINGING CONTRACT.
"AND IT WORKED WHEN WE BOUGHT THAT ENTIRE APARTMENT BUILDING FOR CLYDE HERBETH, SO THAT HE DIDN'T NEED TO PUT UP WITH ANY NEIGHBORS.
"WHAT I'M SAYING IS, THE SCIENCE DOES SEEM TO WORK. THOSE PEOPLE WERE BREACH POINTS, AND NOW THEY'RE NOT."
WHICH BRINGS US BACK TO MACHI, ONE OF THE BIGGEST FOCAL POINTS FOR THE BREACH. POSSIBLY THE BIGGEST OF ALL.
AND HER DREAM IS TO SEE HER MOTHER, RISA, FALL IN LOVE AGAIN.

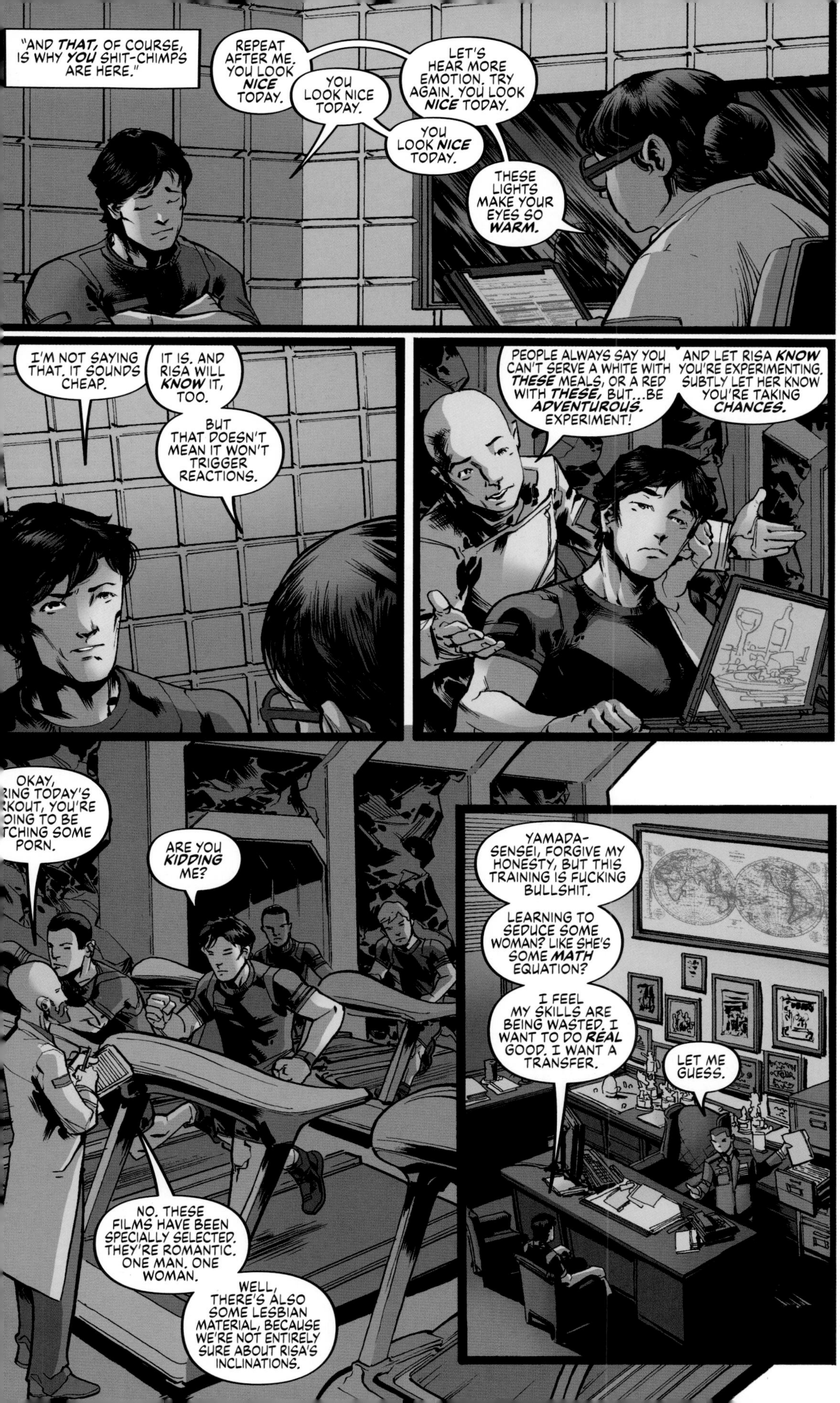
"AND THAT, OF COURSE, IS WHY YOU SHIT-CHIMPS ARE HERE."
REPEAT AFTER ME. YOU LOOK NICE TODAY.
YOU LOOK NICE TODAY.
LET'S HEAR MORE EMOTION. TRY AGAIN. YOU LOOK NICE TODAY.
YOU LOOK NICE TODAY.
THESE LIGHTS MAKE YOUR EYES SO WARM.
I'M NOT SAYING THAT. IT SOUNDS CHEAP.
IT IS. AND RISA WILL KNOW IT, TOO.
BUT THAT DOESN'T MEAN IT WON'T TRIGGER REACTIONS.
PEOPLE ALWAYS SAY YOU CAN'T SERVE A WHITE WITH THESE MEALS, OR A RED WITH THESE, BUT...BE ADVENTUROUS. EXPERIMENT!
AND LET RISA KNOW YOU'RE EXPERIMENTING. SUBTLY LET HER KNOW YOU'RE TAKING CHANCES.
OKAY, RING TODAY'S RKOUT, YOU'RE OING TO BE TCHING SOME PORN.
ARE YOU KIDDING ME?
NO. THESE FILMS HAVE BEEN SPECIALLY SELECTED. THEY'RE ROMANTIC. ONE MAN. ONE WOMAN.
WELL, THERE'S ALSO SOME LESBIAN MATERIAL, BECAUSE WE'RE NOT ENTIRELY SURE ABOUT RISA'S INCLINATIONS.
YAMADA-SENSEI, FORGIVE MY HONESTY, BUT THIS TRAINING IS FUCKING BULLSHIT.
LEARNING TO SEDUCE SOME WOMAN? LIKE SHE'S SOME MATH EQUATION?
I FEEL MY SKILLS ARE BEING WASTED. I WANT TO DO REAL GOOD. I WANT A TRANSFER.
LET ME GUESS.

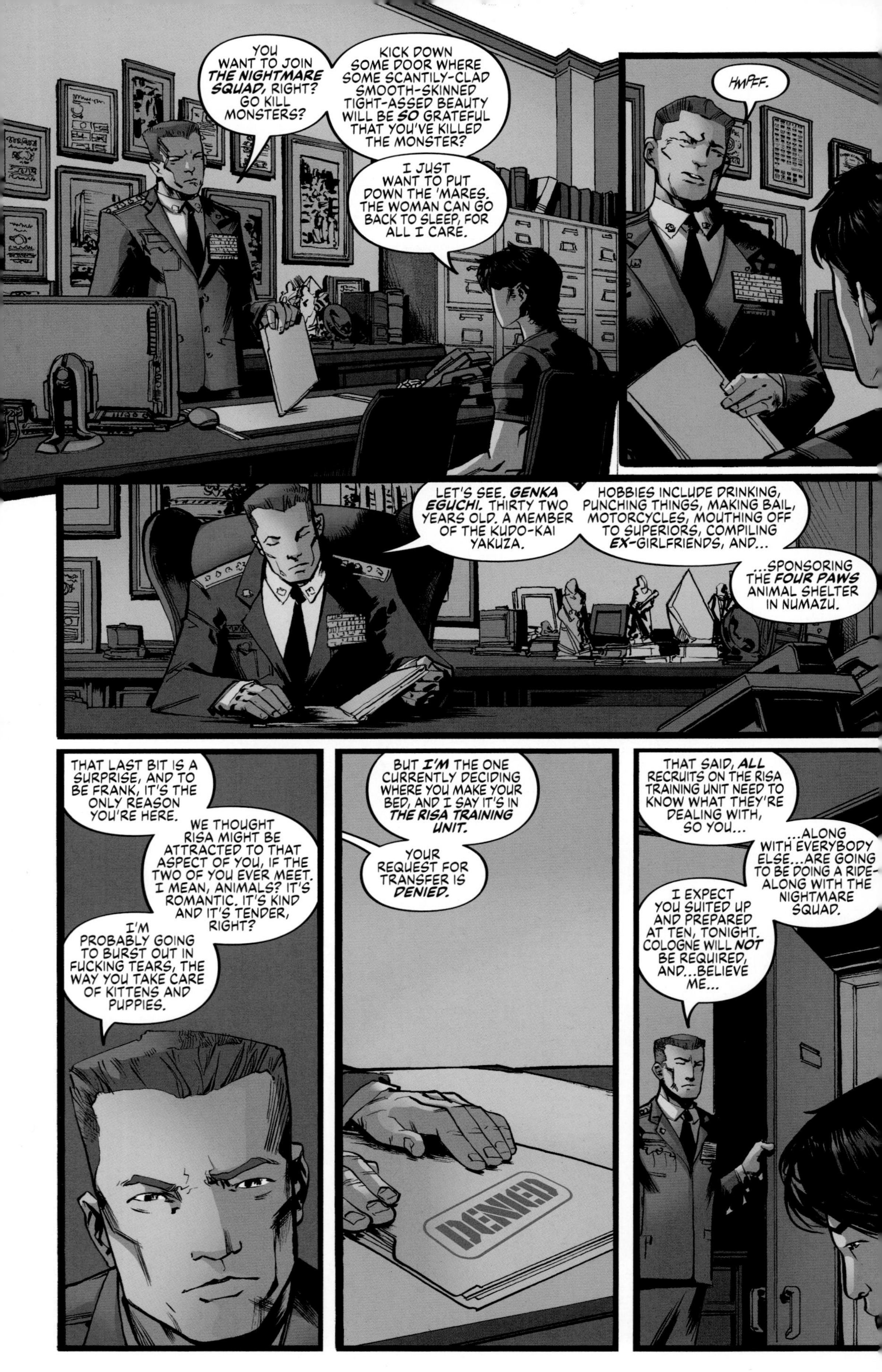

YOU WANT TO JOIN THE NIGHTMARE SQUAD, RIGHT? GO KILL MONSTERS?
KICK DOWN SOME DOOR WHERE SOME SCANTILY-CLAD SMOOTH-SKINNED TIGHT-ASSED BEAUTY WILL BE SO GRATEFUL THAT YOU'VE KILLED THE MONSTER?
I JUST WANT TO PUT DOWN THE 'MARES. THE WOMAN CAN GO BACK TO SLEEP, FOR ALL I CARE.
HMPFF.
LET'S SEE. GENKA EGUCHI. THIRTY TWO YEARS OLD. A MEMBER OF THE KUDO-KAI YAKUZA.
HOBBIES INCLUDE DRINKING, PUNCHING THINGS, MAKING BAIL, MOTORCYCLES, MOUTHING OFF TO SUPERIORS, COMPILING EX-GIRLFRIENDS, AND...
...SPONSORING THE FOUR PAWS ANIMAL SHELTER IN NUMAZU.
THAT LAST BIT IS A SURPRISE, AND TO BE FRANK, IT'S THE ONLY REASON YOU'RE HERE.
WE THOUGHT RISA MIGHT BE ATTRACTED TO THAT ASPECT OF YOU, IF THE TWO OF YOU EVER MEET. I MEAN, ANIMALS? IT'S ROMANTIC. IT'S KIND AND IT'S TENDER, RIGHT?
I'M PROBABLY GOING TO BURST OUT IN FUCKING TEARS, THE WAY YOU TAKE CARE OF KITTENS AND PUPPIES.
BUT I'M THE ONE CURRENTLY DECIDING WHERE YOU MAKE YOUR BED, AND I SAY IT'S IN THE RISA TRAINING UNIT.
YOUR REQUEST FOR TRANSFER IS DENIED.
DENIED
THAT SAID, ALL RECRUITS ON THE RISA TRAINING UNIT NEED TO KNOW WHAT THEY'RE DEALING WITH, SO YOU...
...ALONG WITH EVERYBODY ELSE...ARE GOING TO BE DOING A RIDE-ALONG WITH THE NIGHTMARE SQUAD.
I EXPECT YOU SUITED UP AND PREPARED AT TEN, TONIGHT. COLOGNE WILL NOT BE REQUIRED, AND...BELIEVE ME...

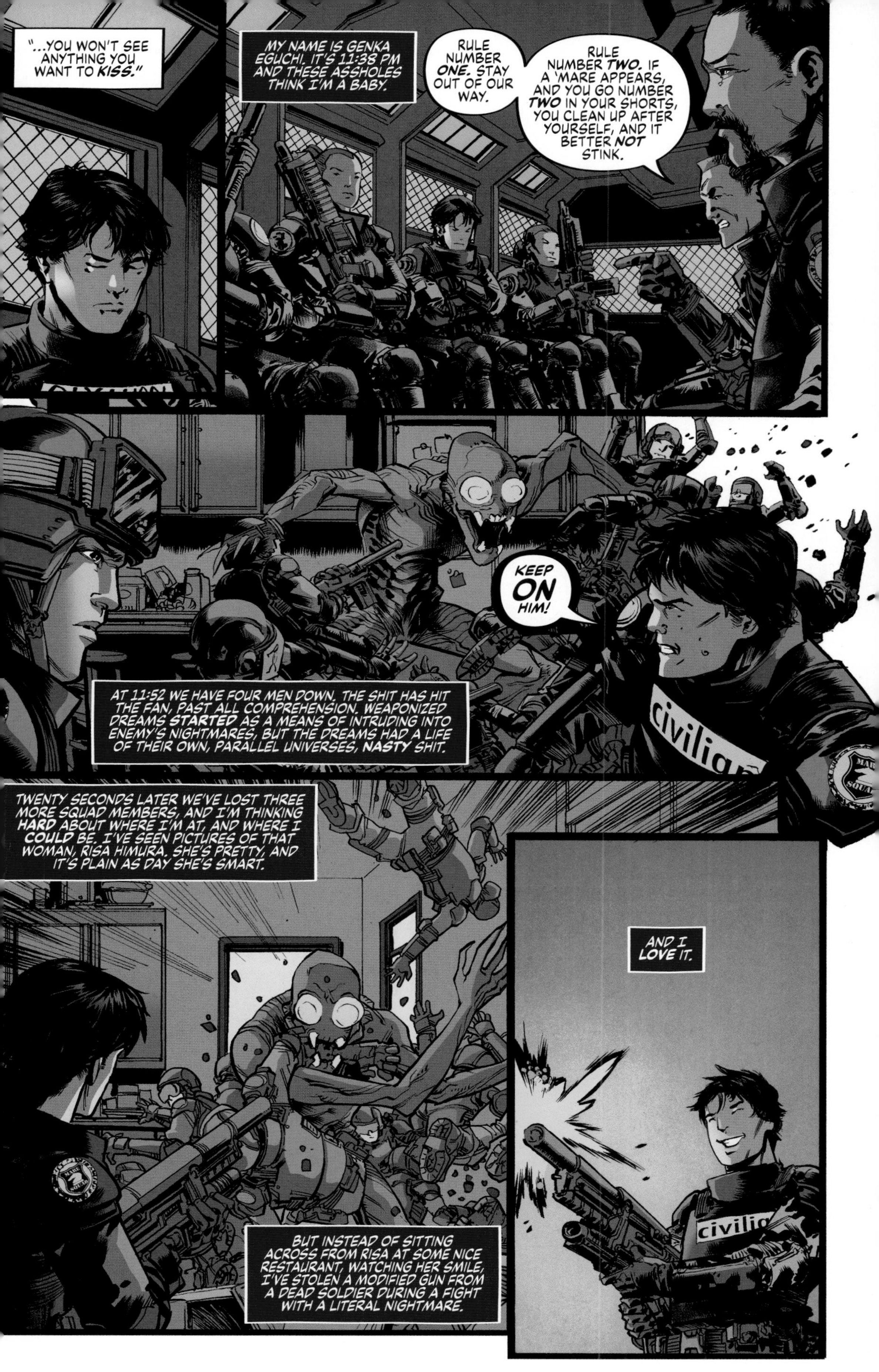
"...YOU WON'T SEE ANYTHING YOU WANT TO KISS."
MY NAME IS GENKA EGUCHI. IT'S 11:38 PM AND THESE ASSHOLES THINK I'M A BABY.
RULE NUMBER ONE. STAY OUT OF OUR WAY.
RULE NUMBER TWO. IF A 'MARE APPEARS, AND YOU GO NUMBER TWO IN YOUR SHORTS, YOU CLEAN UP AFTER YOURSELF, AND IT BETTER NOT STINK.
KEEP ON HIM!
AT 11:52 WE HAVE FOUR MEN DOWN. THE SHIT HAS HIT THE FAN, PAST ALL COMPREHENSION. WEAPONIZED DREAMS STARTED AS A MEANS OF INTRUDING INTO ENEMY'S NIGHTMARES, BUT THE DREAMS HAD A LIFE OF THEIR OWN, PARALLEL UNIVERSES, NASTY SHIT.
civilian
TWENTY SECONDS LATER WE'VE LOST THREE MORE SQUAD MEMBERS, AND I'M THINKING HARD ABOUT WHERE I'M AT, AND WHERE I COULD BE. I'VE SEEN PICTURES OF THAT WOMAN, RISA HIMURA. SHE'S PRETTY, AND IT'S PLAIN AS DAY SHE'S SMART.
BUT INSTEAD OF SITTING ACROSS FROM RISA AT SOME NICE RESTAURANT, WATCHING HER SMILE, I'VE STOLEN A MODIFIED GUN FROM A DEAD SOLDIER DURING A FIGHT WITH A LITERAL NIGHTMARE.
AND I LOVE IT.
civilia

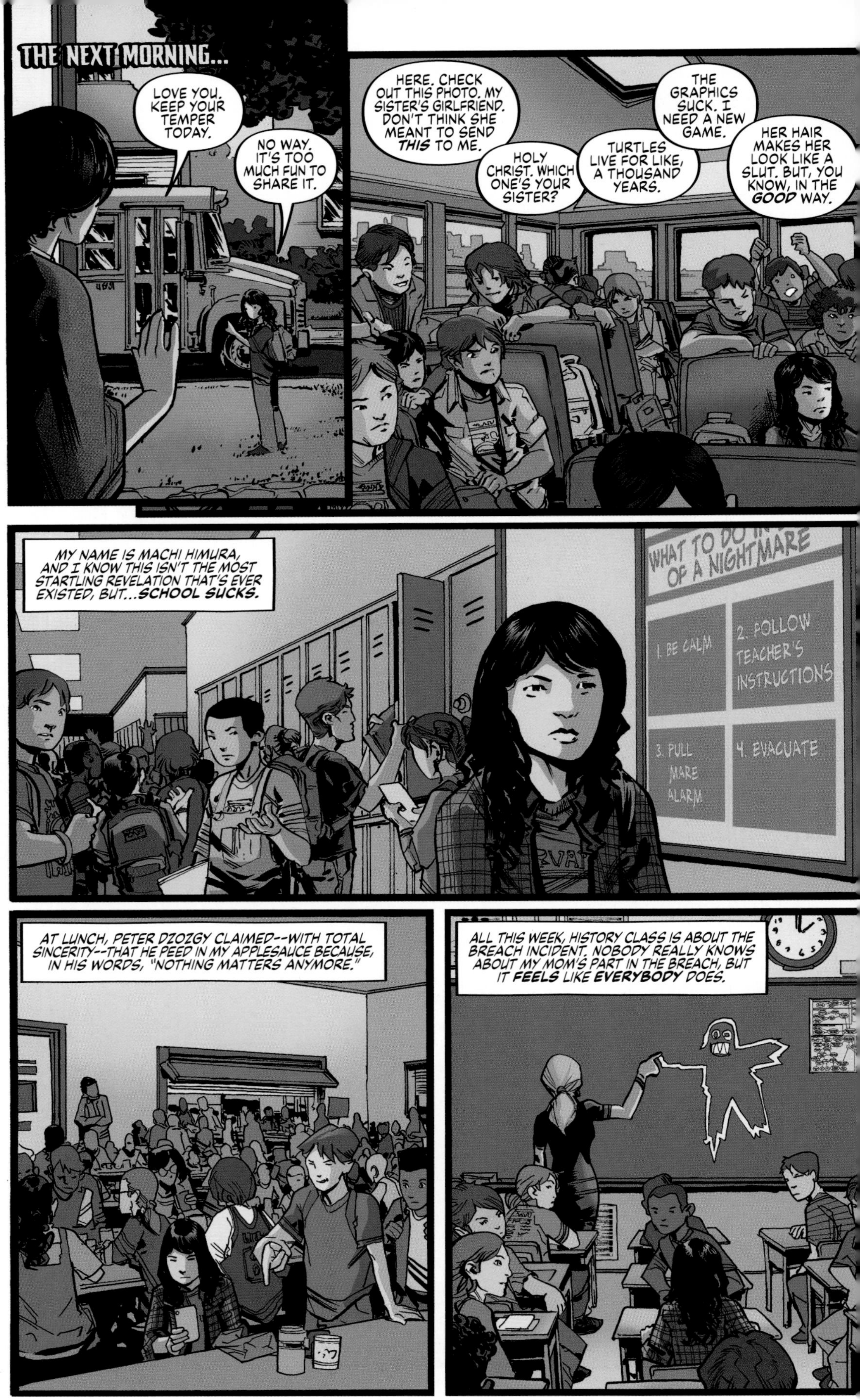
THE NEXT MORNING...
LOVE YOU. KEEP YOUR TEMPER TODAY.
NO WAY. IT'S TOO MUCH FUN TO SHARE IT.
HERE. CHECK OUT THIS PHOTO. MY SISTER'S GIRLFRIEND. DON'T THINK SHE MEANT TO SEND THIS TO ME.
HOLY CHRIST. WHICH ONE'S YOUR SISTER?
TURTLES LIVE FOR LIKE, A THOUSAND YEARS.
THE GRAPHICS SUCK. I NEED A NEW GAME.
HER HAIR MAKES HER LOOK LIKE A SLUT. BUT, YOU KNOW, IN THE GOOD WAY.
MY NAME IS MACHI HIMURA, AND I KNOW THIS ISN'T THE MOST STARTLING REVELATION THAT'S EVER EXISTED, BUT...SCHOOL SUCKS.
WHAT TO DO IN ... OF A NIGHTMARE
1. BE CALM
2. FOLLOW TEACHER'S INSTRUCTIONS
3. PULL MARE ALARM
4. EVACUATE
AT LUNCH, PETER DZOZGY CLAIMED--WITH TOTAL SINCERITY--THAT HE PEED IN MY APPLESAUCE BECAUSE, IN HIS WORDS, "NOTHING MATTERS ANYMORE."
ALL THIS WEEK, HISTORY CLASS IS ABOUT THE BREACH INCIDENT. NOBODY REALLY KNOWS ABOUT MY MOM'S PART IN THE BREACH, BUT IT FEELS LIKE EVERYBODY DOES.

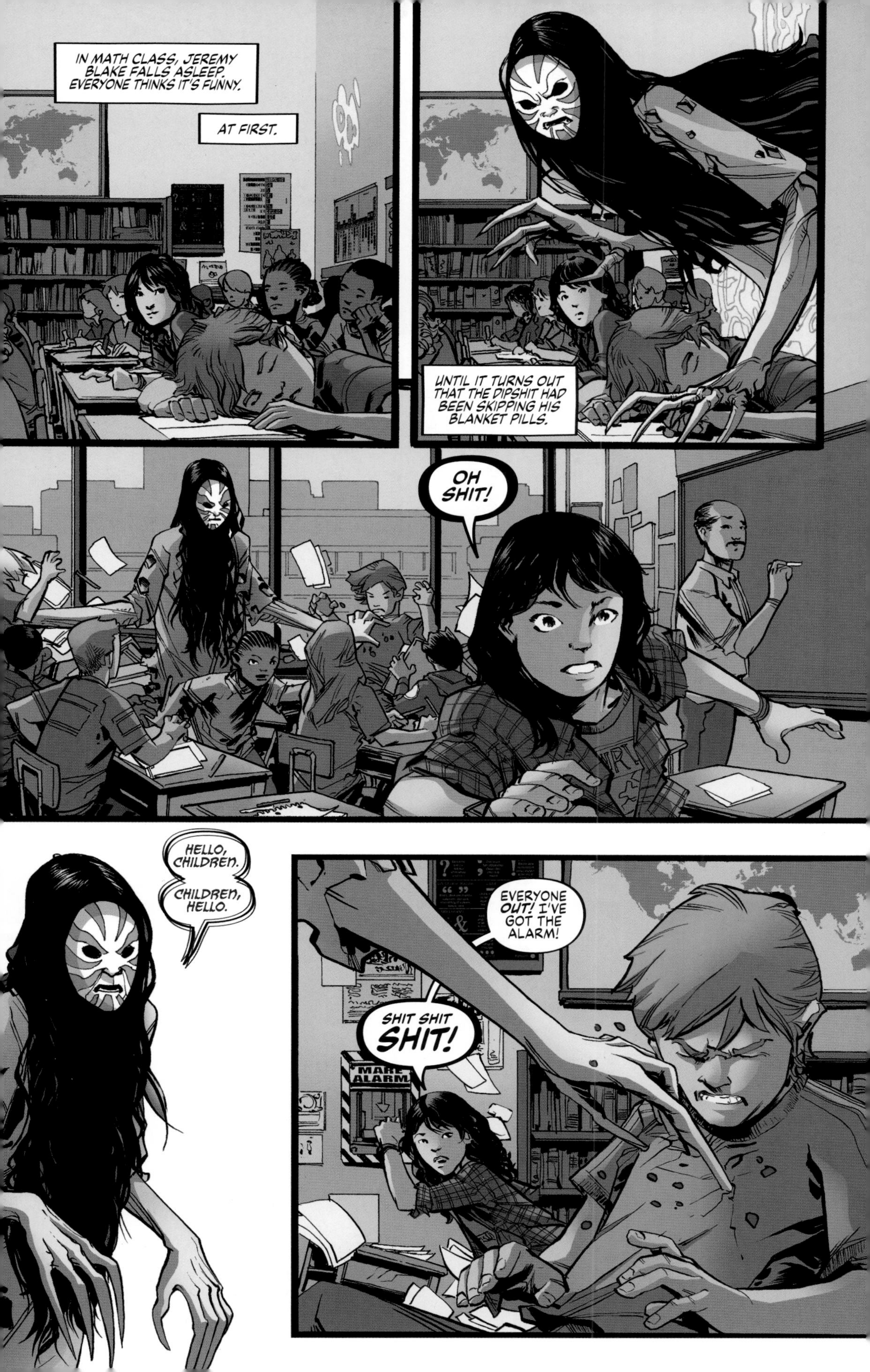
IN MATH CLASS, JEREMY BLAKE FALLS ASLEEP. EVERYONE THINKS IT'S FUNNY.
AT FIRST.
UNTIL IT TURNS OUT THAT THE DIPSHIT HAD BEEN SKIPPING HIS BLANKET PILLS.
OH SHIT!
HELLO, CHILDREN.
CHILDREN, HELLO.
EVERYONE OUT! I'VE GOT THE ALARM!
SHIT SHIT SHIT!
MARE ALARM

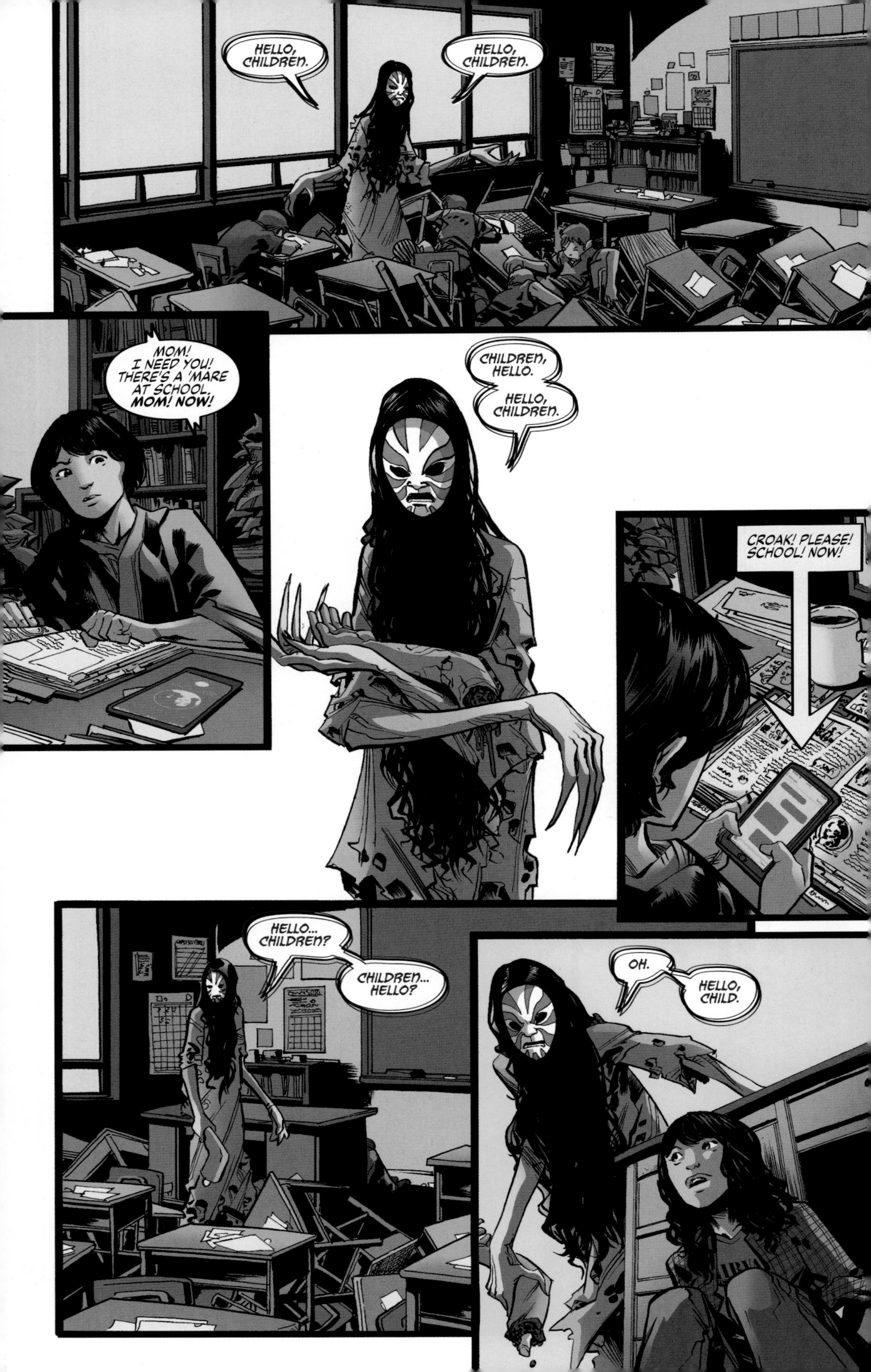
HELLO, CHILDREN.
HELLO, CHILDREN.
MOM! I NEED YOU! THERE'S A 'MARE AT SCHOOL. MOM! NOW!
CHILDREN, HELLO.
HELLO, CHILDREN.
CROAK! PLEASE! SCHOOL! NOW!
HELLO... CHILDREN?
CHILDREN... HELLO?
OH.
HELLO, CHILD.

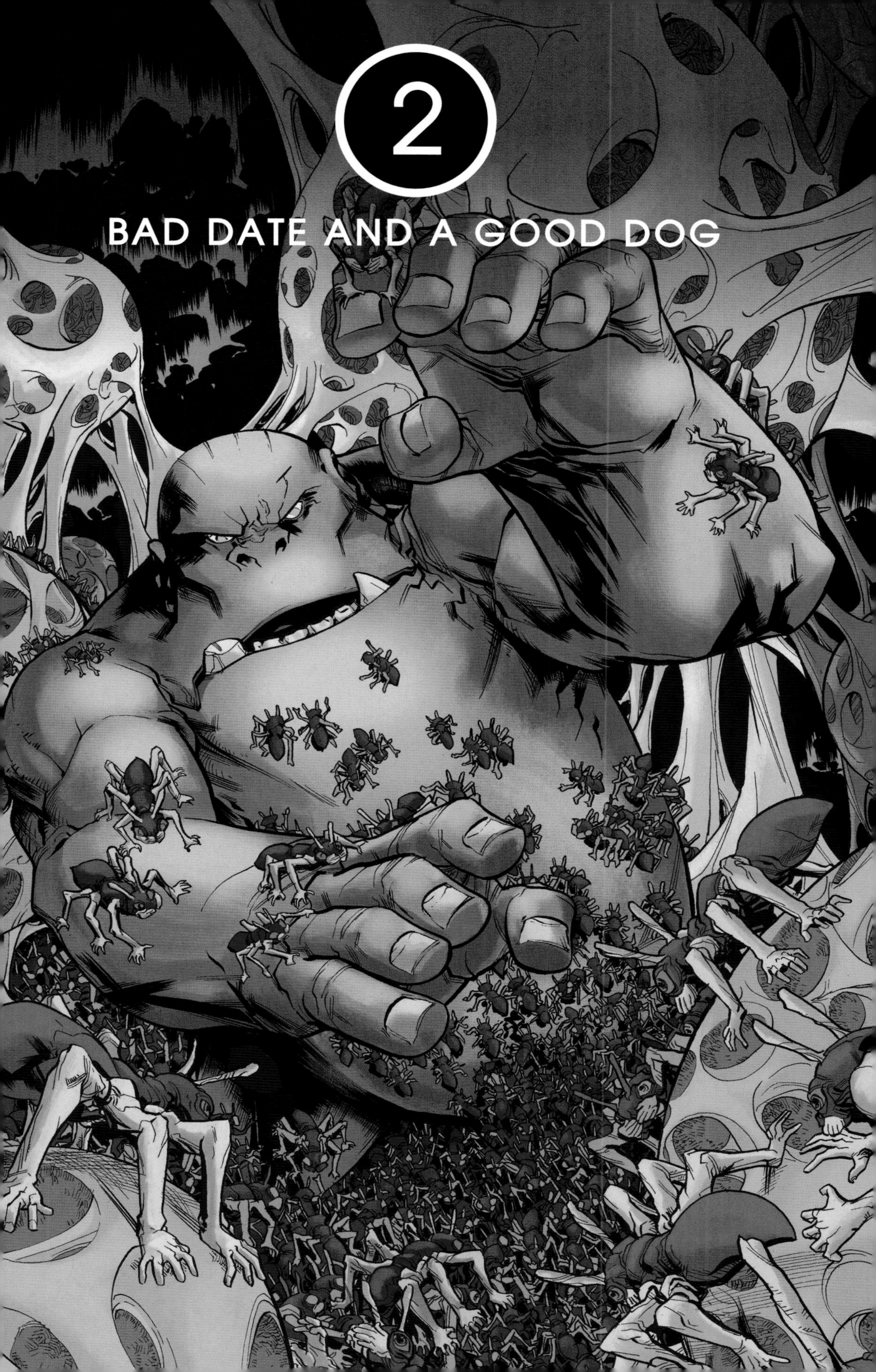
2
BAD DATE AND A GOOD DOG

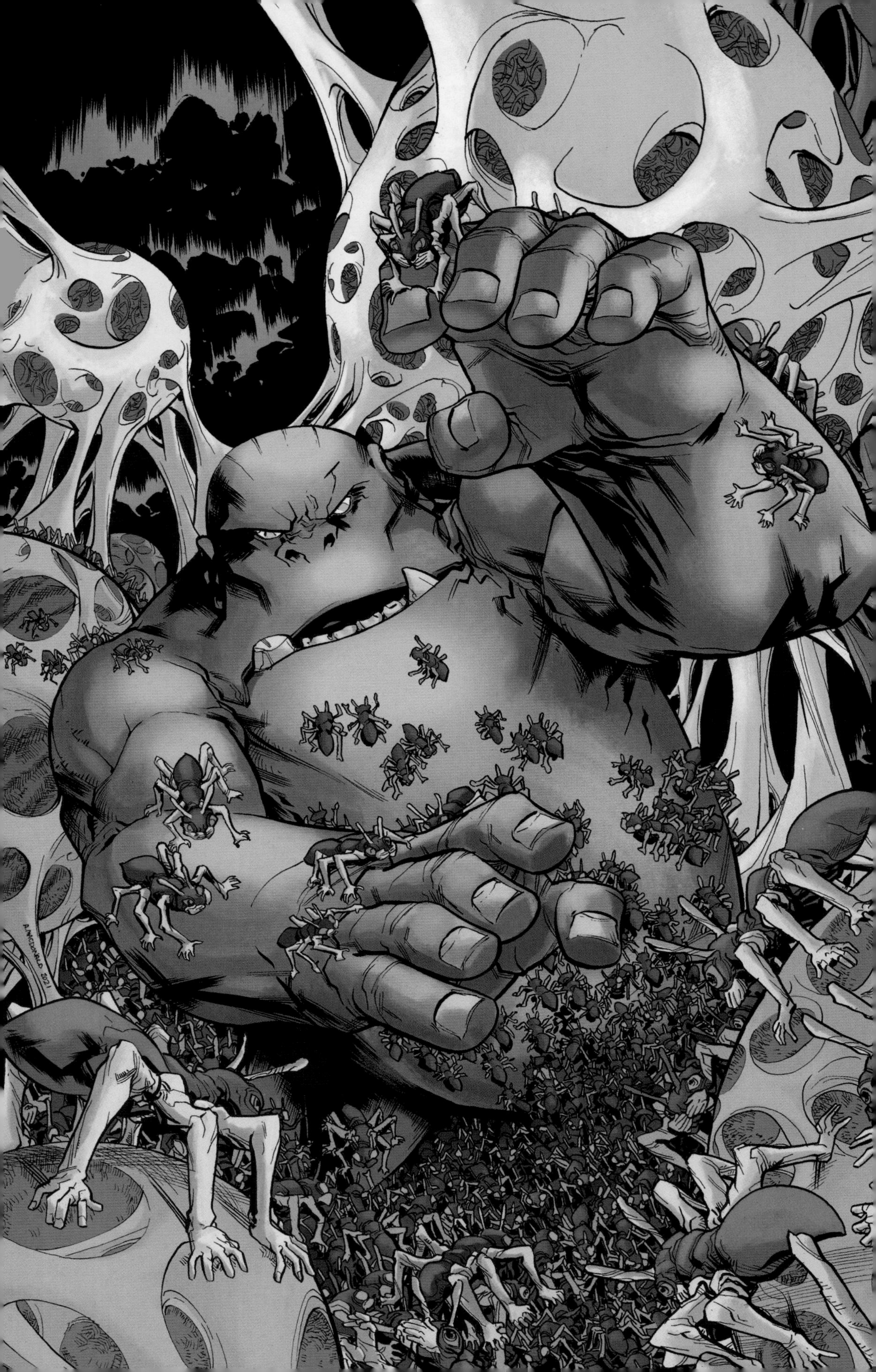
A. MACDONALD 2021

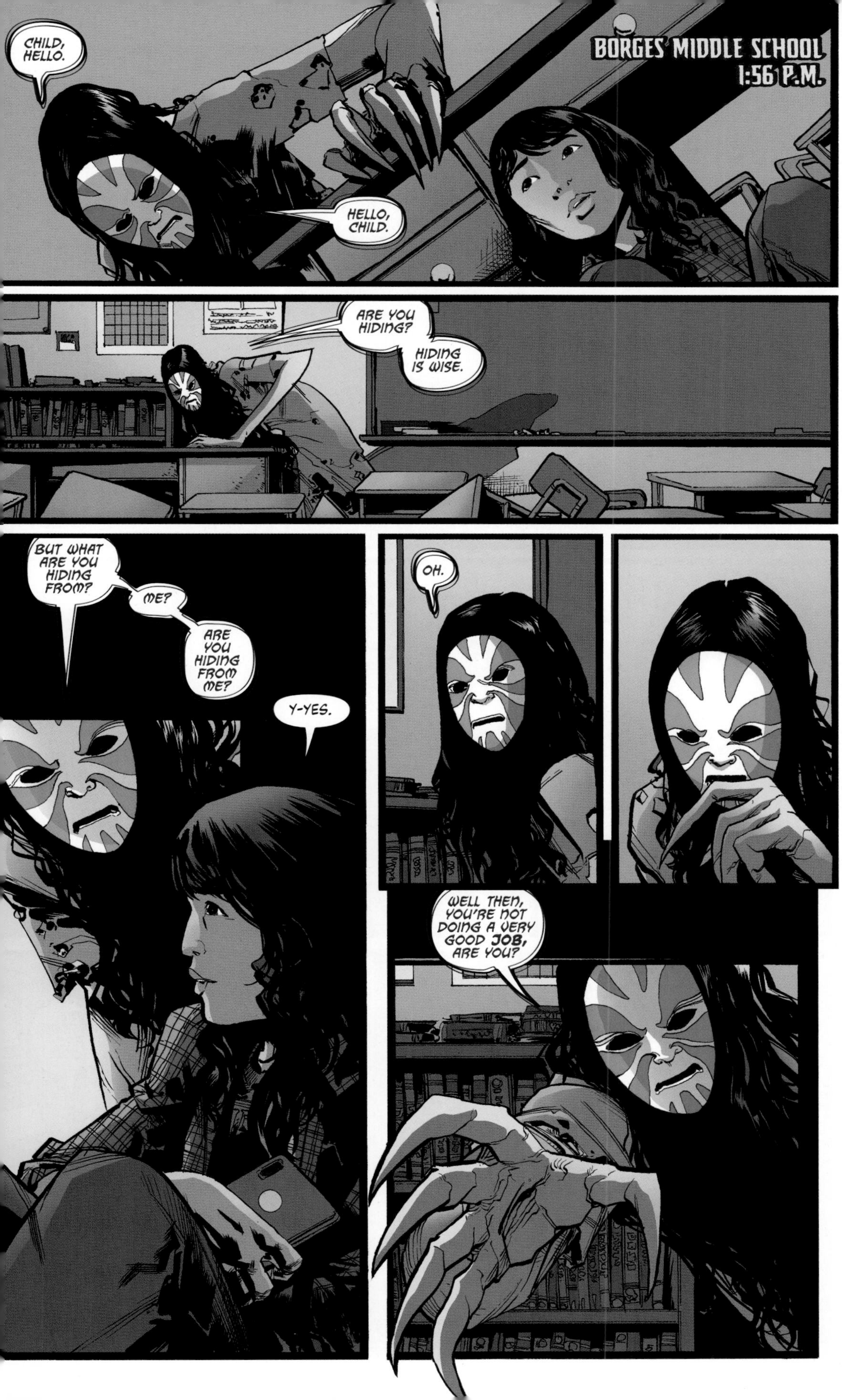

BORGES MIDDLE SCHOOL 1:56 P.M.
CHILD, HELLO.
HELLO, CHILD.
ARE YOU HIDING?
HIDING IS WISE.
BUT WHAT ARE YOU HIDING FROM?
ME?
ARE YOU HIDING FROM ME?
Y-YES.
OH.
WELL THEN, YOU'RE NOT DOING A VERY GOOD JOB, ARE YOU?

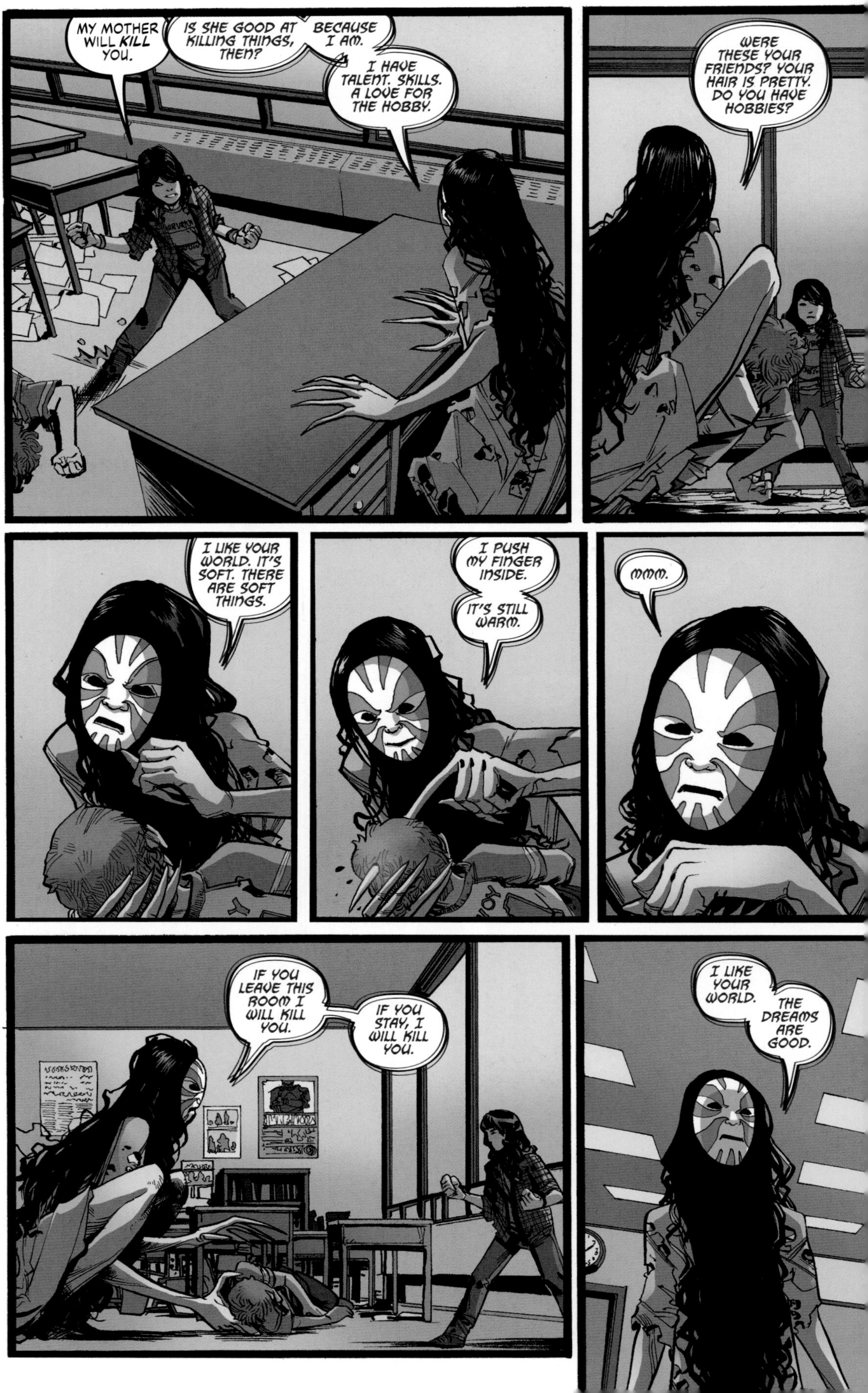
MY MOTHER WILL KILL YOU.
IS SHE GOOD AT KILLING THINGS, THEN?
BECAUSE I AM.
I HAVE TALENT. SKILLS. A LOVE FOR THE HOBBY.
WERE THESE YOUR FRIENDS? YOUR HAIR IS PRETTY. DO YOU HAVE HOBBIES?
I LIKE YOUR WORLD. IT'S SOFT. THERE ARE SOFT THINGS.
I PUSH MY FINGER INSIDE.
IT'S STILL WARM.
MMM.
IF YOU LEAVE THIS ROOM I WILL KILL YOU.
IF YOU STAY, I WILL KILL YOU.
I LIKE YOUR WORLD.
THE DREAMS ARE GOOD.

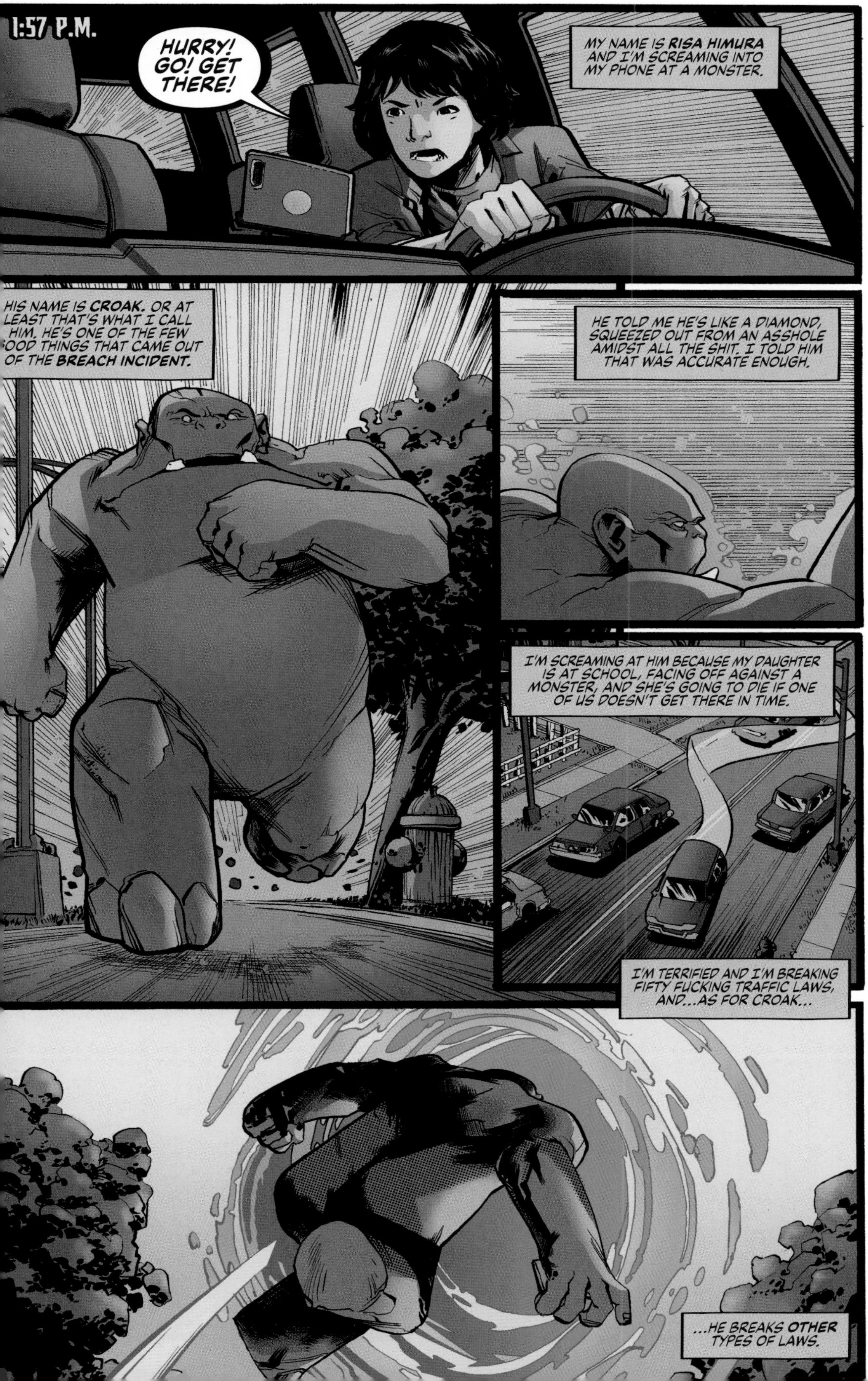
1:57 P.M.
HURRY! GO! GET THERE!
MY NAME IS RISA HIMURA AND I'M SCREAMING INTO MY PHONE AT A MONSTER.
HIS NAME IS CROAK. OR AT LEAST THAT'S WHAT I CALL HIM. HE'S ONE OF THE FEW GOOD THINGS THAT CAME OUT OF THE BREACH INCIDENT.
HE TOLD ME HE'S LIKE A DIAMOND, SQUEEZED OUT FROM AN ASSHOLE AMIDST ALL THE SHIT. I TOLD HIM THAT WAS ACCURATE ENOUGH.
I'M SCREAMING AT HIM BECAUSE MY DAUGHTER IS AT SCHOOL, FACING OFF AGAINST A MONSTER, AND SHE'S GOING TO DIE IF ONE OF US DOESN'T GET THERE IN TIME.
I'M TERRIFIED AND I'M BREAKING FIFTY FUCKING TRAFFIC LAWS, AND...AS FOR CROAK...
...HE BREAKS OTHER TYPES OF LAWS.

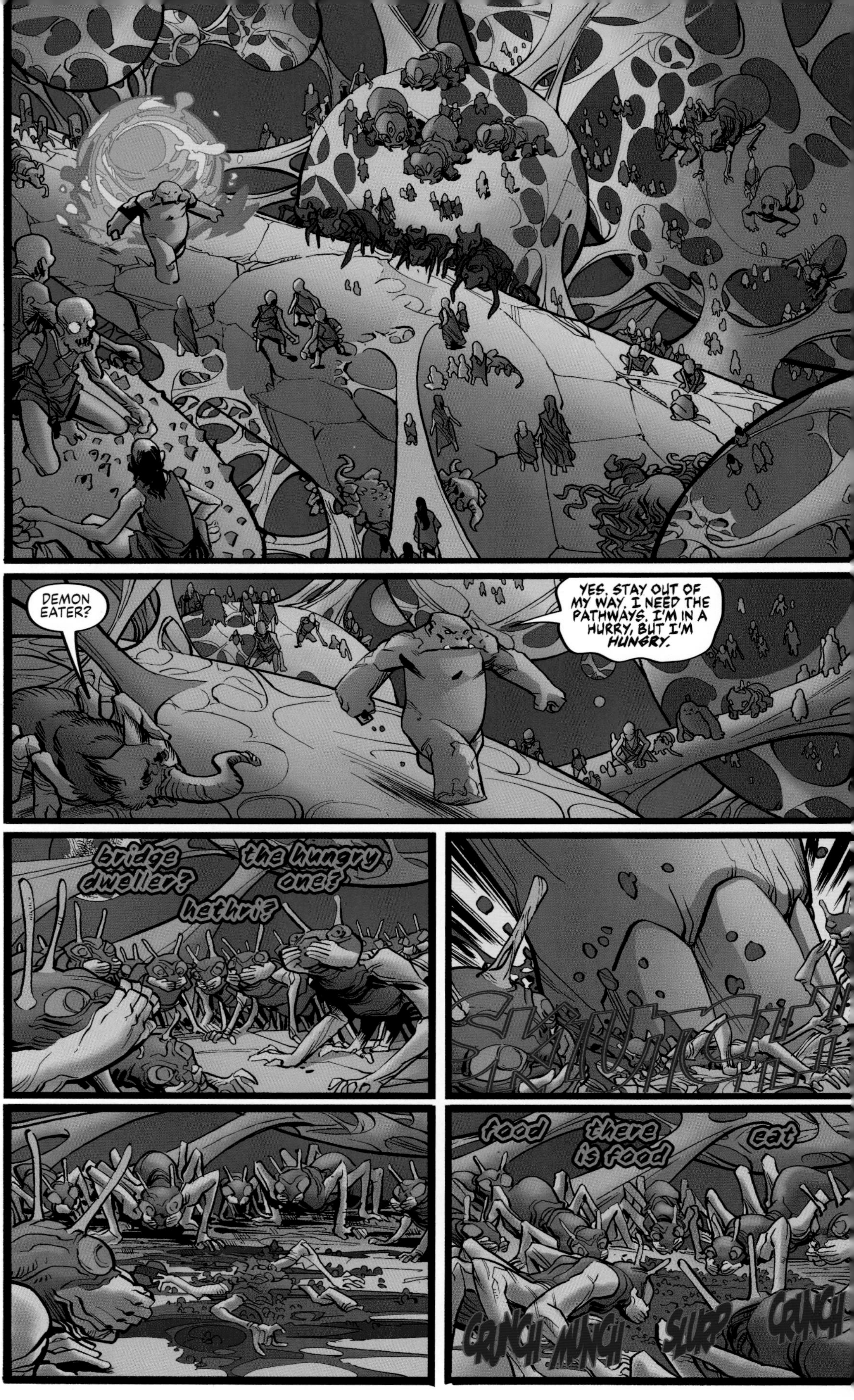
DEMON EATER?
YES. STAY OUT OF MY WAY. I NEED THE PATHWAYS. I'M IN A HURRY, BUT I'M HUNGRY.
bridge dweller?
the hungry one?
hethri?
food
there is food
eat
CRUNCH
MUNCH
SLURP
CRUNCH

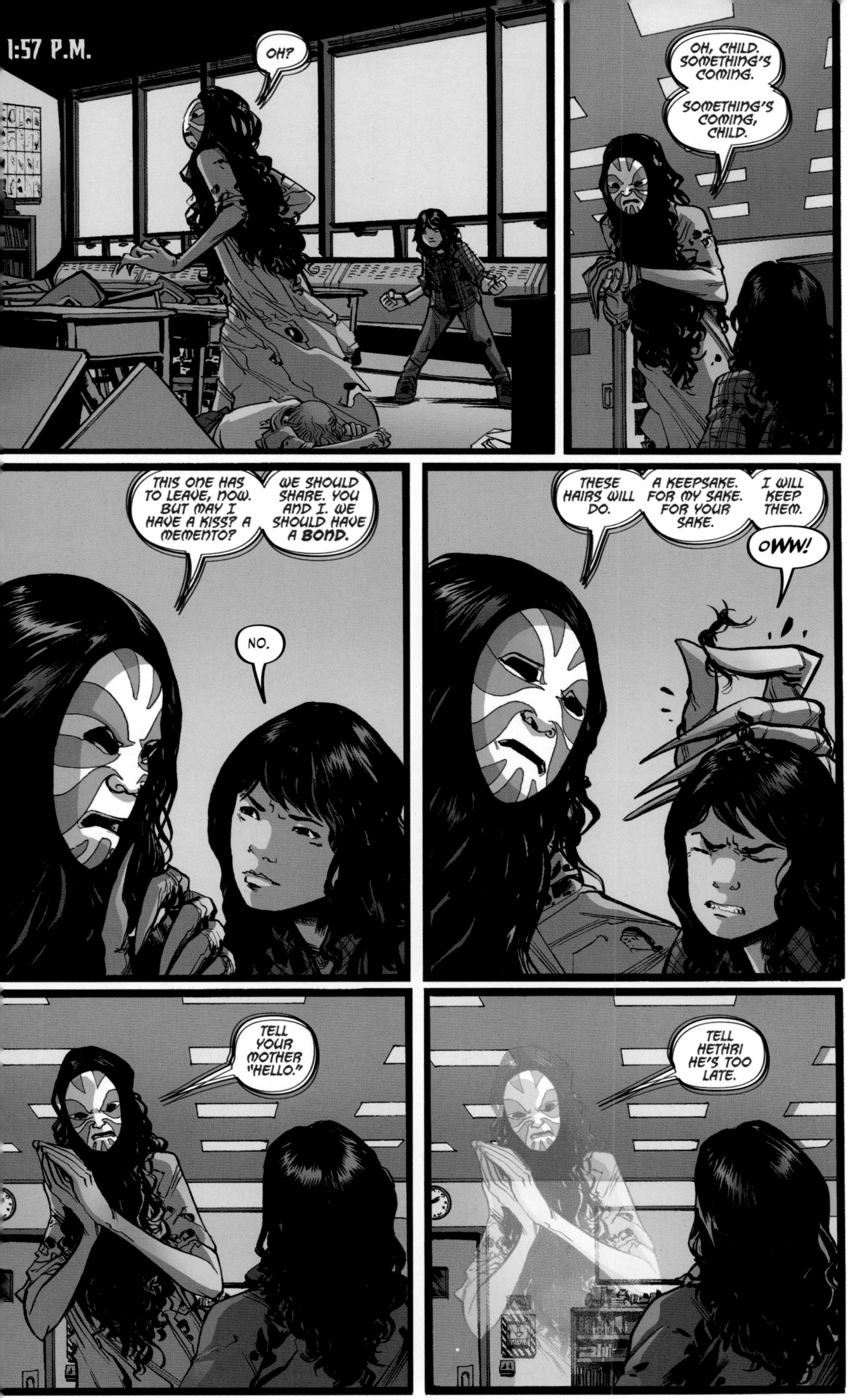
1:57 P.M.
OH?
OH, CHILD. SOMETHING'S COMING.
SOMETHING'S COMING, CHILD.
THIS ONE HAS TO LEAVE, NOW. BUT MAY I HAVE A KISS? A MEMENTO?
WE SHOULD SHARE. YOU AND I. WE SHOULD HAVE A BOND.
NO.
THESE HAIRS WILL DO.
A KEEPSAKE. FOR MY SAKE. FOR YOUR SAKE.
I WILL KEEP THEM.
OWW!
TELL YOUR MOTHER "HELLO."
TELL HETHRI HE'S TOO LATE.

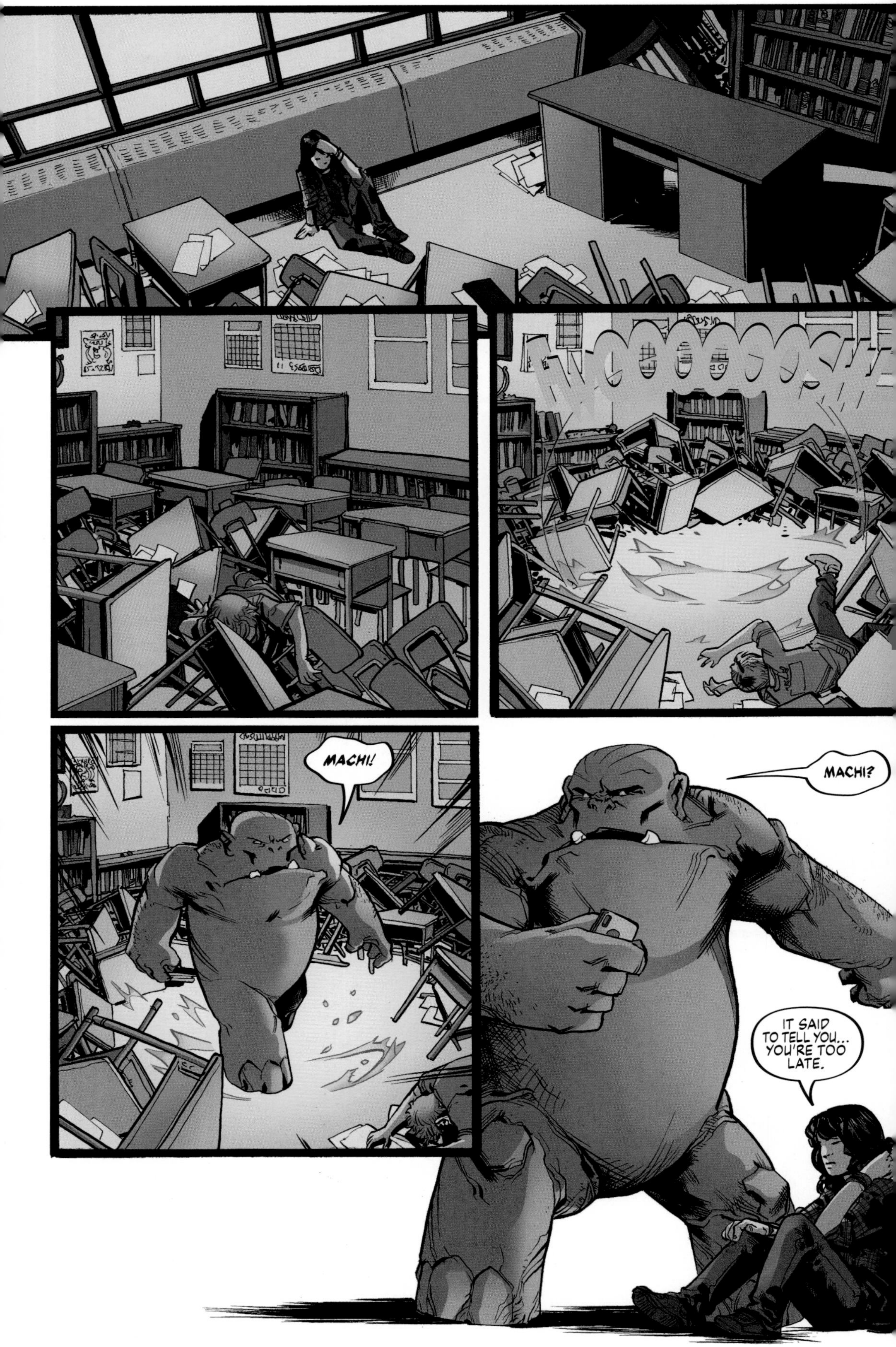
WOOOOOOOSH!
MACHI!
MACHI?
IT SAID TO TELL YOU... YOU'RE TOO LATE.

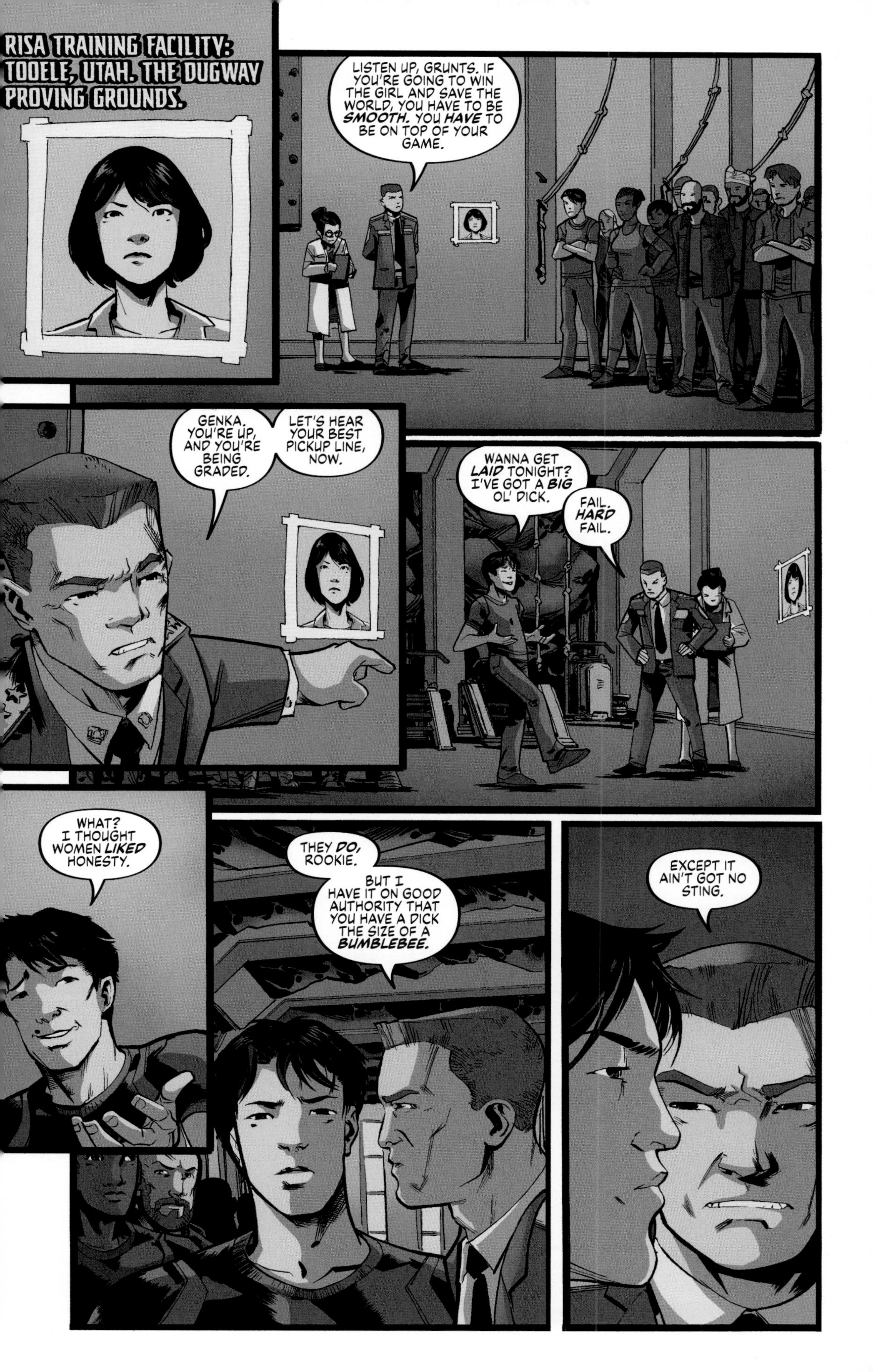
RISA TRAINING FACILITY: TOOELE, UTAH. THE DUGWAY PROVING GROUNDS.
LISTEN UP, GRUNTS. IF YOU'RE GOING TO WIN THE GIRL AND SAVE THE WORLD, YOU HAVE TO BE SMOOTH. YOU HAVE TO BE ON TOP OF YOUR GAME.
GENKA, YOU'RE UP, AND YOU'RE BEING GRADED.
LET'S HEAR YOUR BEST PICKUP LINE, NOW.
WANNA GET LAID TONIGHT? I'VE GOT A BIG OL' DICK.
FAIL. HARD FAIL.
WHAT? I THOUGHT WOMEN LIKED HONESTY.
THEY DO, ROOKIE.
BUT I HAVE IT ON GOOD AUTHORITY THAT YOU HAVE A DICK THE SIZE OF A BUMBLEBEE.
EXCEPT IT AIN'T GOT NO STING.

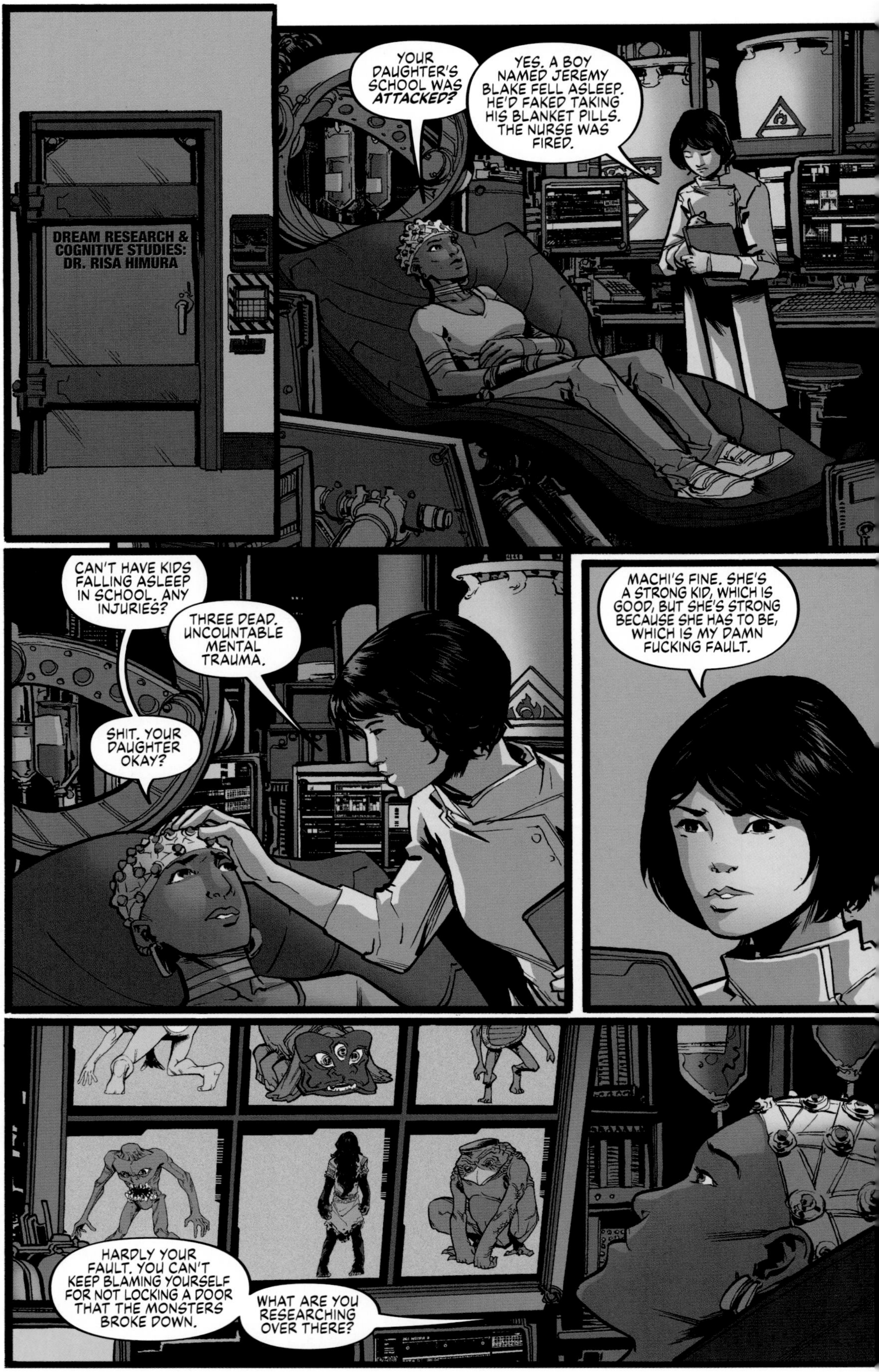
DREAM RESEARCH & COGNITIVE STUDIES: DR. RISA HIMURA
YOUR DAUGHTER'S SCHOOL WAS ATTACKED?
YES. A BOY NAMED JEREMY BLAKE FELL ASLEEP. HE'D FAKED TAKING HIS BLANKET PILLS. THE NURSE WAS FIRED.
CAN'T HAVE KIDS FALLING ASLEEP IN SCHOOL. ANY INJURIES?
THREE DEAD. UNCOUNTABLE MENTAL TRAUMA.
SHIT. YOUR DAUGHTER OKAY?
MACHI'S FINE. SHE'S A STRONG KID, WHICH IS GOOD, BUT SHE'S STRONG BECAUSE SHE HAS TO BE, WHICH IS MY DAMN FUCKING FAULT.
HARDLY YOUR FAULT. YOU CAN'T KEEP BLAMING YOURSELF FOR NOT LOCKING A DOOR THAT THE MONSTERS BROKE DOWN.
WHAT ARE YOU RESEARCHING OVER THERE?

"I'M TRYING TO FIND OUT WHAT TYPE OF MONSTER WAS AT THE SCHOOL.

SHIRIME: "BUTTOCK'S EYE" MONSTER. CONFIRMED SIGHTINGS: 1534

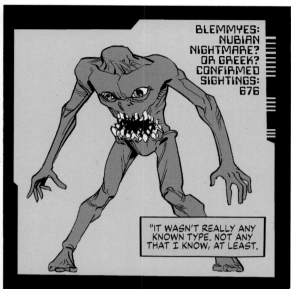

BLEMMYES: NUBIAN NIGHTMARE? OR GREEK? CONFIRMED SIGHTINGS: 676

"IT WASN'T REALLY ANY KNOWN TYPE. NOT ANY THAT I KNOW, AT LEAST.

PONTIANAK: MALAYSIAN/INDONESIAN: GHOSTS OF WOMEN WHO DIED IN CHILDBIRTH. CONFIRMED SIGHTINGS: 14,812

"IT WAS A CLASSIC 'PONTIANAK' TYPE, BUT...WITH VARIATIONS."

DIFFERENCES? I HAVEN'T HEARD MUCH IN THE WAY OF PONTIANAK VARIATIONS.

THAT'S WHAT MACHI SAYS SHE SAW, THOUGH.

A PONTIANAK. BUT WITH A KABUKI MASK. WORN OVER ITS HAIR.

A PONTIANAK WITH A KABUKI MASK? THAT'S A MIX OF TWO DIFFERENT CULTURES. THAT...THAT IS UNUSUAL.

YEAH. I HOPE WE'RE NOT DEALING WITH SOMETHING NEW.

WE STILL CAN'T HANDLE THE OLD.

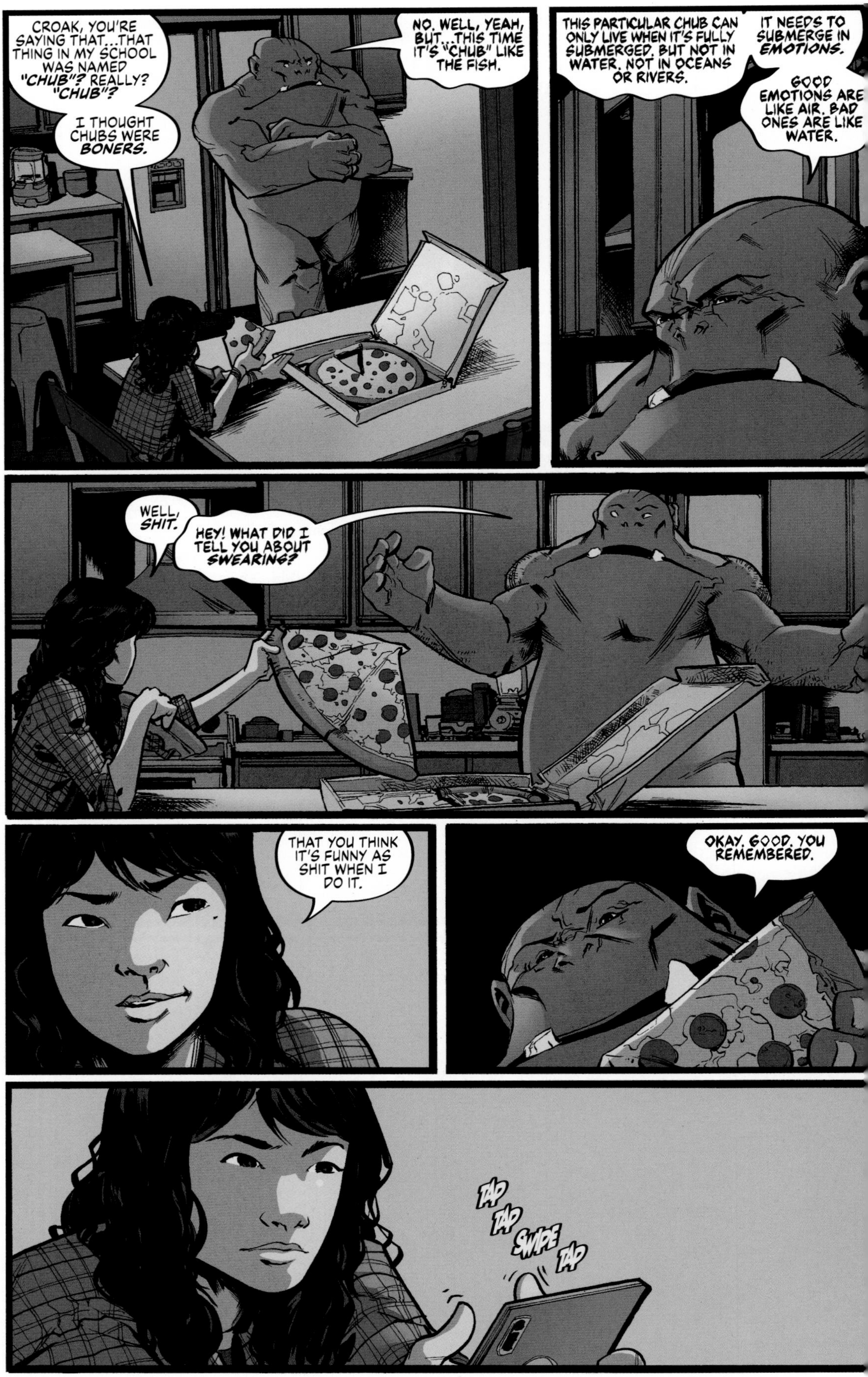
CROAK, YOU'RE SAYING THAT...THAT THING IN MY SCHOOL WAS NAMED "CHUB"? REALLY? "CHUB"?
I THOUGHT CHUBS WERE BONERS.
NO. WELL, YEAH, BUT...THIS TIME IT'S "CHUB" LIKE THE FISH.
THIS PARTICULAR CHUB CAN ONLY LIVE WHEN IT'S FULLY SUBMERGED. BUT NOT IN WATER. NOT IN OCEANS OR RIVERS.
IT NEEDS TO SUBMERGE IN EMOTIONS.
GOOD EMOTIONS ARE LIKE AIR. BAD ONES ARE LIKE WATER.
WELL, SHIT.
HEY! WHAT DID I TELL YOU ABOUT SWEARING?
THAT YOU THINK IT'S FUNNY AS SHIT WHEN I DO IT.
OKAY. GOOD. YOU REMEMBERED.
TAP
TAP
SWIPE
TAP

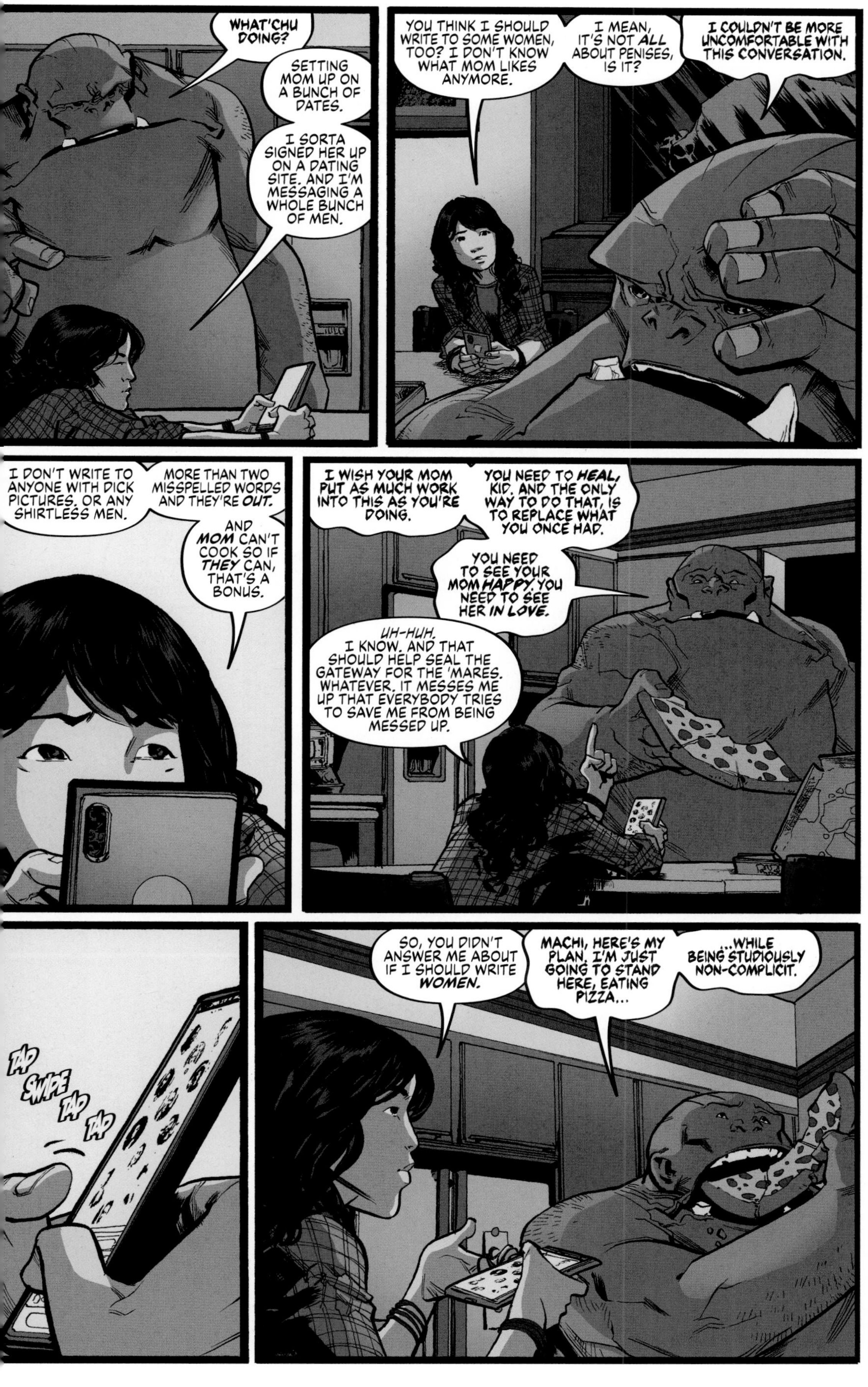
WHAT'CHU DOING?
SETTING MOM UP ON A BUNCH OF DATES.
I SORTA SIGNED HER UP ON A DATING SITE. AND I'M MESSAGING A WHOLE BUNCH OF MEN.
YOU THINK I SHOULD WRITE TO SOME WOMEN, TOO? I DON'T KNOW WHAT MOM LIKES ANYMORE.
I MEAN, IT'S NOT ALL ABOUT PENISES, IS IT?
I COULDN'T BE MORE UNCOMFORTABLE WITH THIS CONVERSATION.
I DON'T WRITE TO ANYONE WITH DICK PICTURES. OR ANY SHIRTLESS MEN.
MORE THAN TWO MISSPELLED WORDS AND THEY'RE OUT.
AND MOM CAN'T COOK SO IF THEY CAN, THAT'S A BONUS.
I WISH YOUR MOM PUT AS MUCH WORK INTO THIS AS YOU'RE DOING.
YOU NEED TO HEAL, KID. AND THE ONLY WAY TO DO THAT, IS TO REPLACE WHAT YOU ONCE HAD.
YOU NEED TO SEE YOUR MOM HAPPY. YOU NEED TO SEE HER IN LOVE.
UH-HUH. I KNOW. AND THAT SHOULD HELP SEAL THE GATEWAY FOR THE 'MARES. WHATEVER. IT MESSES ME UP THAT EVERYBODY TRIES TO SAVE ME FROM BEING MESSED UP.
TAP
SWIPE
TAP
TAP
SO, YOU DIDN'T ANSWER ME ABOUT IF I SHOULD WRITE WOMEN.
MACHI, HERE'S MY PLAN. I'M JUST GOING TO STAND HERE, EATING PIZZA...
...WHILE BEING STUDIOUSLY NON-COMPLICIT.

RISA TRAINING FACILITY. TOOELE, UTAH.

HERE'S WHAT WE GOT, PEOPLE. YESTERDAY, A NEW TYPE OF 'MARE APPEARED AND ALMOST TOOK DOWN MACHI WHEN *WE* WERE ALL SITTING AROUND DIDDLING OURSELVES AND PLAYING KISSY-FACE WITH PILLOWS.

SO HERE'S WHAT WE'RE GOING TO DO.

"WE'RE RAMPING UP ON THE TRAINING. CONDENSING THE COURSE. FINAL EXAMS ARE IN TWO WEEKS. PREPARE TO GET ABOUT FOUR MINUTES OF SLEEP A DAY UNTIL THEN. BUT HEY..."

...WHO WANTS TO DREAM THEIR DAYS AWAY, ANYWAY?

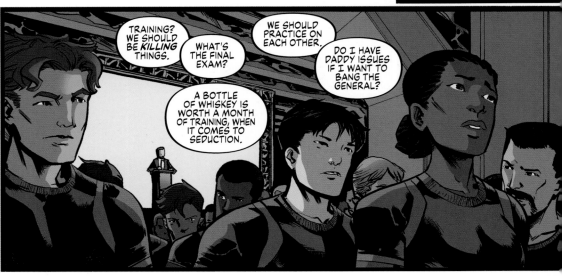

TRAINING? WE SHOULD BE *KILLING* THINGS.

WHAT'S THE FINAL EXAM?

WE SHOULD PRACTICE ON EACH OTHER.

DO I HAVE DADDY ISSUES IF I WANT TO BANG THE GENERAL?

A BOTTLE OF WHISKEY IS WORTH A MONTH OF TRAINING, WHEN IT COMES TO SEDUCTION.

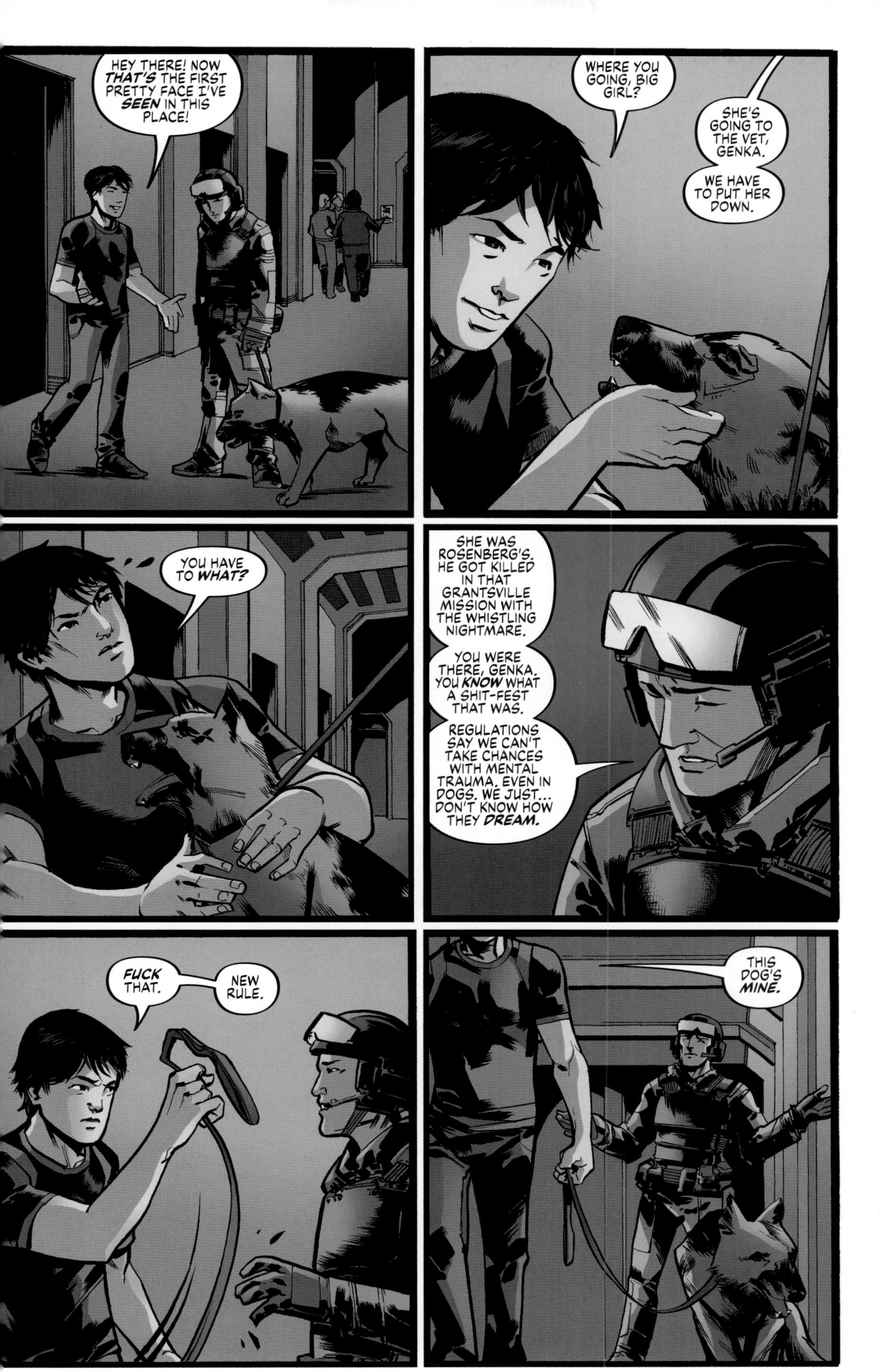
HEY THERE! NOW *THAT'S* THE FIRST PRETTY FACE I'VE *SEEN* IN THIS PLACE!
WHERE YOU GOING, BIG GIRL?
SHE'S GOING TO THE VET, GENKA.
WE HAVE TO PUT HER DOWN.
YOU HAVE TO *WHAT?*
SHE WAS ROSENBERG'S. HE GOT KILLED IN THAT GRANTSVILLE MISSION WITH THE WHISTLING NIGHTMARE.
YOU WERE THERE, GENKA. YOU *KNOW* WHAT A SHIT-FEST THAT WAS.
REGULATIONS SAY WE CAN'T TAKE CHANCES WITH MENTAL TRAUMA, EVEN IN DOGS. WE JUST... DON'T KNOW HOW THEY *DREAM.*
FUCK THAT.
NEW RULE.
THIS DOG'S *MINE.*

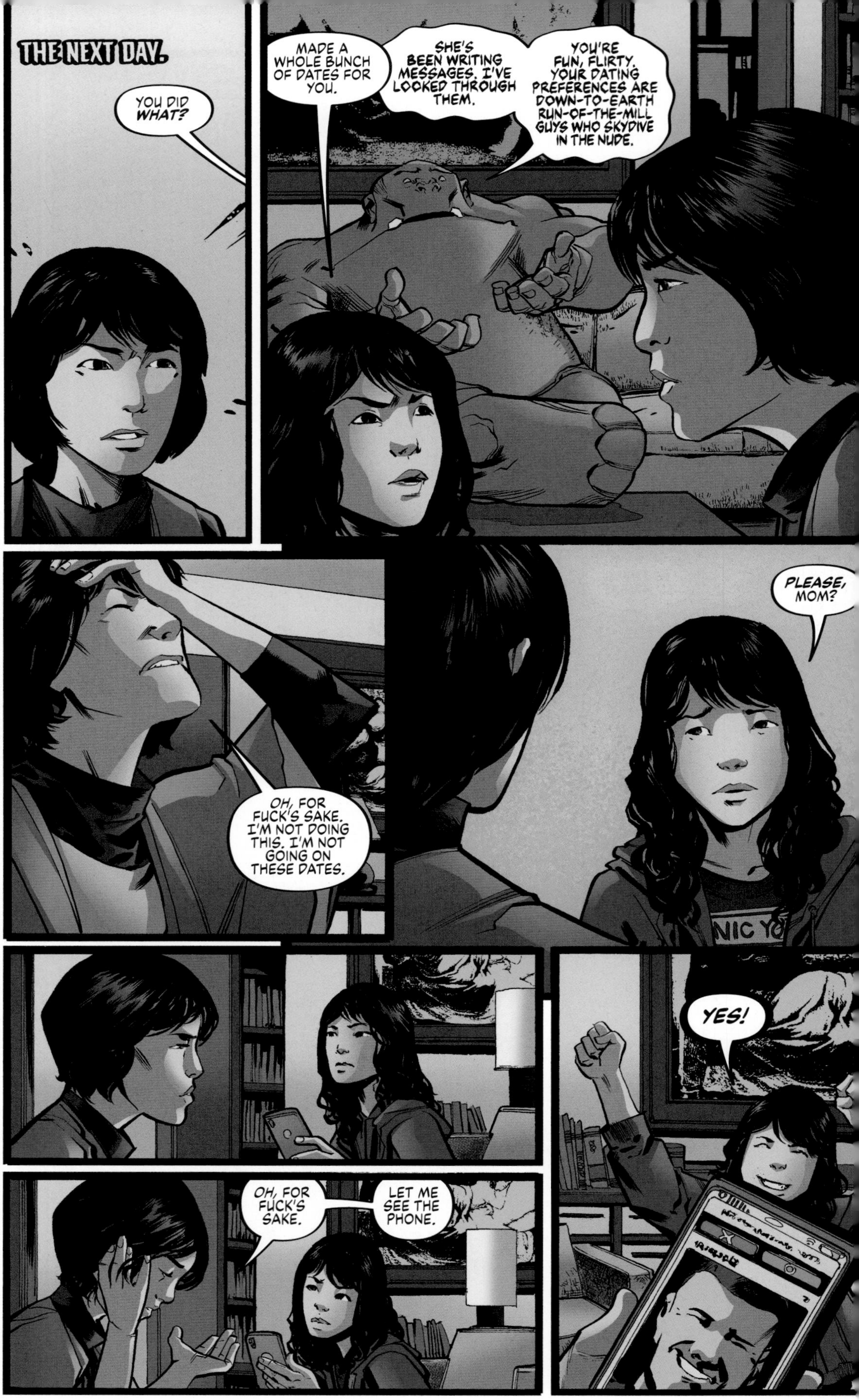
THE NEXT DAY.
YOU DID WHAT?
MADE A WHOLE BUNCH OF DATES FOR YOU.
SHE'S BEEN WRITING MESSAGES. I'VE LOOKED THROUGH THEM.
YOU'RE FUN, FLIRTY. YOUR DATING PREFERENCES ARE DOWN-TO-EARTH RUN-OF-THE-MILL GUYS WHO SKYDIVE IN THE NUDE.
OH, FOR FUCK'S SAKE. I'M NOT DOING THIS. I'M NOT GOING ON THESE DATES.
PLEASE, MOM?
OH, FOR FUCK'S SAKE.
LET ME SEE THE PHONE.
YES!

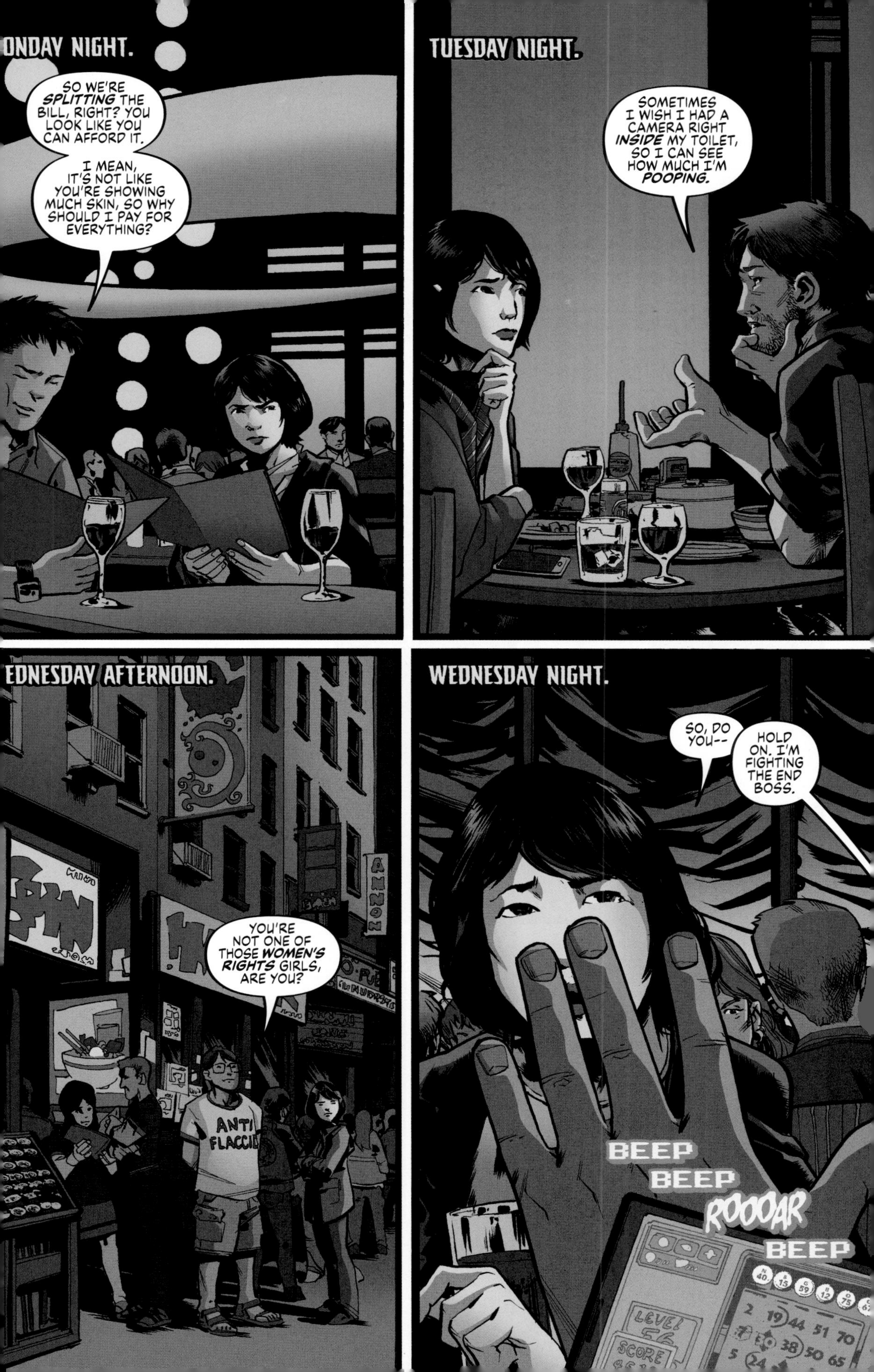
ONDAY NIGHT.
SO WE'RE SPLITTING THE BILL, RIGHT? YOU LOOK LIKE YOU CAN AFFORD IT.
I MEAN, IT'S NOT LIKE YOU'RE SHOWING MUCH SKIN, SO WHY SHOULD I PAY FOR EVERYTHING?
TUESDAY NIGHT.
SOMETIMES I WISH I HAD A CAMERA RIGHT INSIDE MY TOILET, SO I CAN SEE HOW MUCH I'M POOPING.
EDNESDAY AFTERNOON.
YOU'RE NOT ONE OF THOSE WOMEN'S RIGHTS GIRLS, ARE YOU?
ANTI FLACCID
WEDNESDAY NIGHT.
SO, DO YOU--
HOLD ON. I'M FIGHTING THE END BOSS.
BEEP
BEEP
ROOOAR
BEEP
LEVEL 56
SCORE

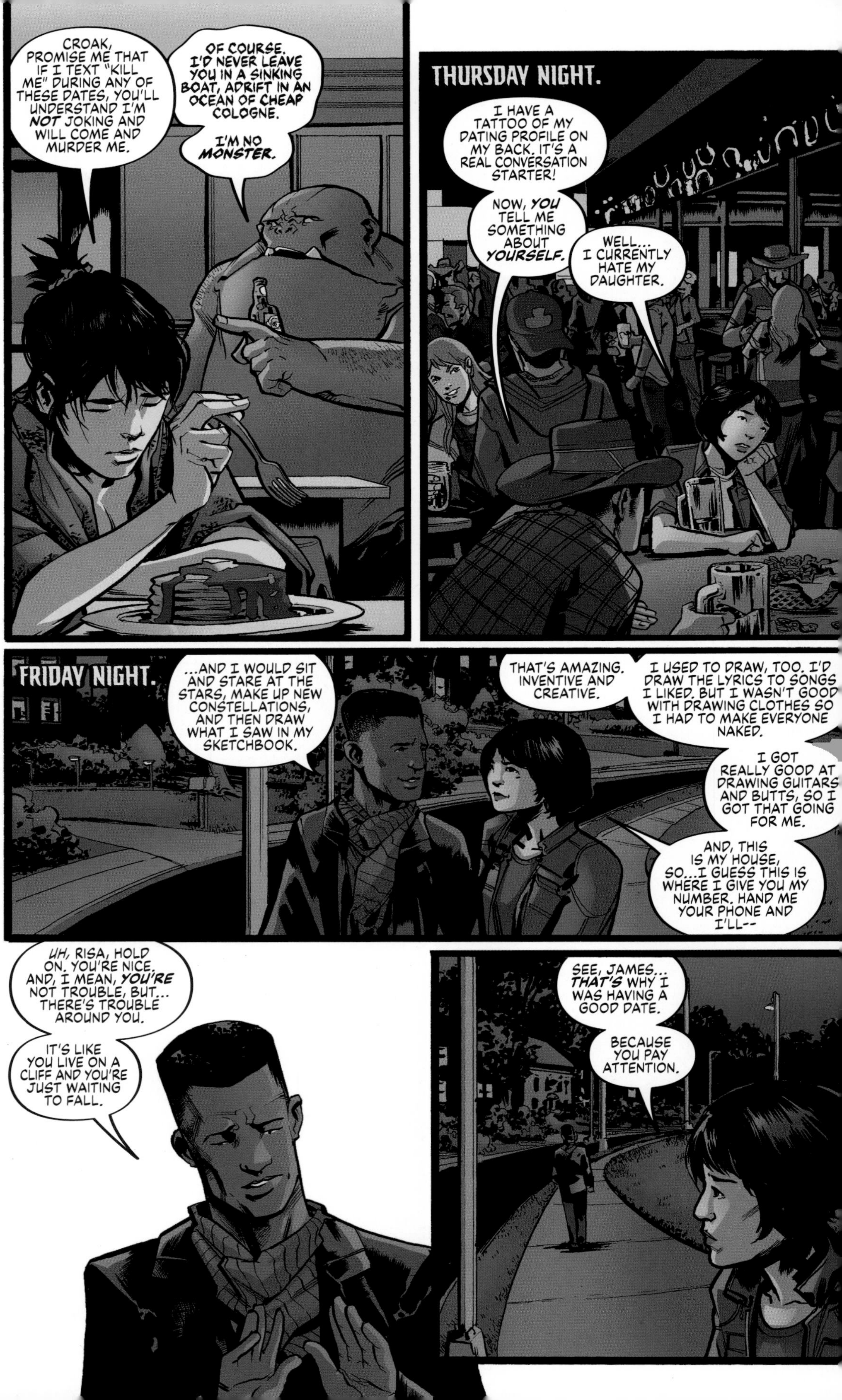
CROAK, PROMISE ME THAT IF I TEXT "KILL ME" DURING ANY OF THESE DATES, YOU'LL UNDERSTAND I'M NOT JOKING AND WILL COME AND MURDER ME.
OF COURSE. I'D NEVER LEAVE YOU IN A SINKING BOAT, ADRIFT IN AN OCEAN OF CHEAP COLOGNE.
I'M NO MONSTER.
THURSDAY NIGHT.
I HAVE A TATTOO OF MY DATING PROFILE ON MY BACK. IT'S A REAL CONVERSATION STARTER!
NOW, YOU TELL ME SOMETHING ABOUT YOURSELF.
WELL... I CURRENTLY HATE MY DAUGHTER.
FRIDAY NIGHT.
...AND I WOULD SIT AND STARE AT THE STARS, MAKE UP NEW CONSTELLATIONS, AND THEN DRAW WHAT I SAW IN MY SKETCHBOOK.
THAT'S AMAZING. INVENTIVE AND CREATIVE.
I USED TO DRAW, TOO. I'D DRAW THE LYRICS TO SONGS I LIKED. BUT I WASN'T GOOD WITH DRAWING CLOTHES SO I HAD TO MAKE EVERYONE NAKED.
I GOT REALLY GOOD AT DRAWING GUITARS AND BUTTS, SO I GOT THAT GOING FOR ME.
AND, THIS IS MY HOUSE, SO...I GUESS THIS IS WHERE I GIVE YOU MY NUMBER. HAND ME YOUR PHONE AND I'LL--
UH, RISA, HOLD ON. YOU'RE NICE. AND, I MEAN, YOU'RE NOT TROUBLE, BUT... THERE'S TROUBLE AROUND YOU.
IT'S LIKE YOU LIVE ON A CLIFF AND YOU'RE JUST WAITING TO FALL.
SEE, JAMES... THAT'S WHY I WAS HAVING A GOOD DATE.
BECAUSE YOU PAY ATTENTION.

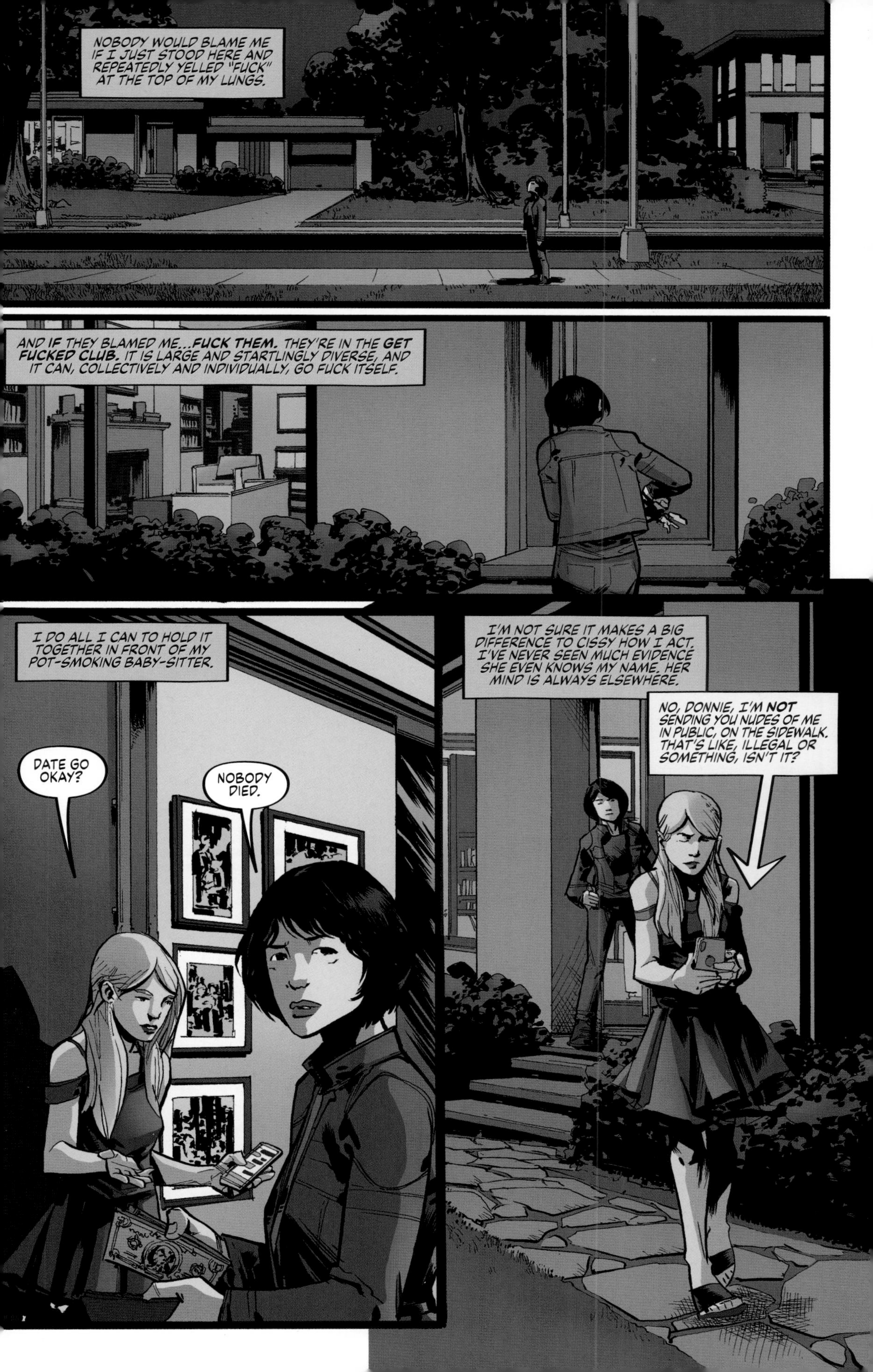
NOBODY WOULD BLAME ME IF I JUST STOOD HERE AND REPEATEDLY YELLED "FUCK" AT THE TOP OF MY LUNGS.
AND IF THEY BLAMED ME...FUCK THEM. THEY'RE IN THE GET FUCKED CLUB. IT IS LARGE AND STARTLINGLY DIVERSE, AND IT CAN, COLLECTIVELY AND INDIVIDUALLY, GO FUCK ITSELF.
I DO ALL I CAN TO HOLD IT TOGETHER IN FRONT OF MY POT-SMOKING BABY-SITTER.
DATE GO OKAY?
NOBODY DIED.
I'M NOT SURE IT MAKES A BIG DIFFERENCE TO CISSY HOW I ACT. I'VE NEVER SEEN MUCH EVIDENCE SHE EVEN KNOWS MY NAME. HER MIND IS ALWAYS ELSEWHERE.
NO, DONNIE, I'M NOT SENDING YOU NUDES OF ME IN PUBLIC, ON THE SIDEWALK. THAT'S LIKE, ILLEGAL OR SOMETHING, ISN'T IT?

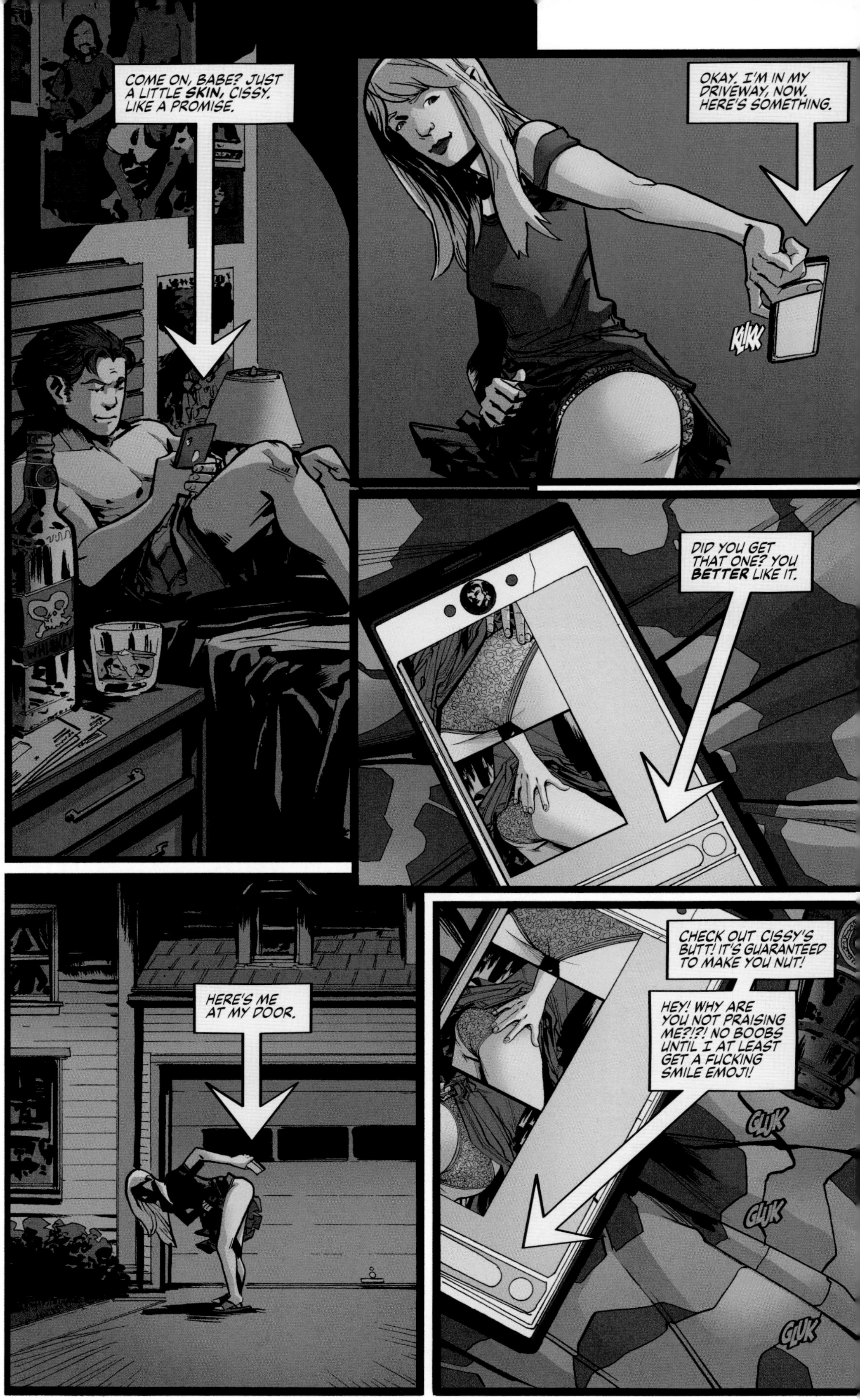
COME ON, BABE? JUST A LITTLE **SKIN**, CISSY. LIKE A PROMISE.
OKAY. I'M IN MY DRIVEWAY, NOW. HERE'S SOMETHING.
KLIKK
DID YOU GET THAT ONE? YOU **BETTER** LIKE IT.
HERE'S ME AT MY DOOR.
CHECK OUT CISSY'S BUTT! IT'S GUARANTEED TO MAKE YOU NUT!
HEY! WHY ARE YOU NOT PRAISING ME?!?! NO BOOBS UNTIL I AT LEAST GET A FUCKING SMILE EMOJI!
GLUK
GLUK
GLUK

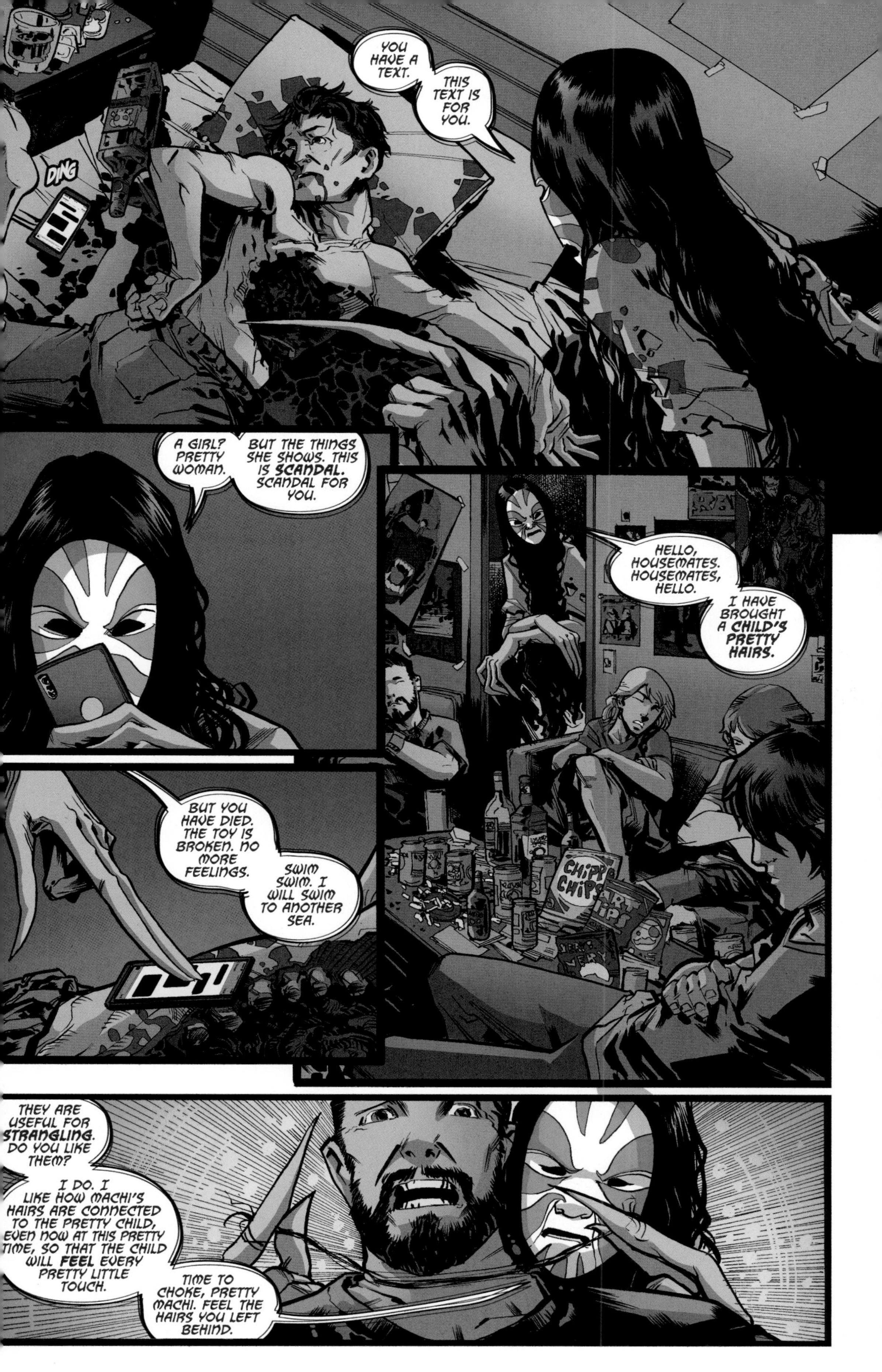
YOU HAVE A TEXT.
THIS TEXT IS FOR YOU.
DING
A GIRL? PRETTY WOMAN.
BUT THE THINGS SHE SHOWS. THIS IS SCANDAL. SCANDAL FOR YOU.
BUT YOU HAVE DIED. THE TOY IS BROKEN. NO MORE FEELINGS.
SWIM SWIM. I WILL SWIM TO ANOTHER SEA.
HELLO, HOUSEMATES. HOUSEMATES, HELLO.
I HAVE BROUGHT A CHILD'S PRETTY HAIRS.
THEY ARE USEFUL FOR STRANGLING. DO YOU LIKE THEM?
I DO. I LIKE HOW MACHI'S HAIRS ARE CONNECTED TO THE PRETTY CHILD, EVEN NOW AT THIS PRETTY TIME, SO THAT THE CHILD WILL FEEL EVERY PRETTY LITTLE TOUCH.
TIME TO CHOKE, PRETTY MACHI. FEEL THE HAIRS YOU LEFT BEHIND.

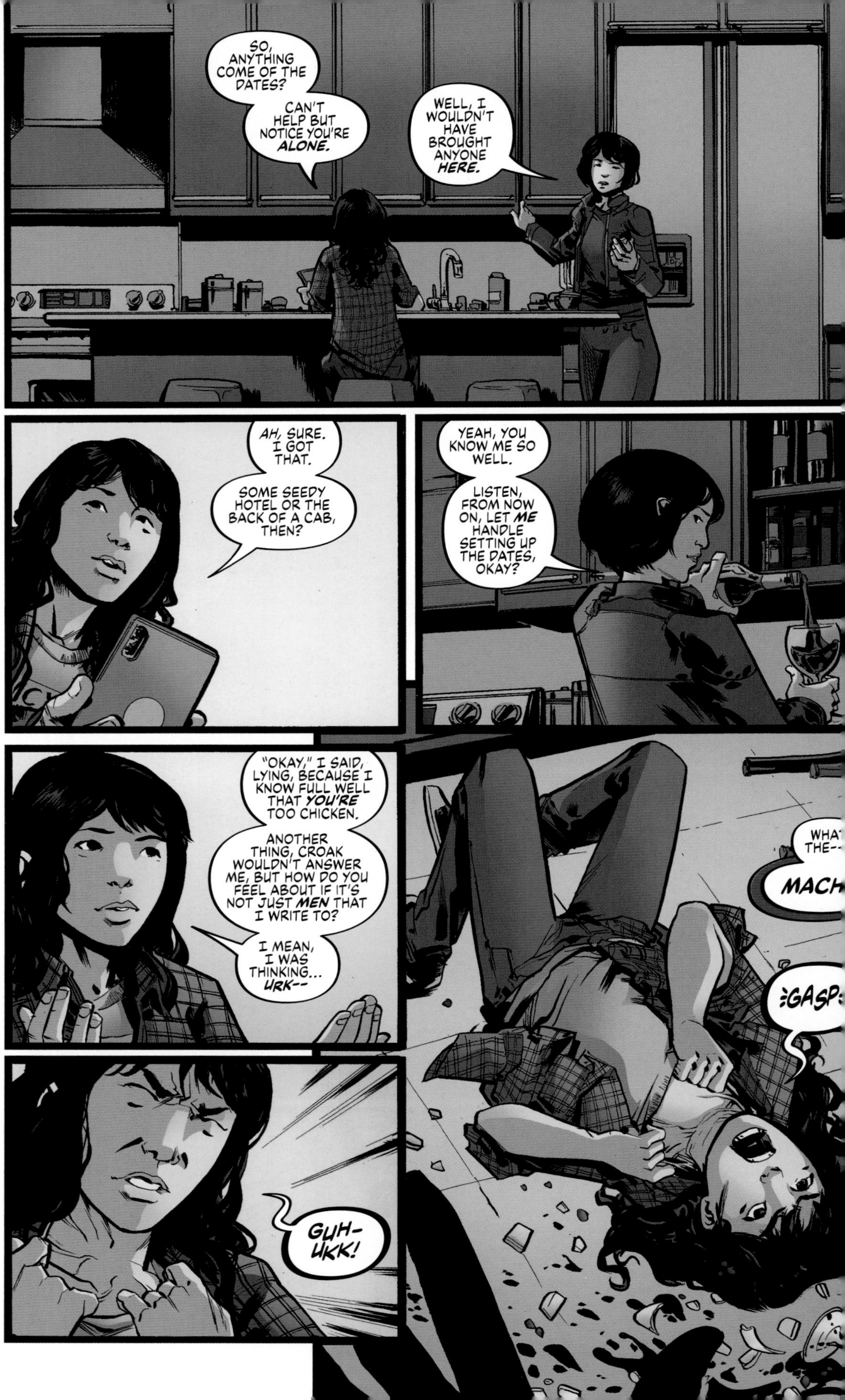
SO, ANYTHING COME OF THE DATES?
CAN'T HELP BUT NOTICE YOU'RE *ALONE.*
WELL, I WOULDN'T HAVE BROUGHT ANYONE *HERE.*
AH, SURE. I GOT THAT.
SOME SEEDY HOTEL OR THE BACK OF A CAB, THEN?
YEAH, YOU KNOW ME SO WELL.
LISTEN, FROM NOW ON, LET *ME* HANDLE SETTING UP THE DATES, OKAY?
"OKAY," I SAID, LYING, BECAUSE I KNOW FULL WELL THAT *YOU'RE* TOO CHICKEN.
ANOTHER THING, CROAK WOULDN'T ANSWER ME, BUT HOW DO YOU FEEL ABOUT IF IT'S NOT *JUST MEN* THAT I WRITE TO?
I MEAN, I WAS THINKING... *URK--*
GUH-UKK!
WHA THE--
MACH
GASP

3

THE FOX CONSULTATION

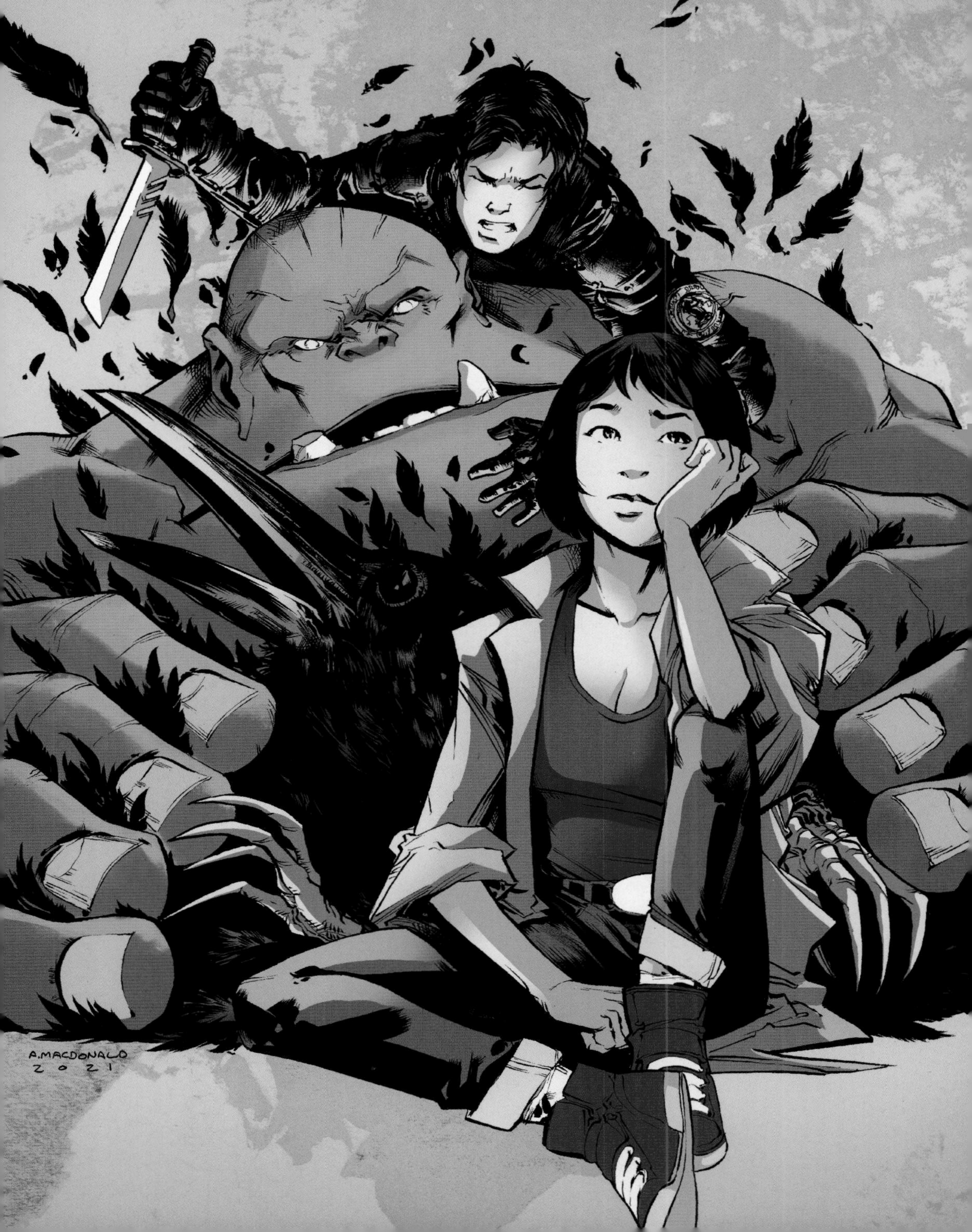
A.MACDONALD
2021

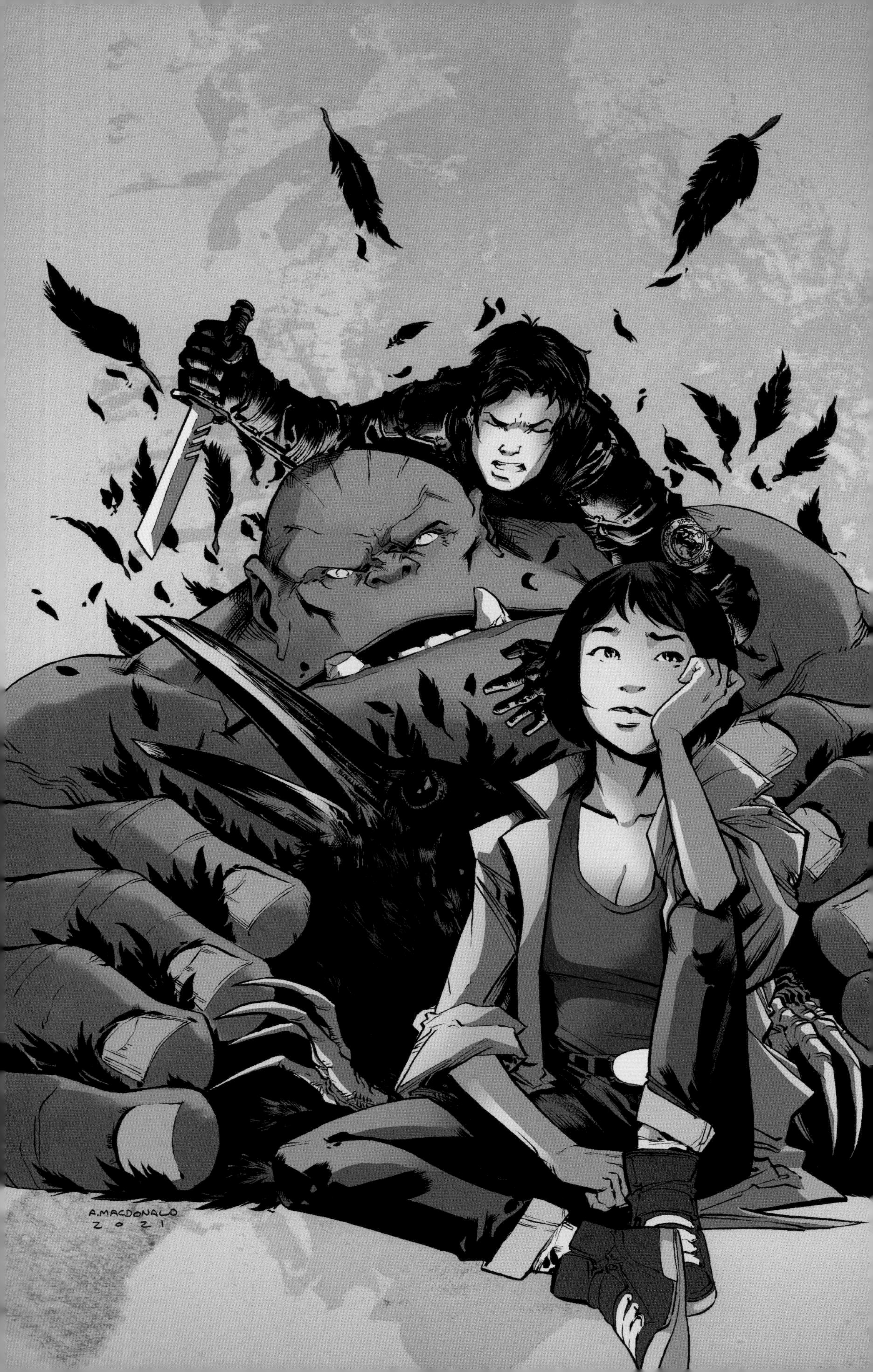
A.MACDONALD
2021

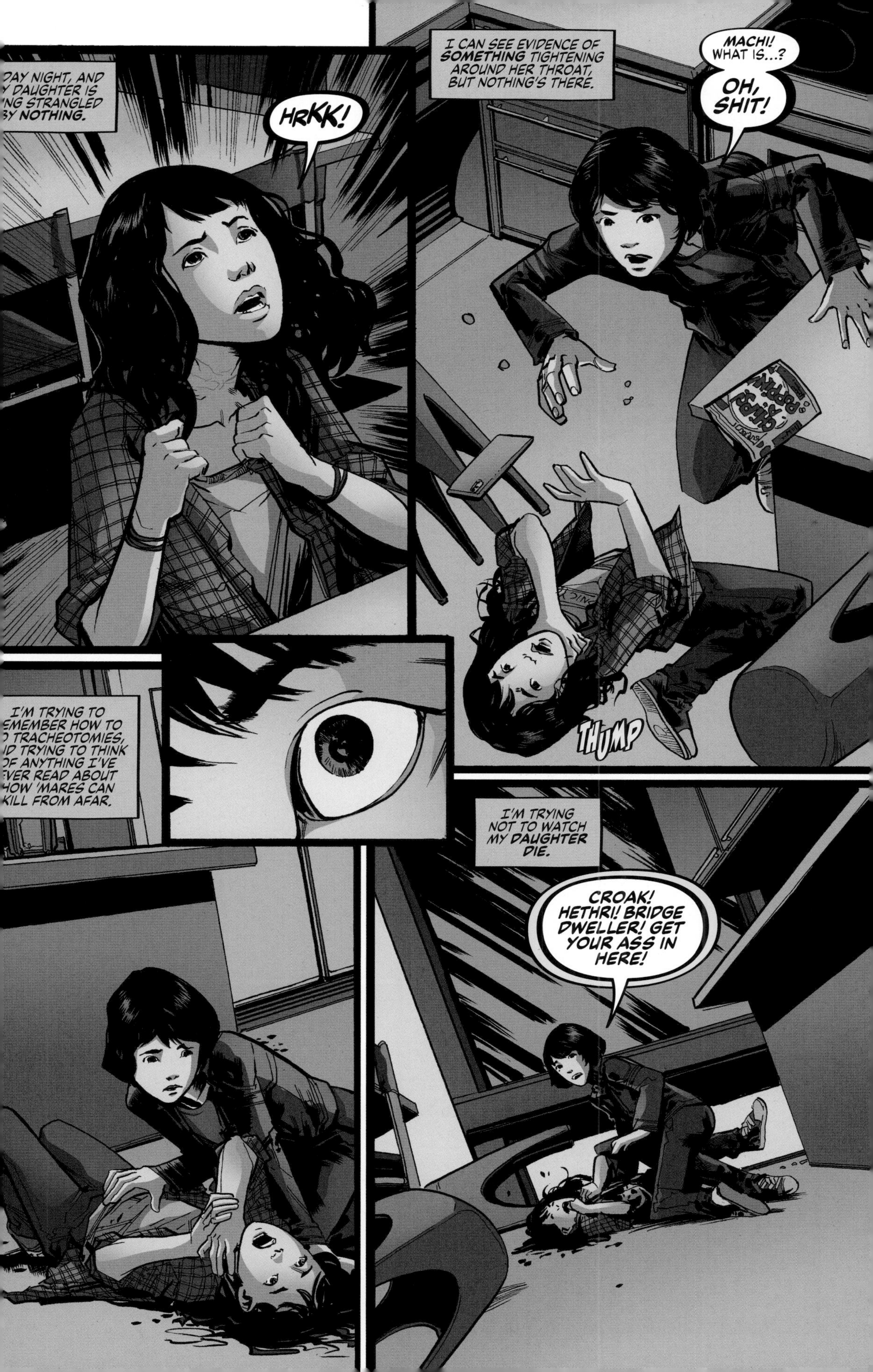
DAY NIGHT, AND
Y DAUGHTER IS
NG STRANGLED
BY NOTHING.
HRKK!
I CAN SEE EVIDENCE OF SOMETHING TIGHTENING AROUND HER THROAT, BUT NOTHING'S THERE.
MACHI! WHAT IS...?
OH, SHIT!
THUMP
I'M TRYING TO
EMEMBER HOW TO
D TRACHEOTOMIES,
ID TRYING TO THINK
OF ANYTHING I'VE
EVER READ ABOUT
HOW 'MARES CAN
KILL FROM AFAR.
I'M TRYING NOT TO WATCH MY DAUGHTER DIE.
CROAK! HETHRI! BRIDGE DWELLER! GET YOUR ASS IN HERE!

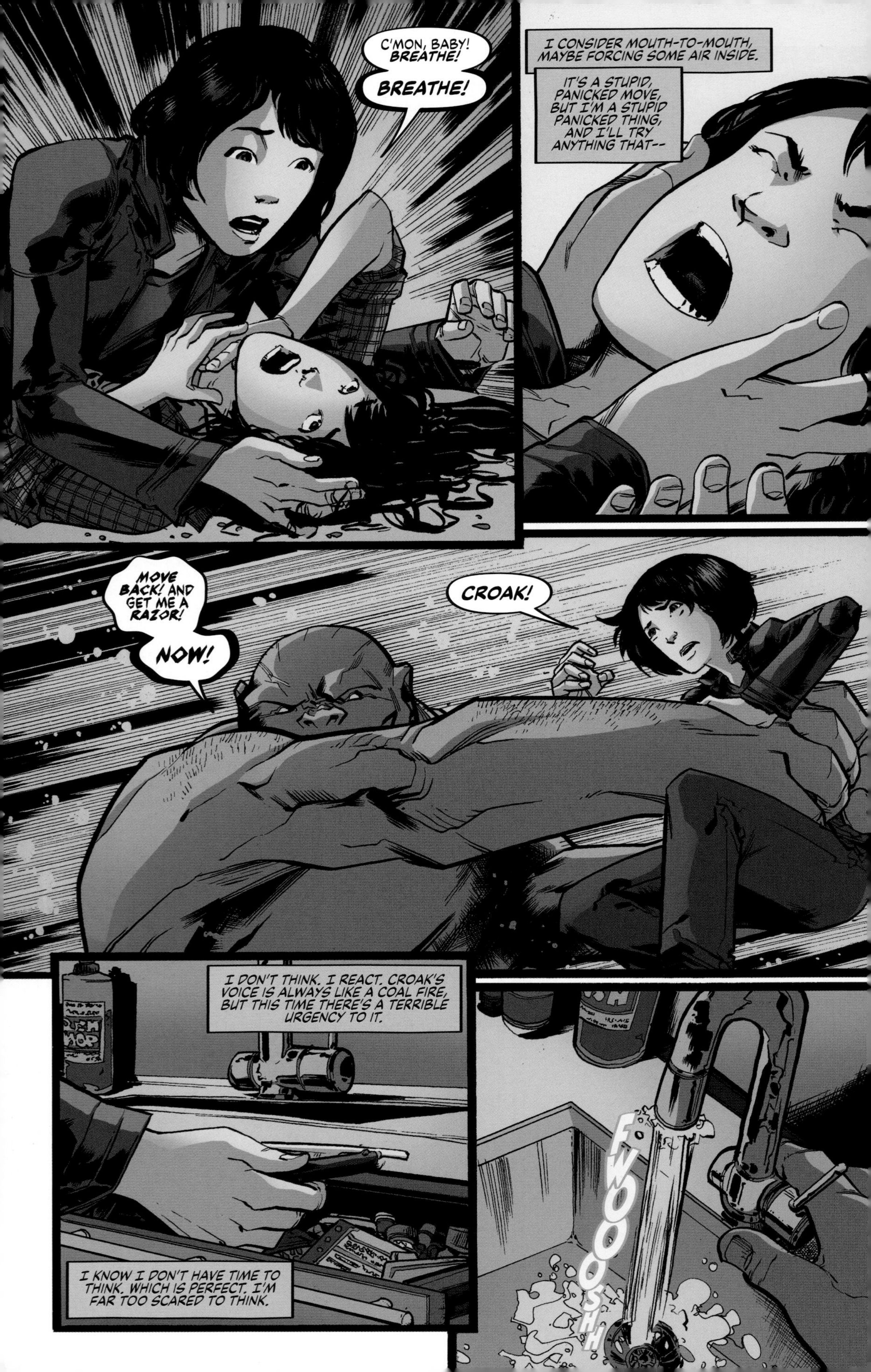
C'MON, BABY! BREATHE!
BREATHE!
I CONSIDER MOUTH-TO-MOUTH, MAYBE FORCING SOME AIR INSIDE.
IT'S A STUPID, PANICKED MOVE, BUT I'M A STUPID PANICKED THING, AND I'LL TRY ANYTHING THAT--
MOVE BACK! AND GET ME A RAZOR!
NOW!
CROAK!
I DON'T THINK. I REACT. CROAK'S VOICE IS ALWAYS LIKE A COAL FIRE, BUT THIS TIME THERE'S A TERRIBLE URGENCY TO IT.
I KNOW I DON'T HAVE TIME TO THINK. WHICH IS PERFECT. I'M FAR TOO SCARED TO THINK.
FWOOOOSHH

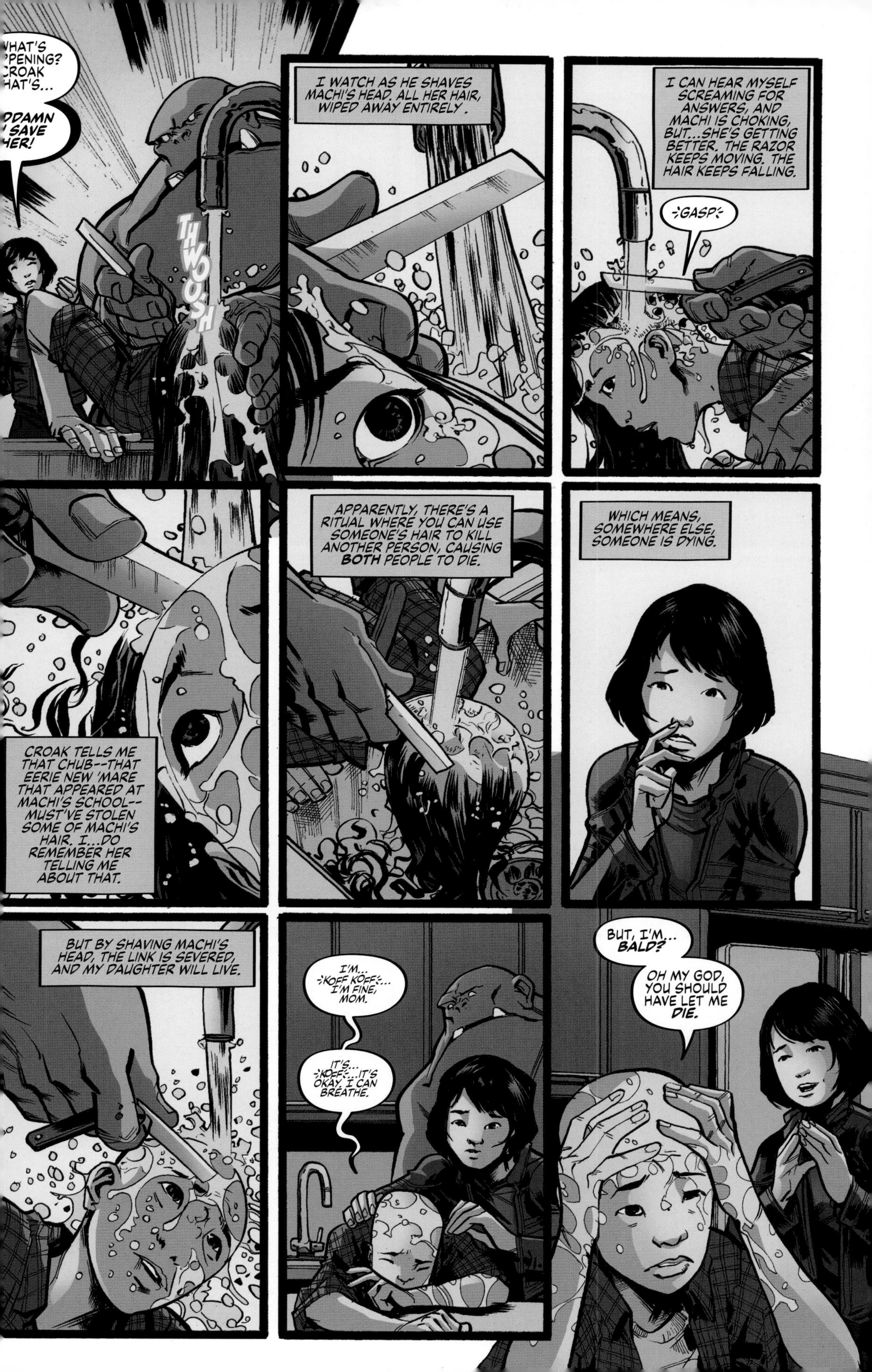

WHAT'S PPENING? CROAK HAT'S...
DDAMN SAVE HER!
THWOOSH
I WATCH AS HE SHAVES MACHI'S HEAD. ALL HER HAIR, WIPED AWAY ENTIRELY.
I CAN HEAR MYSELF SCREAMING FOR ANSWERS, AND MACHI IS CHOKING, BUT...SHE'S GETTING BETTER. THE RAZOR KEEPS MOVING. THE HAIR KEEPS FALLING.
GASP
CROAK TELLS ME THAT CHUB--THAT EERIE NEW 'MARE THAT APPEARED AT MACHI'S SCHOOL--MUST'VE STOLEN SOME OF MACHI'S HAIR. I...DO REMEMBER HER TELLING ME ABOUT THAT.
APPARENTLY, THERE'S A RITUAL WHERE YOU CAN USE SOMEONE'S HAIR TO KILL ANOTHER PERSON, CAUSING BOTH PEOPLE TO DIE.
WHICH MEANS, SOMEWHERE ELSE, SOMEONE IS DYING.
BUT BY SHAVING MACHI'S HEAD, THE LINK IS SEVERED, AND MY DAUGHTER WILL LIVE.
I'M... KOFF KOFF... I'M FINE, MOM.
IT'S... KOFF... IT'S OKAY. I CAN BREATHE.
BUT, I'M... BALD?
OH MY GOD, YOU SHOULD HAVE LET ME DIE.

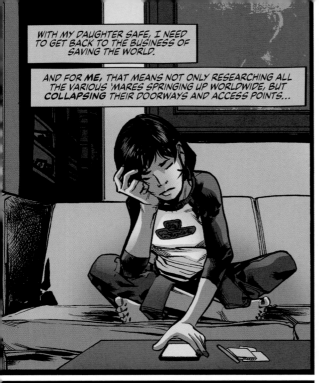

WITH MY DAUGHTER SAFE, I NEED TO GET BACK TO THE BUSINESS OF SAVING THE WORLD.

AND FOR ME, THAT MEANS NOT ONLY RESEARCHING ALL THE VARIOUS 'MARES SPRINGING UP WORLDWIDE, BUT COLLAPSING THEIR DOORWAYS AND ACCESS POINTS...

...BY FINDING ONE GOOD MAN IN THIS STUPID WORLD.

FRIDAY NIGHT? SUR RICK! LOOKIN FORWARD T IT.

I THINK ABOUT ALL THE PRESSURE I PUT ON THESE DATES, THE TENSION OF MEETING SOMEONE NEW, AND HOW UNFAIR IT IS THAT I'VE BEEN PUT IN THIS SITUATION.

LUNCH ON THURSDAY WOULD BE PERFECT, ALEX.

BUT THEN I THINK TO MYSELF THAT, YOU KNOW, MOST WOMEN PROBABLY DON'T FEEL ANY DIFFERENT ABOUT DATING.

MEET YOU AT THE BAR, THEN, DEONDRE!

EVERY MAN YOU MEET IN THE GROCERY STORE, OR AT WORK, OR THROUGH SOME DATING APP, EVERY ONE OF THEM COULD POTENTIALLY BE BORING. MUNDANE. NO SPARK.

AND, OF COURSE, THEY COULD ALL BE DANGEROUS.

WHAT TIME DOES THE MOVIE START, KOJI?

BUT ONE OF THESE MEN COULD, AT LEAST IN SOME WAY, SAVE SOMEONE'S WORLD.

KLIK

CHRIST, FREAK GIRL. MY **BALLS** ARE HAIRIER THAN YOUR **HEAD**.

WELL, HERE GOES NOTHING. MY NAME IS **MACHI HIMURA**. I'M IN SEVENTH GRADE AT BORGES MIDDLE SCHOOL AND...HOORAY...TODAY I AM BALD.

CAN I WRITE SOMETHING ON YOUR HEAD?

THERE'S AN IDEA I'VE BEEN CONSIDERING LATELY. EVERY DAY, HERE AT CESSPOOL MIDDLE SCHOOL, I TRY TO FIT IN. I TRY TO BE NICE. AND IT NEVER WORKS.

AND THERE'S THAT EINSTEIN QUOTE ABOUT HOW "THE DEFINITION OF INSANITY IS DOING THE SAME THING OVER AND OVER AGAIN, BUT EXPECTING DIFFERENT RESULTS."

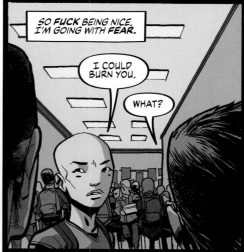

SO **FUCK** BEING NICE. I'M GOING WITH **FEAR**.

I COULD BURN YOU.

WHAT?

I KNOW MORE ABOUT DREAMS AND 'MARES THAN ALMOST ANYONE ON EARTH.

IT'S LIKE A FIRE IN MY HEAD, SIZZLING THROUGH MY BRAIN, AND IF I **LET** IT, IF I **WANTED** TO...

...I COULD BURN YOU ALL TO A FUCKING **CRISP**.

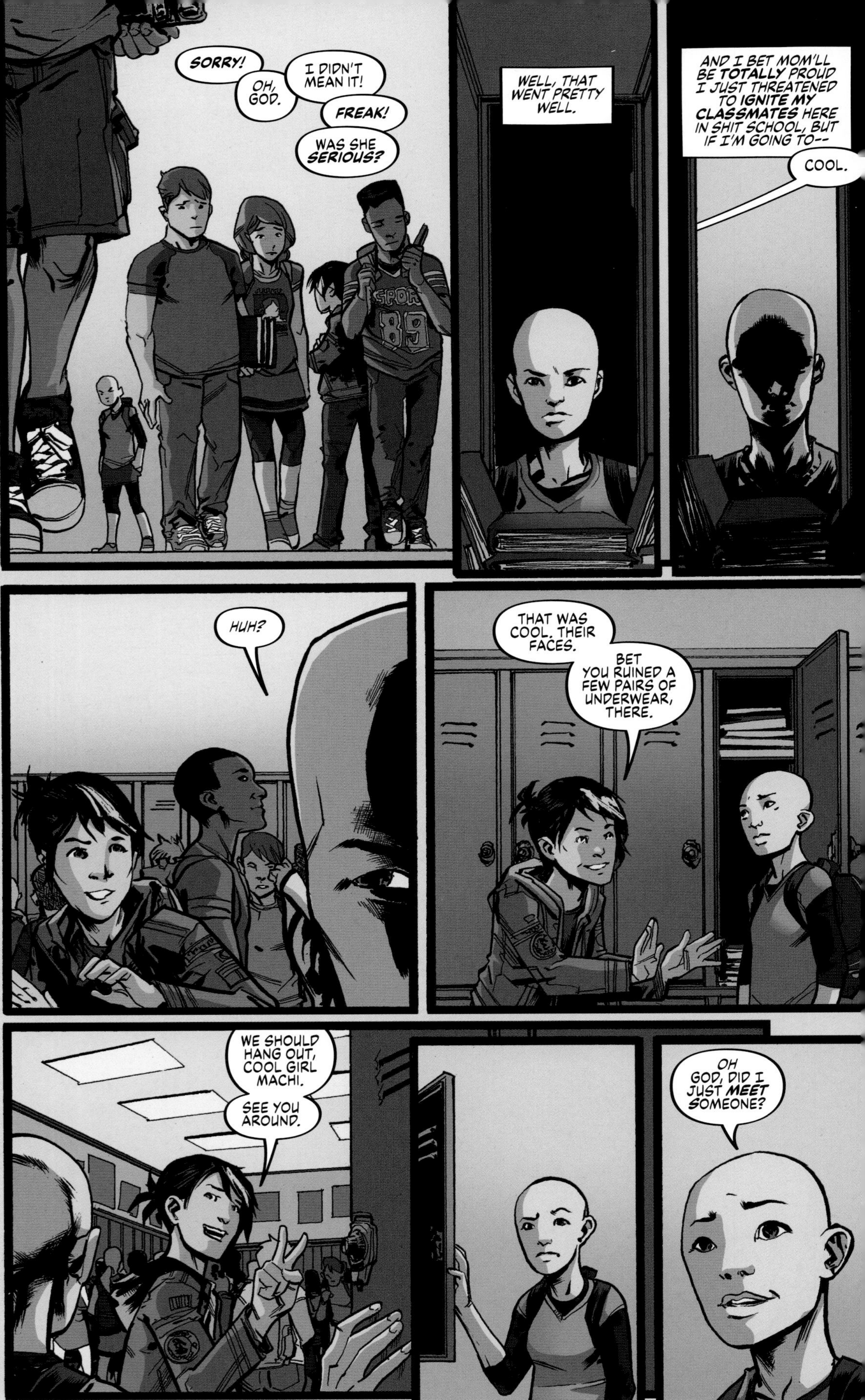
SORRY!
OH, GOD.
I DIDN'T MEAN IT!
FREAK!
WAS SHE SERIOUS?
WELL, THAT WENT PRETTY WELL.
AND I BET MOM'LL BE TOTALLY PROUD I JUST THREATENED TO IGNITE MY CLASSMATES HERE IN SHIT SCHOOL, BUT IF I'M GOING TO--
COOL.
HUH?
THAT WAS COOL. THEIR FACES.
BET YOU RUINED A FEW PAIRS OF UNDERWEAR, THERE.
WE SHOULD HANG OUT, COOL GIRL MACHI.
SEE YOU AROUND.
OH GOD, DID I JUST MEET SOMEONE?

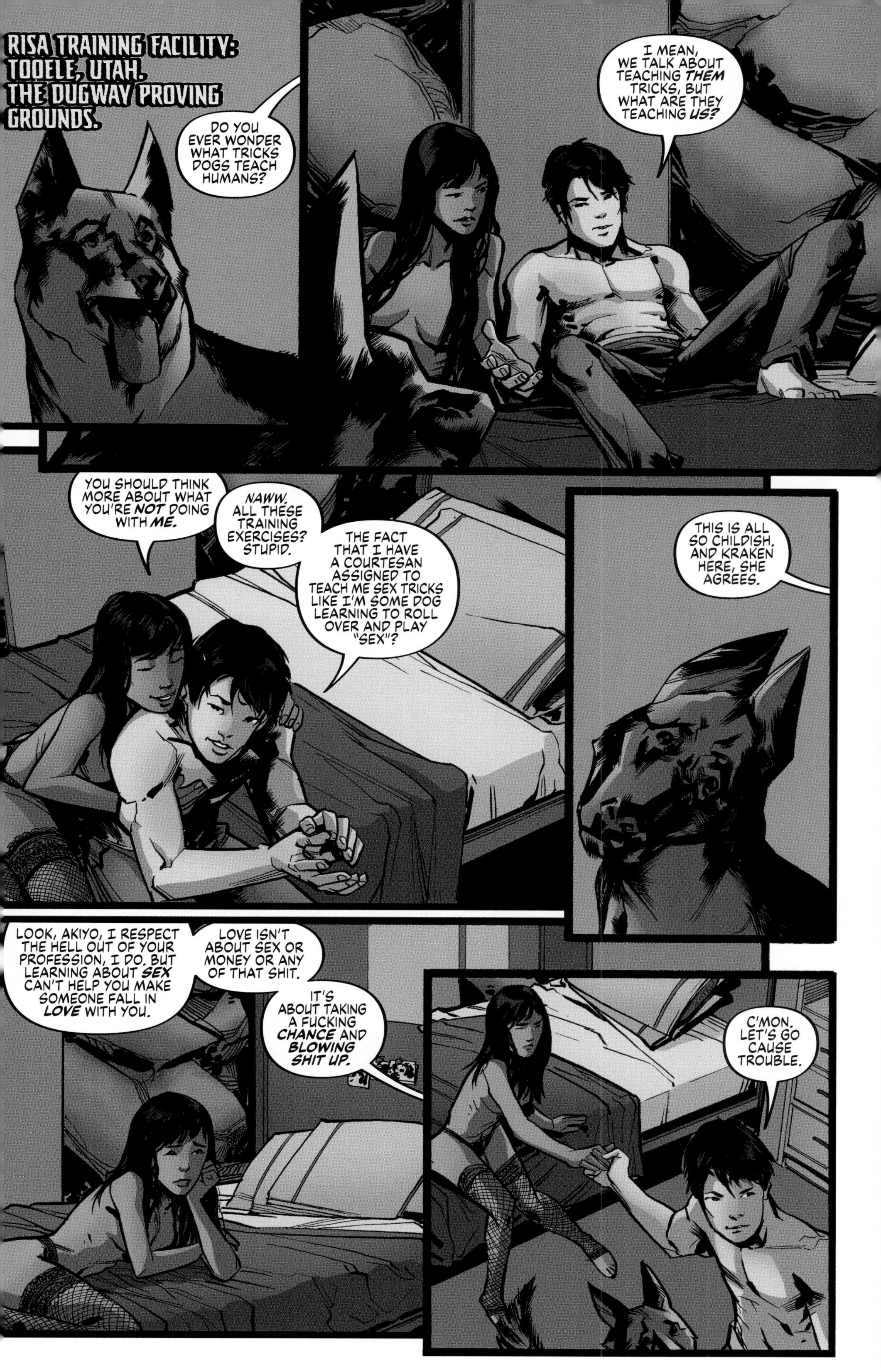

RISA TRAINING FACILITY: TOOELE, UTAH. THE DUGWAY PROVING GROUNDS.
DO YOU EVER WONDER WHAT TRICKS DOGS TEACH HUMANS?
I MEAN, WE TALK ABOUT TEACHING *THEM* TRICKS, BUT WHAT ARE THEY TEACHING *US?*
YOU SHOULD THINK MORE ABOUT WHAT YOU'RE *NOT* DOING WITH *ME.*
NAWW. ALL THESE TRAINING EXERCISES? STUPID.
THE FACT THAT I HAVE A COURTESAN ASSIGNED TO TEACH ME SEX TRICKS LIKE I'M SOME DOG LEARNING TO ROLL OVER AND PLAY "SEX"?
THIS IS ALL SO CHILDISH. AND KRAKEN HERE, SHE AGREES.
LOOK, AKIYO, I RESPECT THE HELL OUT OF YOUR PROFESSION, I DO. BUT LEARNING ABOUT *SEX* CAN'T HELP YOU MAKE SOMEONE FALL IN *LOVE* WITH YOU.
LOVE ISN'T ABOUT SEX OR MONEY OR ANY OF THAT SHIT.
IT'S ABOUT TAKING A FUCKING *CHANCE* AND *BLOWING SHIT UP.*
C'MON. LET'S GO CAUSE TROUBLE.

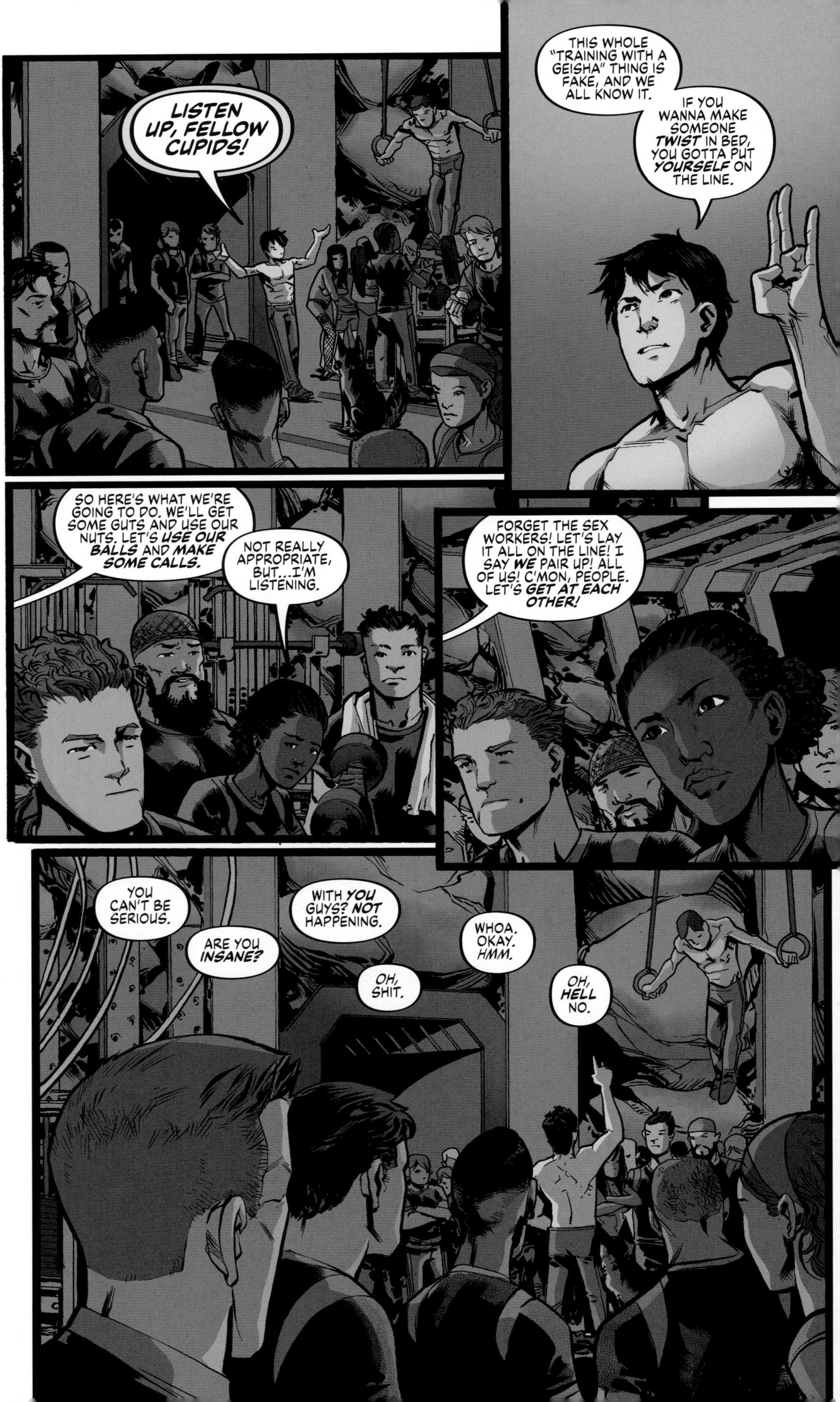
LISTEN UP, FELLOW CUPIDS!
THIS WHOLE "TRAINING WITH A GEISHA" THING IS FAKE, AND WE ALL KNOW IT.
IF YOU WANNA MAKE SOMEONE TWIST IN BED, YOU GOTTA PUT YOURSELF ON THE LINE.
SO HERE'S WHAT WE'RE GOING TO DO. WE'LL GET SOME GUTS AND USE OUR NUTS. LET'S USE OUR BALLS AND MAKE SOME CALLS.
NOT REALLY APPROPRIATE, BUT...I'M LISTENING.
FORGET THE SEX WORKERS! LET'S LAY IT ALL ON THE LINE! I SAY WE PAIR UP! ALL OF US! C'MON, PEOPLE. LET'S GET AT EACH OTHER!
YOU CAN'T BE SERIOUS.
ARE YOU INSANE?
WITH YOU GUYS? NOT HAPPENING.
OH, SHIT.
WHOA. OKAY. HMM.
OH, HELL NO.

WAIT A MOMENT.

HUH? GENERAL YAMADA?

HELLO, SIR!

SIR!

AT EASE, AT EASE.

OR RATHER, NOT AT EASE.

IN FACT, LET'S RAMP UP THE FUCKING TENSION, LITERALLY.

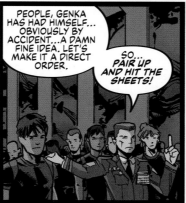

PEOPLE, GENKA HAS HAD HIMSELF... OBVIOUSLY BY ACCIDENT...A DAMN FINE IDEA. LET'S MAKE IT A DIRECT ORDER.

SO... PAIR UP AND HIT THE SHEETS!

SIR, IF I MAY. PAIRING UP IS...WELL, THERE ARE TWENTY-FIVE MEN AND ONLY FIVE WOMEN.

WELL, HOLE-LEE HELL. WE GOT OURSELVES AN OUTRIGHT MATH-E-MATICAL GENIUS, HERE!

LISTEN, YOU'RE TRAINING YOURSELVES TO GET OUT THERE AND SEDUCE RISA HIMURA!

AND THERE IS ONLY, BY MY COUNT, EXACTLY ONE RISA HIMURA IN A WORLD OF SEVERAL BILLION PEOPLE!

NOW HOW YOU GOING TO DO THAT...

...IF YOU STUB YOUR GODDAMN DICK ON A ONE-IN-FIVE CHANCE?

...

SIR, YES SIR!

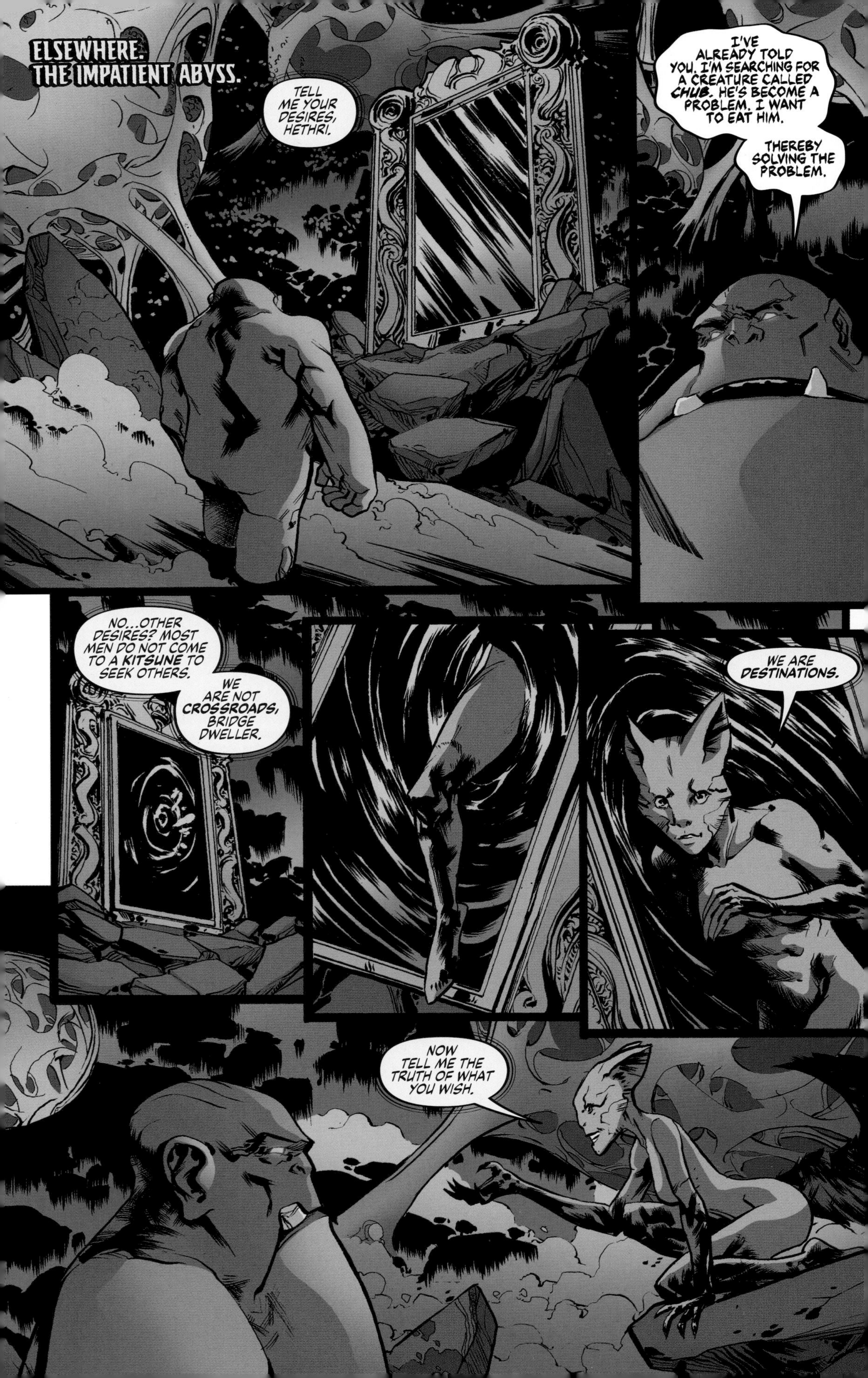
ELSEWHERE. THE IMPATIENT ABYSS.
TELL ME YOUR DESIRES, HETHRI.
I'VE ALREADY TOLD YOU. I'M SEARCHING FOR A CREATURE CALLED CHUB. HE'S BECOME A PROBLEM. I WANT TO EAT HIM.
THEREBY SOLVING THE PROBLEM.
NO...OTHER DESIRES? MOST MEN DO NOT COME TO A KITSUNE TO SEEK OTHERS.
WE ARE NOT CROSSROADS, BRIDGE DWELLER.
WE ARE DESTINATIONS.
NOW TELL ME THE TRUTH OF WHAT YOU WISH.

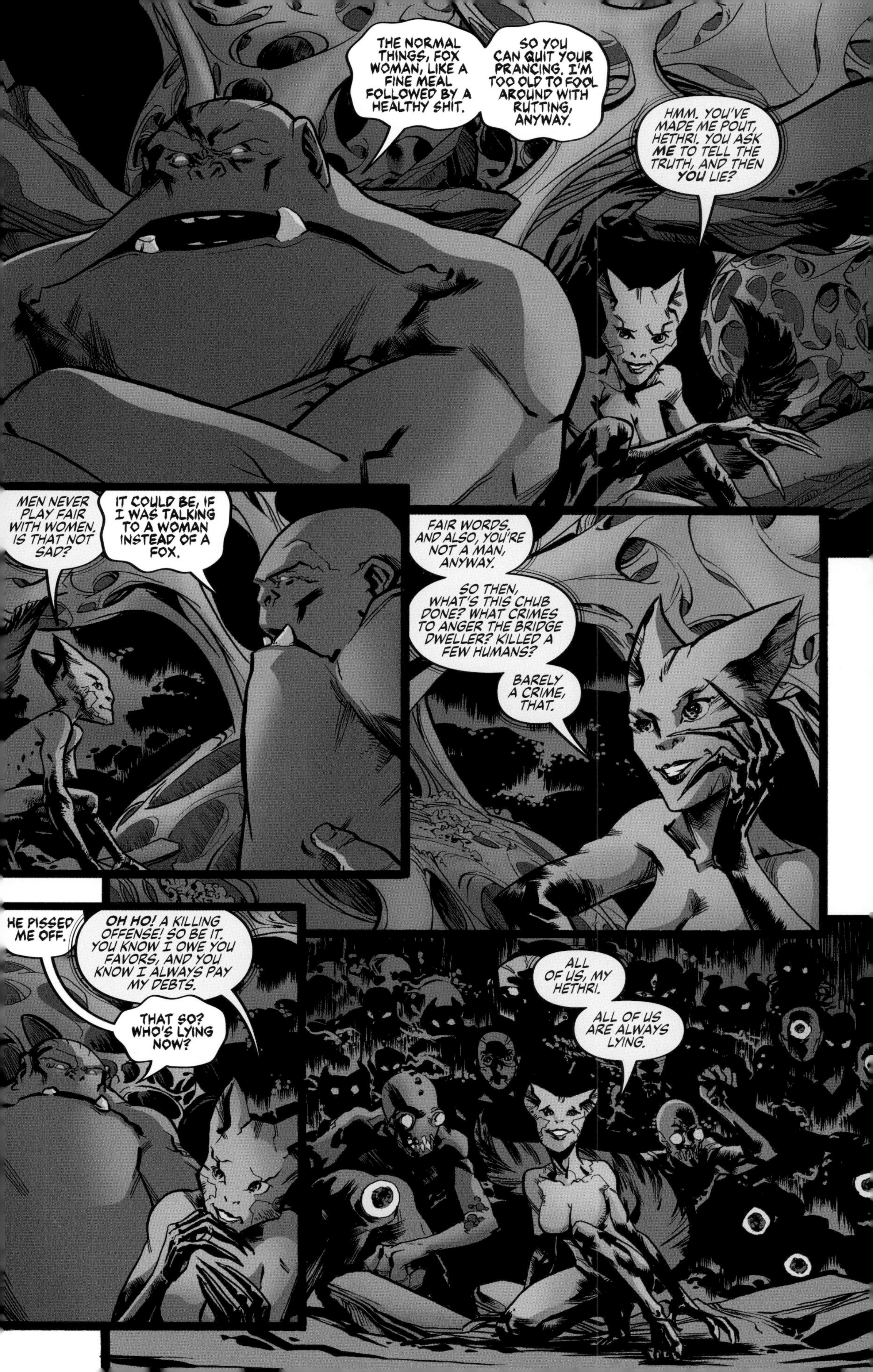
THE NORMAL THINGS, FOX WOMAN, LIKE A FINE MEAL FOLLOWED BY A HEALTHY SHIT.
SO YOU CAN QUIT YOUR PRANCING. I'M TOO OLD TO FOOL AROUND WITH RUTTING, ANYWAY.
HMM. YOU'VE MADE ME POUT, HETHRI. YOU ASK **ME** TO TELL THE TRUTH, AND THEN **YOU** LIE?
MEN NEVER PLAY FAIR WITH WOMEN. IS THAT NOT SAD?
IT COULD BE, IF I WAS TALKING TO A WOMAN INSTEAD OF A FOX.
FAIR WORDS, AND ALSO, YOU'RE NOT A MAN, ANYWAY.
SO THEN, WHAT'S THIS CHUB DONE? WHAT CRIMES TO ANGER THE BRIDGE DWELLER? KILLED A FEW HUMANS?
BARELY A CRIME, THAT.
HE PISSED ME OFF.
OH HO! A KILLING OFFENSE! SO BE IT. YOU KNOW I OWE YOU FAVORS, AND YOU KNOW I ALWAYS PAY MY DEBTS.
THAT SO? WHO'S LYING NOW?
ALL OF US, MY HETHRI.
ALL OF US ARE ALWAYS LYING.

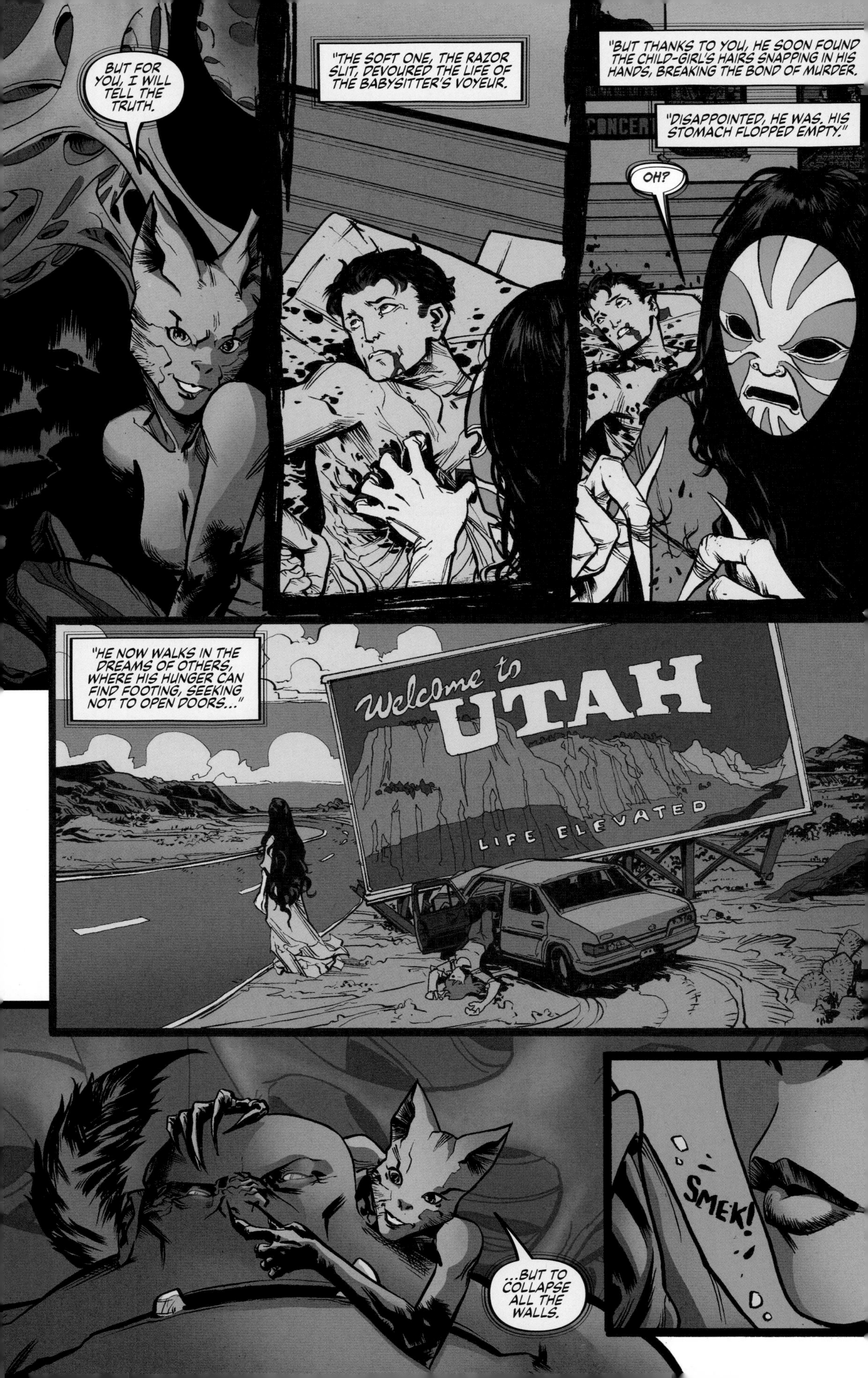
BUT FOR YOU, I WILL TELL THE TRUTH.
"THE SOFT ONE, THE RAZOR SLIT, DEVOURED THE LIFE OF THE BABYSITTER'S VOYEUR.
"BUT THANKS TO YOU, HE SOON FOUND THE CHILD-GIRL'S HAIRS SNAPPING IN HIS HANDS, BREAKING THE BOND OF MURDER.
"DISAPPOINTED, HE WAS. HIS STOMACH FLOPPED EMPTY."
OH?
"HE NOW WALKS IN THE DREAMS OF OTHERS, WHERE HIS HUNGER CAN FIND FOOTING, SEEKING NOT TO OPEN DOORS..."
Welcome to UTAH
LIFE ELEVATED
...BUT TO COLLAPSE ALL THE WALLS.
SMEK!

I FEEL LIKE I'M GOING TO COLLAPSE.

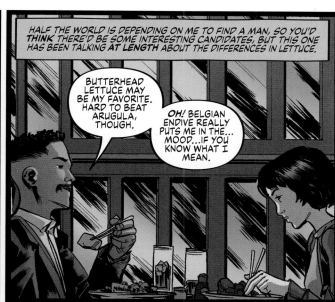

HALF THE WORLD IS DEPENDING ON ME TO FIND A MAN, SO YOU'D **THINK** THERE'D BE SOME INTERESTING CANDIDATES, BUT THIS ONE HAS BEEN TALKING **AT LENGTH** ABOUT THE DIFFERENCES IN LETTUCE.

BUTTERHEAD LETTUCE MAY BE MY FAVORITE. HARD TO BEAT ARUGULA, THOUGH.

OH! BELGIAN ENDIVE REALLY PUTS ME IN THE... MOOD...IF YOU KNOW WHAT I MEAN.

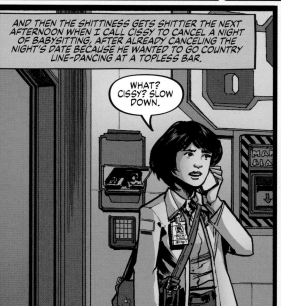

AND THEN THE SHITTINESS GETS SHITTIER THE NEXT AFTERNOON WHEN I CALL CISSY TO CANCEL A NIGHT OF BABYSITTING, AFTER ALREADY CANCELING THE NIGHT'S DATE BECAUSE HE WANTED TO GO COUNTRY LINE-DANCING AT A TOPLESS BAR.

WHAT? CISSY? SLOW DOWN.

AND THAT'S WHEN I FIND OUT THAT A 'MARE RIPPED CISSY'S BOYFRIEND APART, ALONG WITH EVERY LAST ONE OF HIS ROOMMATES.

WHEN I MENTION THE MURDERS TO CROAK, HE TELLS ME IT WAS THAT ASSHOLE, **CHUB.** SO CROAK ALREADY **KNEW** ABOUT THE ATTACKS BUT DIDN'T SEE FIT TO TELL **ME.**

YOU CAN'T KEEP THESE **SECRETS** FROM ME!

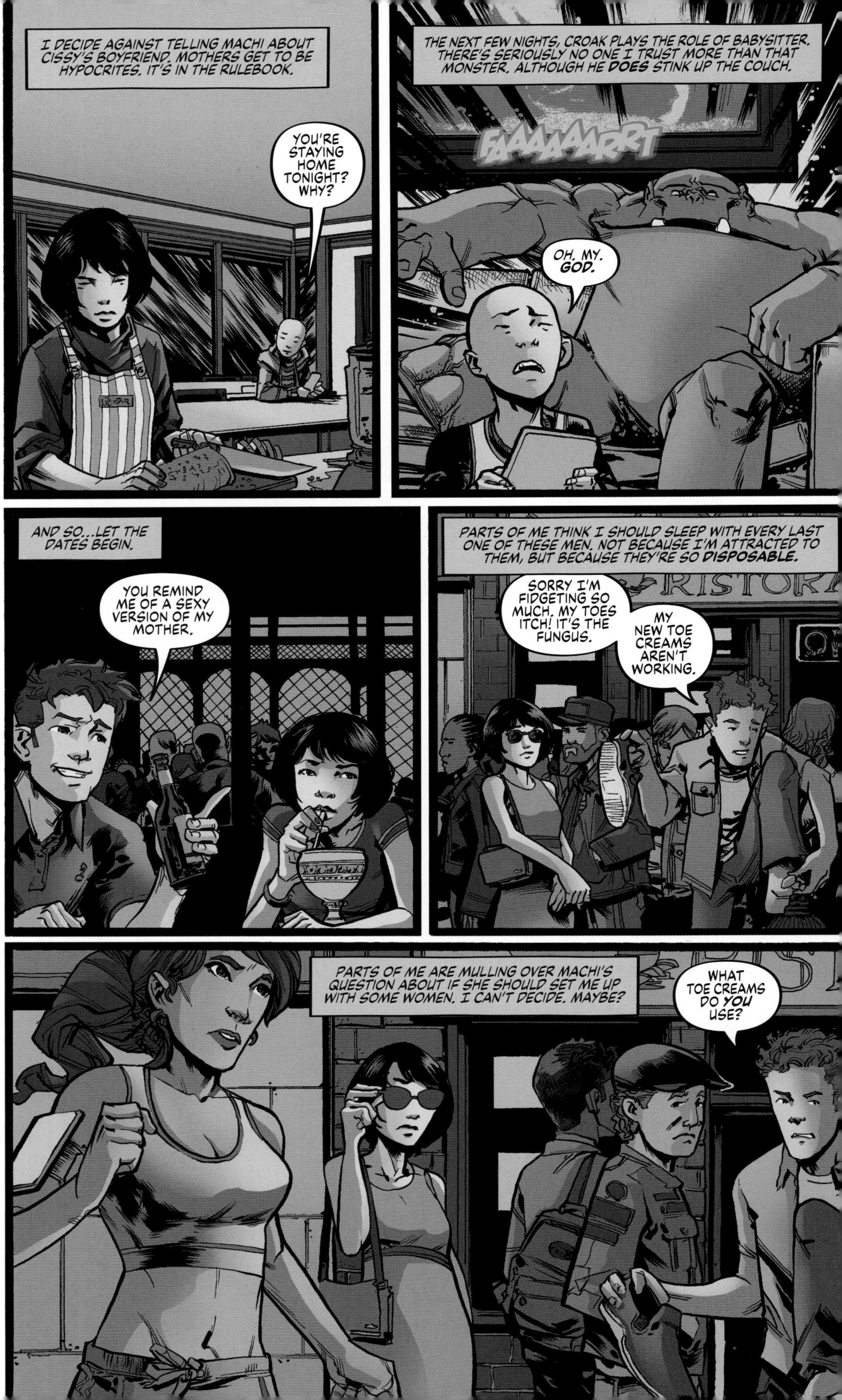
I DECIDE AGAINST TELLING MACHI ABOUT CISSY'S BOYFRIEND. MOTHERS GET TO BE HYPOCRITES. IT'S IN THE RULEBOOK.
YOU'RE STAYING HOME TONIGHT? WHY?
THE NEXT FEW NIGHTS, CROAK PLAYS THE ROLE OF BABYSITTER. THERE'S SERIOUSLY NO ONE I TRUST MORE THAN THAT MONSTER. ALTHOUGH HE DOES STINK UP THE COUCH.
FAAAAAARRT
OH. MY. GOD.
AND SO...LET THE DATES BEGIN.
YOU REMIND ME OF A SEXY VERSION OF MY MOTHER.
PARTS OF ME THINK I SHOULD SLEEP WITH EVERY LAST ONE OF THESE MEN. NOT BECAUSE I'M ATTRACTED TO THEM, BUT BECAUSE THEY'RE SO DISPOSABLE.
SORRY I'M FIDGETING SO MUCH. MY TOES ITCH! IT'S THE FUNGUS.
MY NEW TOE CREAMS AREN'T WORKING.
PARTS OF ME ARE MULLING OVER MACHI'S QUESTION ABOUT IF SHE SHOULD SET ME UP WITH SOME WOMEN. I CAN'T DECIDE. MAYBE?
WHAT TOE CREAMS DO YOU USE?

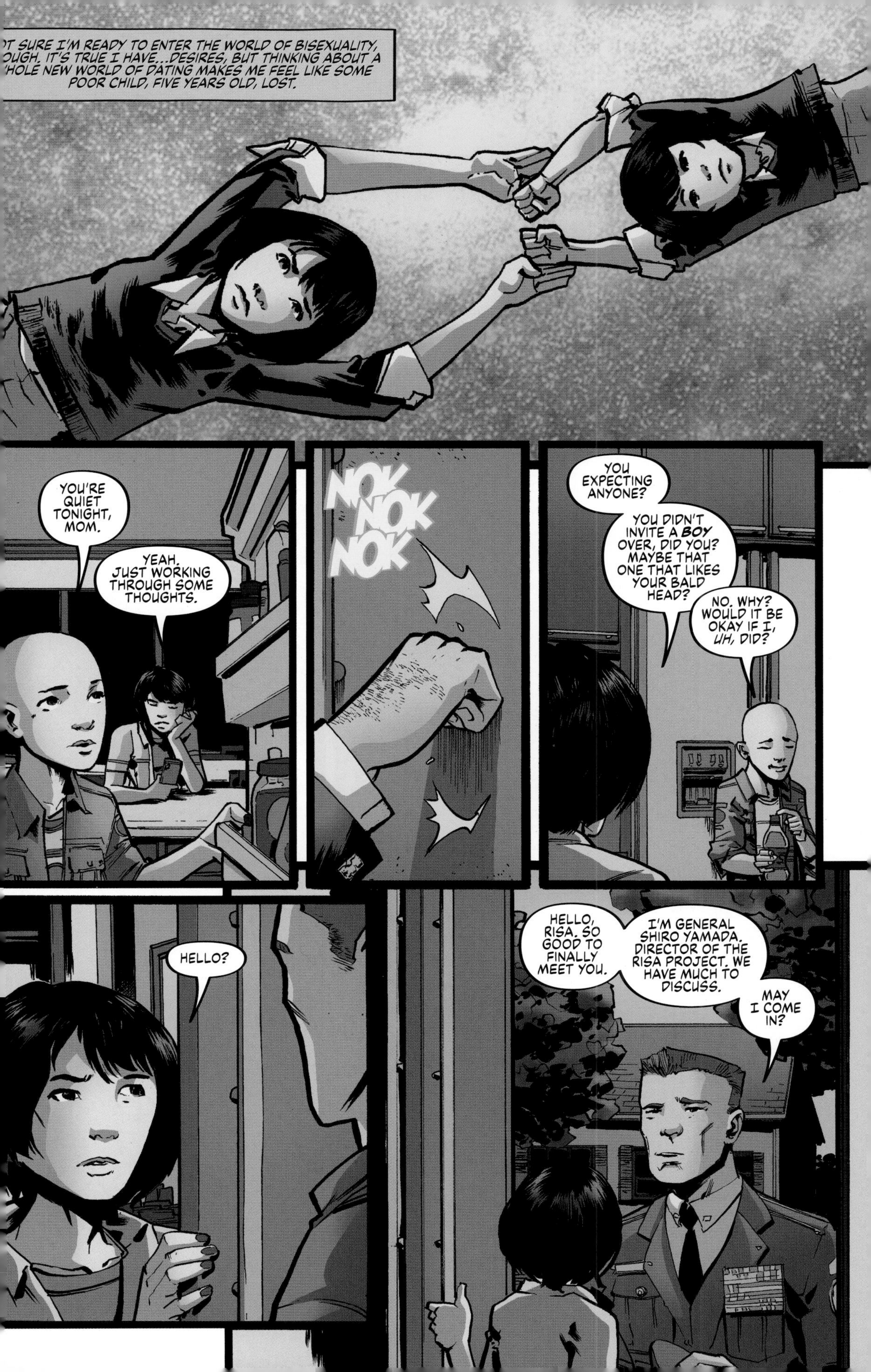

OT SURE I'M READY TO ENTER THE WORLD OF BISEXUALITY, OUGH. IT'S TRUE I HAVE...DESIRES, BUT THINKING ABOUT A HOLE NEW WORLD OF DATING MAKES ME FEEL LIKE SOME POOR CHILD, FIVE YEARS OLD, LOST.
YOU'RE QUIET TONIGHT, MOM.
YEAH. JUST WORKING THROUGH SOME THOUGHTS.
NOK NOK NOK
YOU EXPECTING ANYONE?
YOU DIDN'T INVITE A BOY OVER, DID YOU? MAYBE THAT ONE THAT LIKES YOUR BALD HEAD?
NO. WHY? WOULD IT BE OKAY IF I, UH, DID?
HELLO?
HELLO, RISA. SO GOOD TO FINALLY MEET YOU.
I'M GENERAL SHIRO YAMADA. DIRECTOR OF THE RISA PROJECT. WE HAVE MUCH TO DISCUSS.
MAY I COME IN?

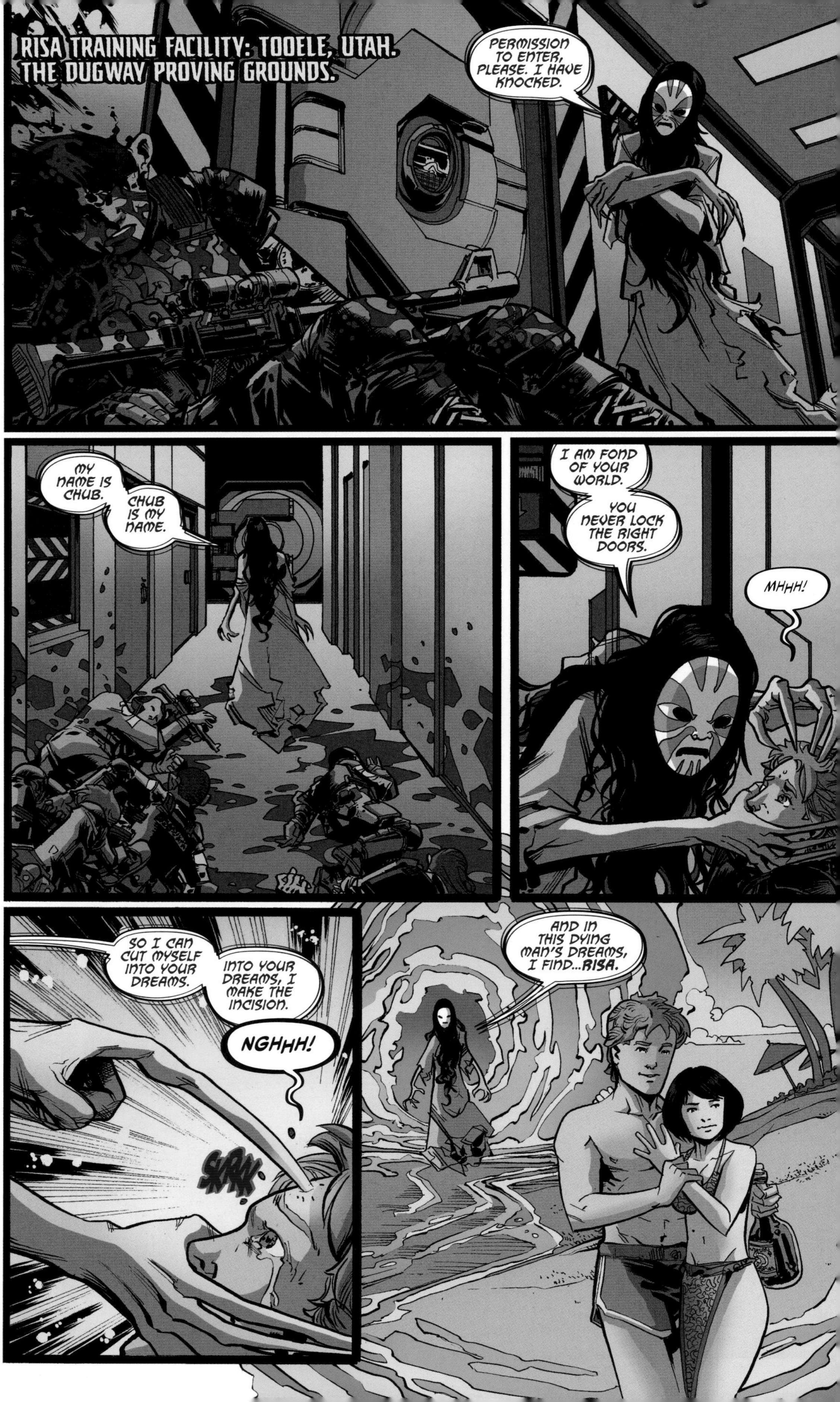
RISA TRAINING FACILITY: TOOELE, UTAH.
THE DUGWAY PROVING GROUNDS.
PERMISSION TO ENTER, PLEASE. I HAVE KNOCKED.
MY NAME IS CHUB.
CHUB IS MY NAME.
I AM FOND OF YOUR WORLD.
YOU NEVER LOCK THE RIGHT DOORS.
MHHH!
SO I CAN CUT MYSELF INTO YOUR DREAMS.
INTO YOUR DREAMS, I MAKE THE INCISION.
NGHHH!
SKRK
AND IN THIS DYING MAN'S DREAMS, I FIND...RISA.

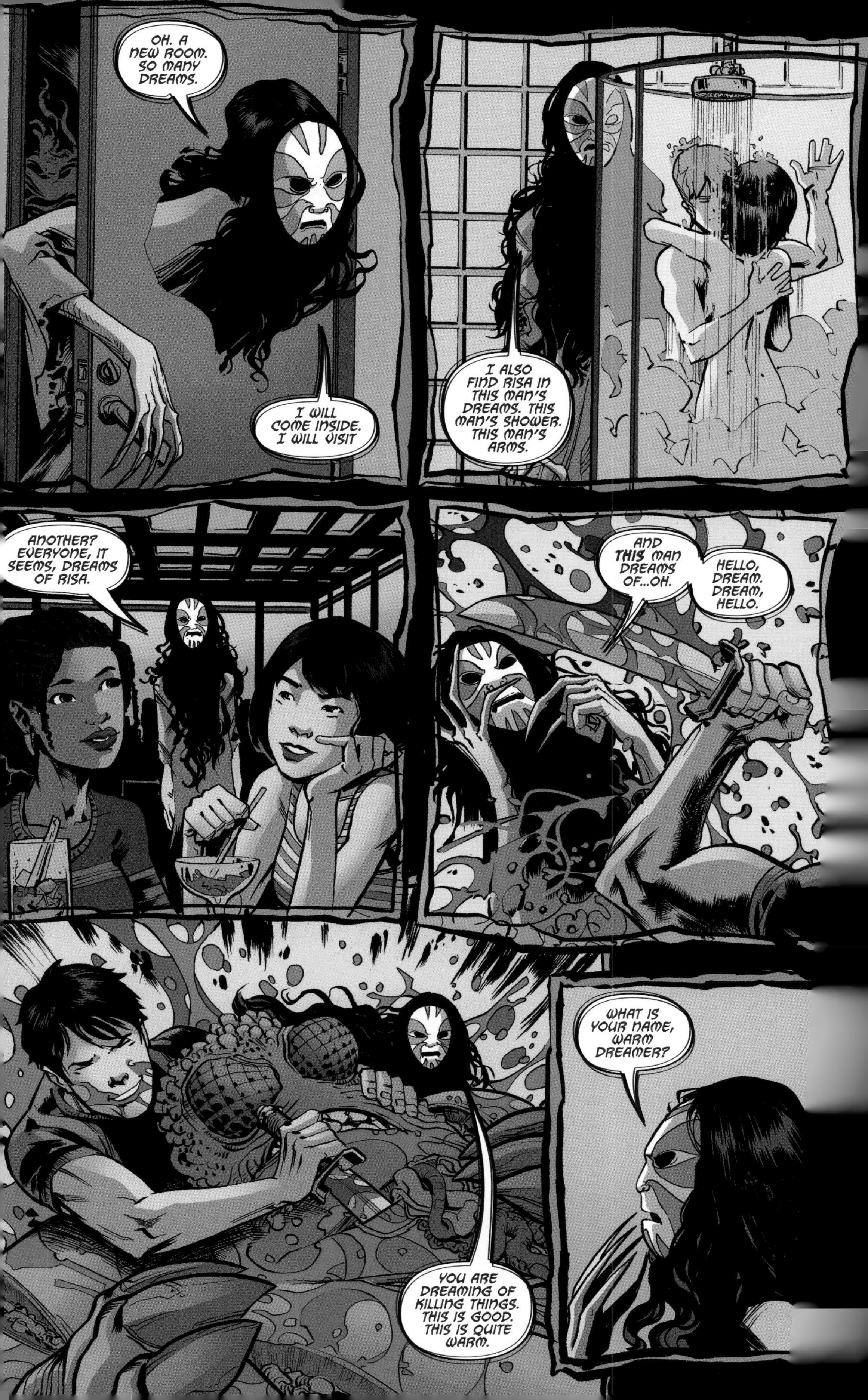
OH. A NEW ROOM. SO MANY DREAMS.
I WILL COME INSIDE. I WILL VISIT
I ALSO FIND RISA IN THIS MAN'S DREAMS. THIS MAN'S SHOWER. THIS MAN'S ARMS.
ANOTHER? EVERYONE, IT SEEMS, DREAMS OF RISA.
AND THIS MAN DREAMS OF...OH.
HELLO, DREAM. DREAM, HELLO.
YOU ARE DREAMING OF KILLING THINGS. THIS IS GOOD. THIS IS QUITE WARM.
WHAT IS YOUR NAME, WARM DREAMER?

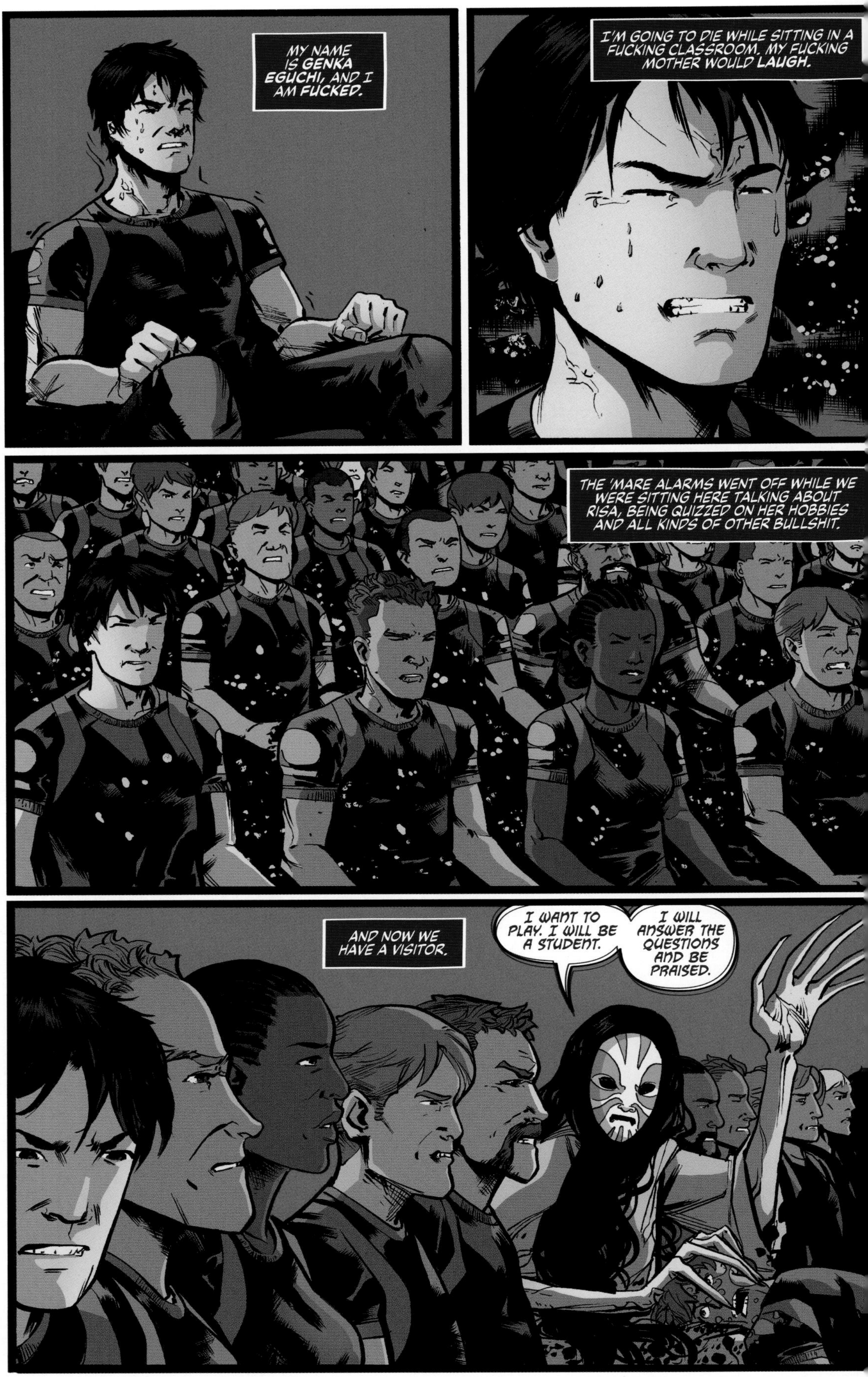
MY NAME IS GENKA EGUCHI, AND I AM FUCKED.
I'M GOING TO DIE WHILE SITTING IN A FUCKING CLASSROOM. MY FUCKING MOTHER WOULD LAUGH.
THE 'MARE ALARMS WENT OFF WHILE WE WERE SITTING HERE TALKING ABOUT RISA, BEING QUIZZED ON HER HOBBIES AND ALL KINDS OF OTHER BULLSHIT.
AND NOW WE HAVE A VISITOR.
I WANT TO PLAY. I WILL BE A STUDENT.
I WILL ANSWER THE QUESTIONS AND BE PRAISED.

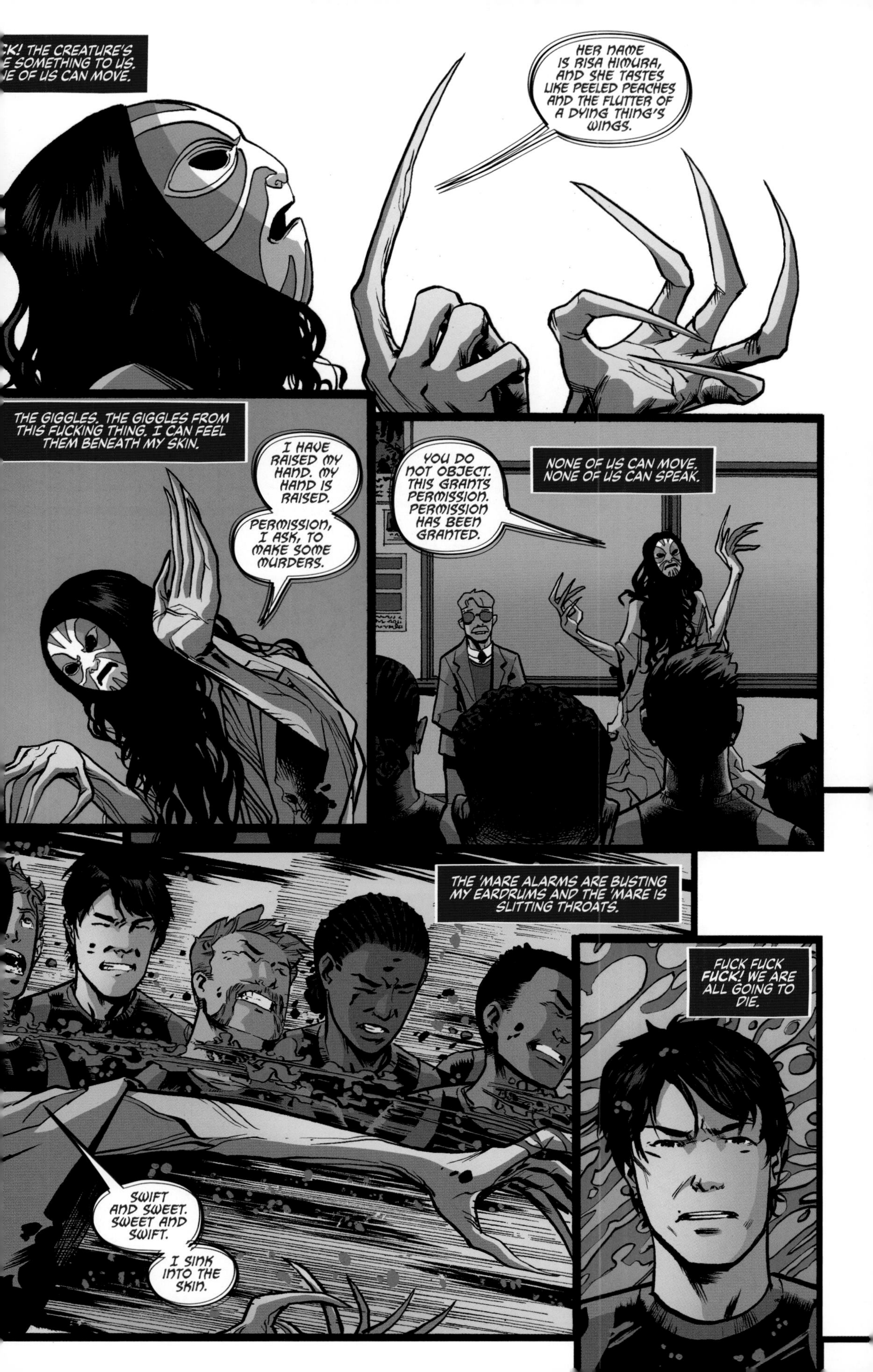
CK! THE CREATURE'S
E SOMETHING TO US.
NE OF US CAN MOVE.
HER NAME IS RISA HIMURA, AND SHE TASTES LIKE PEELED PEACHES AND THE FLUTTER OF A DYING THING'S WINGS.
THE GIGGLES. THE GIGGLES FROM THIS FUCKING THING. I CAN FEEL THEM BENEATH MY SKIN.
I HAVE RAISED MY HAND. MY HAND IS RAISED.
PERMISSION, I ASK, TO MAKE SOME MURDERS.
YOU DO NOT OBJECT. THIS GRANTS PERMISSION. PERMISSION HAS BEEN GRANTED.
NONE OF US CAN MOVE. NONE OF US CAN SPEAK.
THE 'MARE ALARMS ARE BUSTING MY EARDRUMS AND THE 'MARE IS SLITTING THROATS.
SWIFT AND SWEET. SWEET AND SWIFT.
I SINK INTO THE SKIN.
FUCK FUCK FUCK! WE ARE ALL GOING TO DIE.

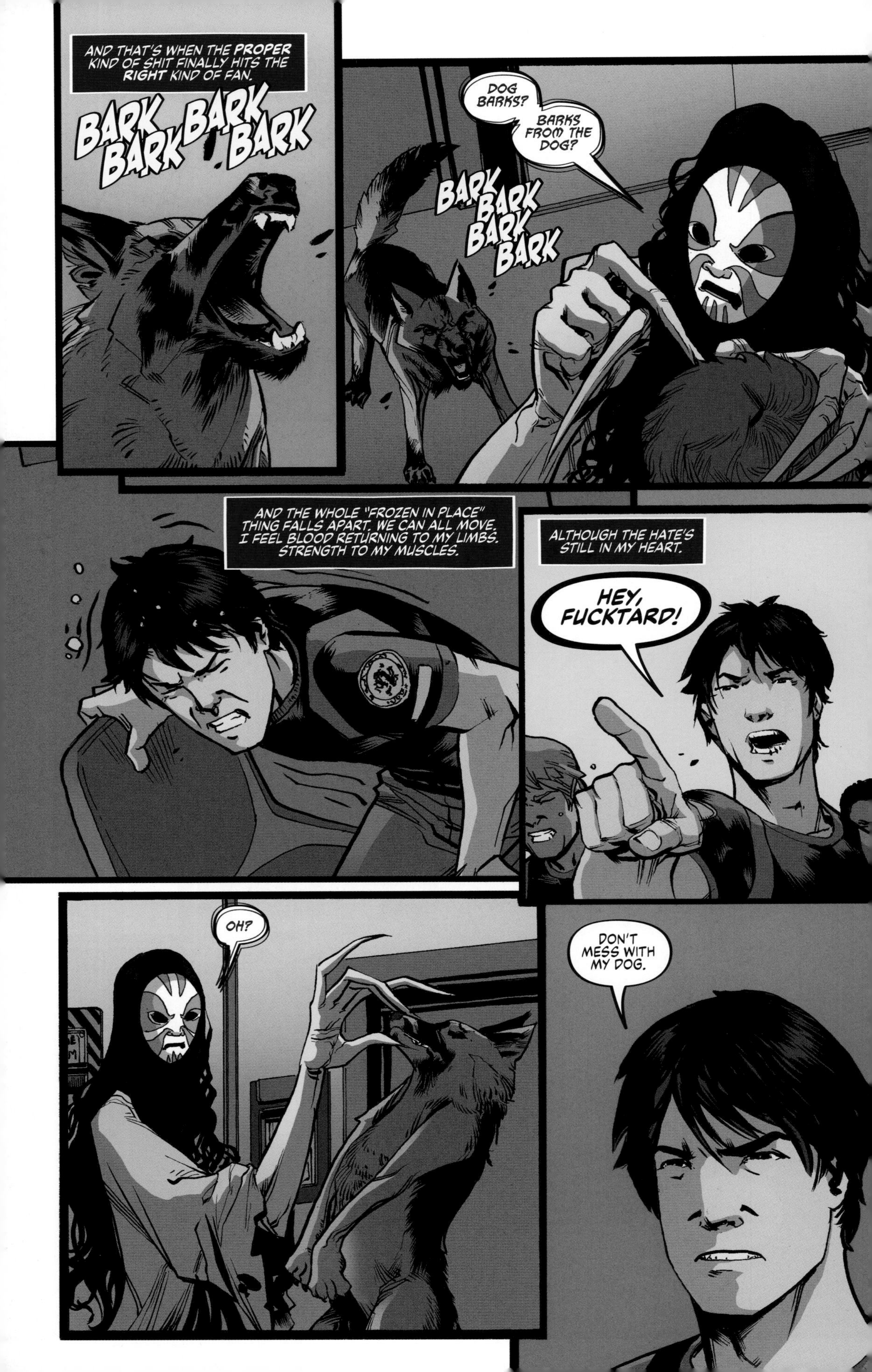
AND THAT'S WHEN THE PROPER KIND OF SHIT FINALLY HITS THE RIGHT KIND OF FAN.
BARK BARK BARK BARK
DOG BARKS?
BARKS FROM THE DOG?
BARK BARK BARK BARK
AND THE WHOLE "FROZEN IN PLACE" THING FALLS APART. WE CAN ALL MOVE. I FEEL BLOOD RETURNING TO MY LIMBS. STRENGTH TO MY MUSCLES.
ALTHOUGH THE HATE'S STILL IN MY HEART.
HEY, FUCKTARD!
OH?
DON'T MESS WITH MY DOG.

4
THE DOG IS FINE

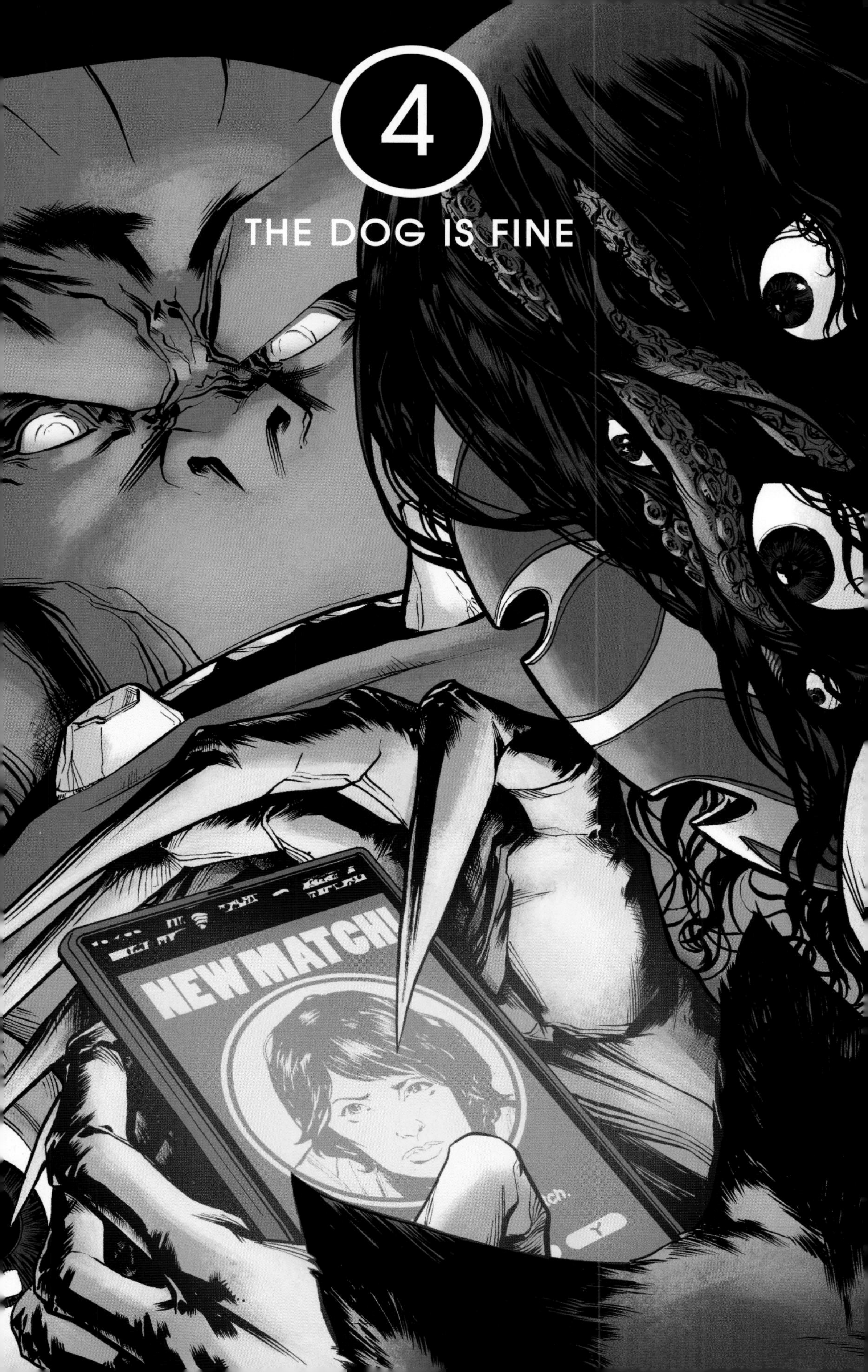
NEW MATCH

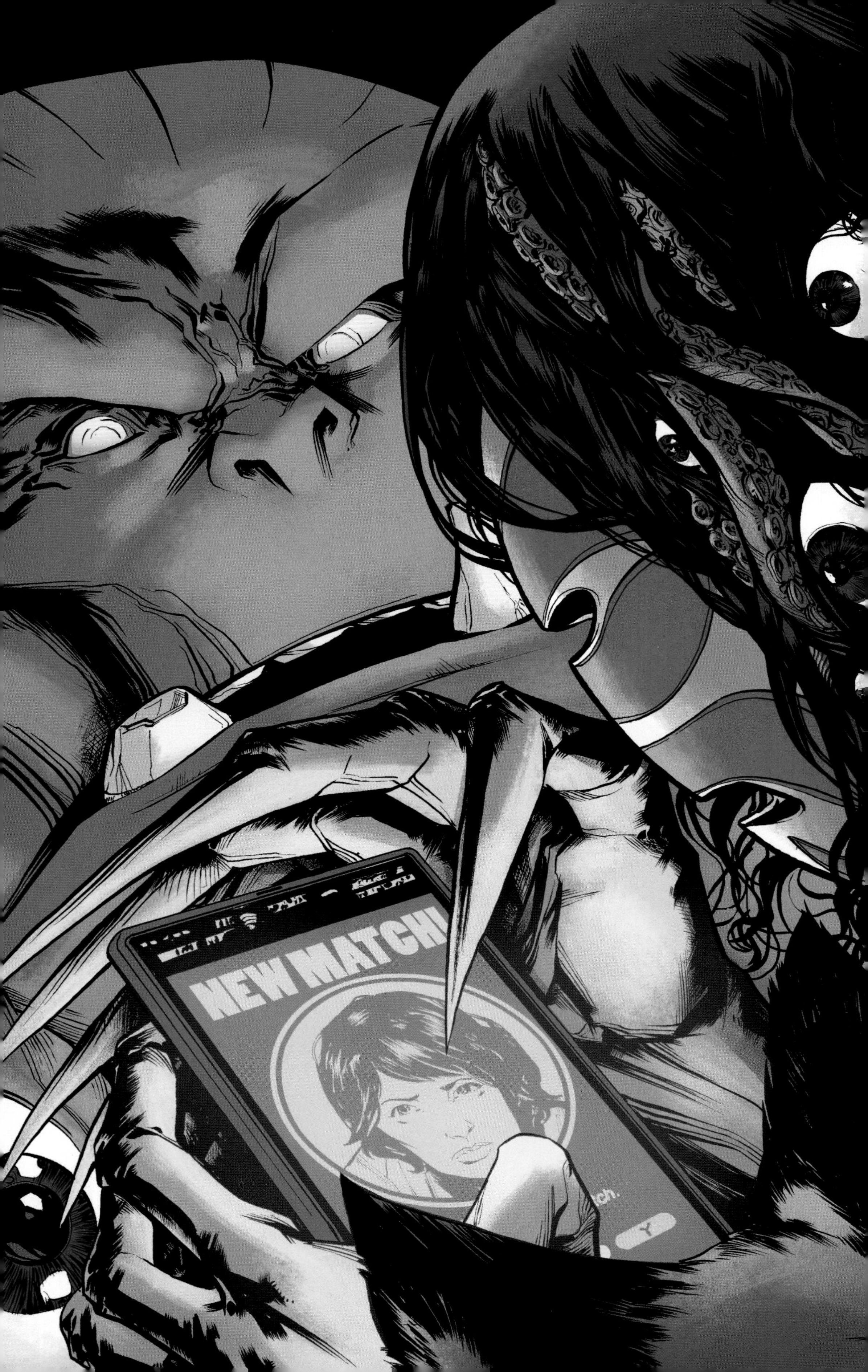
NEW MATCH!

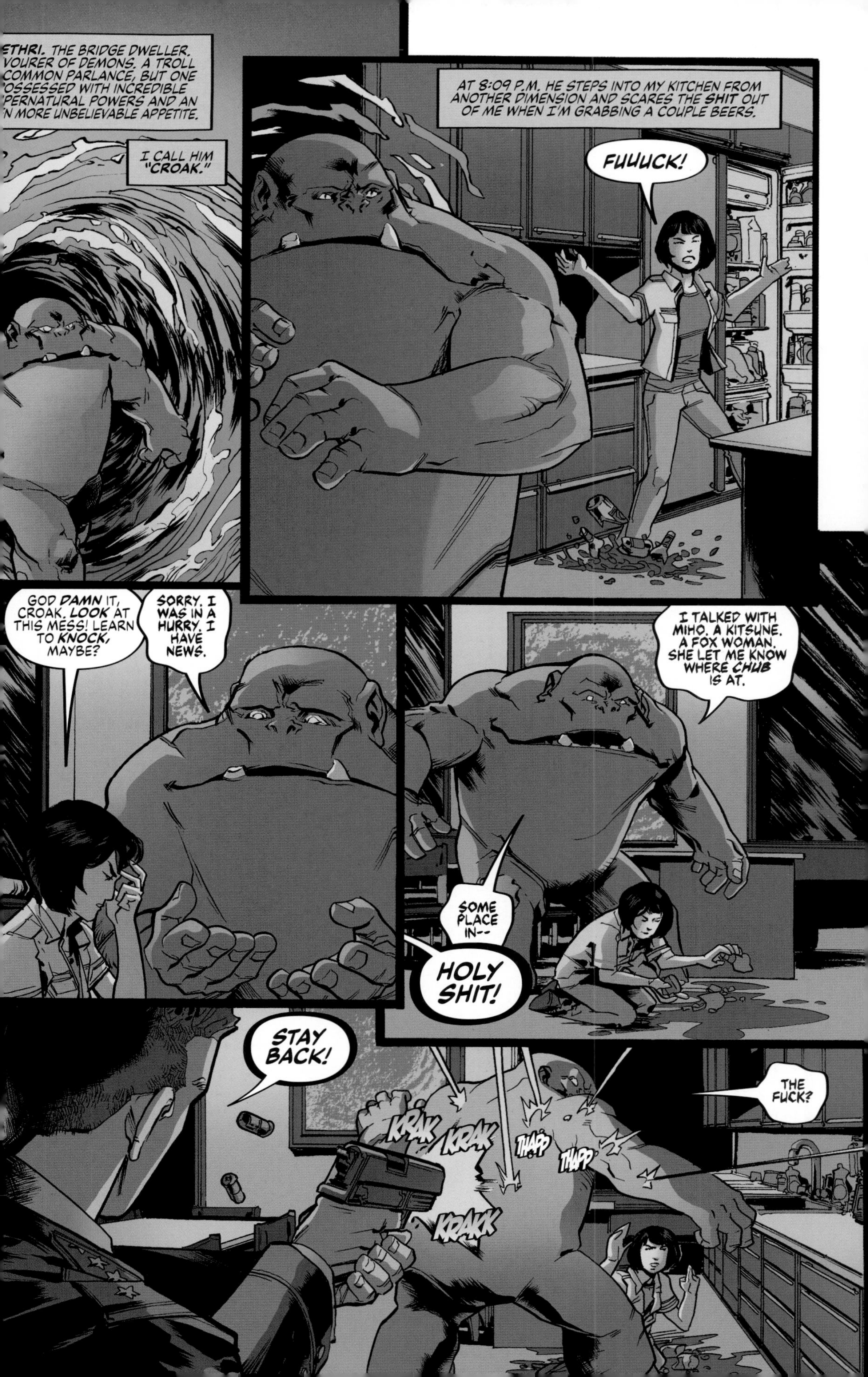
ETHRI. THE BRIDGE DWELLER. VOURER OF DEMONS. A TROLL COMMON PARLANCE, BUT ONE OSSESSED WITH INCREDIBLE PERNATURAL POWERS AND AN N MORE UNBELIEVABLE APPETITE.
I CALL HIM "CROAK."
AT 8:09 P.M. HE STEPS INTO MY KITCHEN FROM ANOTHER DIMENSION AND SCARES THE SHIT OUT OF ME WHEN I'M GRABBING A COUPLE BEERS.
FUUUCK!
GOD DAMN IT, CROAK. LOOK AT THIS MESS! LEARN TO KNOCK, MAYBE?
SORRY. I WAS IN A HURRY. I HAVE NEWS.
I TALKED WITH MIHO. A KITSUNE. A FOX WOMAN. SHE LET ME KNOW WHERE CHUB IS AT.
SOME PLACE IN--
HOLY SHIT!
STAY BACK!
KRAK
KRAK
THAPP
THAPP
KRAKK
THE FUCK?

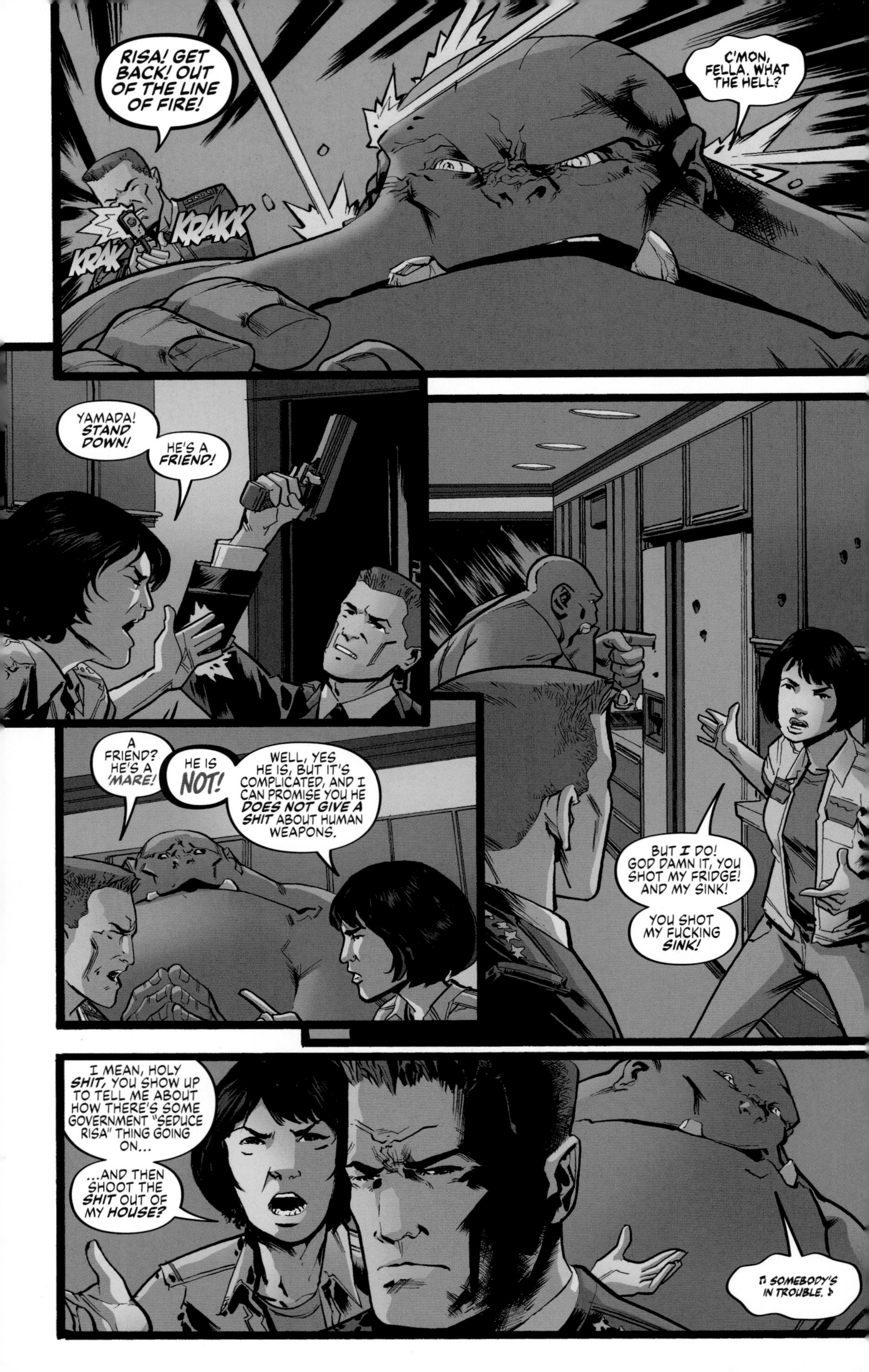
RISA! GET BACK! OUT OF THE LINE OF FIRE!
KRAK
KRAKK
C'MON, FELLA. WHAT THE HELL?
YAMADA! STAND DOWN!
HE'S A FRIEND!
A FRIEND? HE'S A 'MARE!
HE IS NOT!
WELL, YES HE IS, BUT IT'S COMPLICATED, AND I CAN PROMISE YOU HE DOES NOT GIVE A SHIT ABOUT HUMAN WEAPONS.
BUT I DO! GOD DAMN IT, YOU SHOT MY FRIDGE! AND MY SINK!
YOU SHOT MY FUCKING SINK!
I MEAN, HOLY SHIT, YOU SHOW UP TO TELL ME ABOUT HOW THERE'S SOME GOVERNMENT "SEDUCE RISA" THING GOING ON...
...AND THEN SHOOT THE SHIT OUT OF MY HOUSE?
♫ SOMEBODY'S IN TROUBLE. ♪

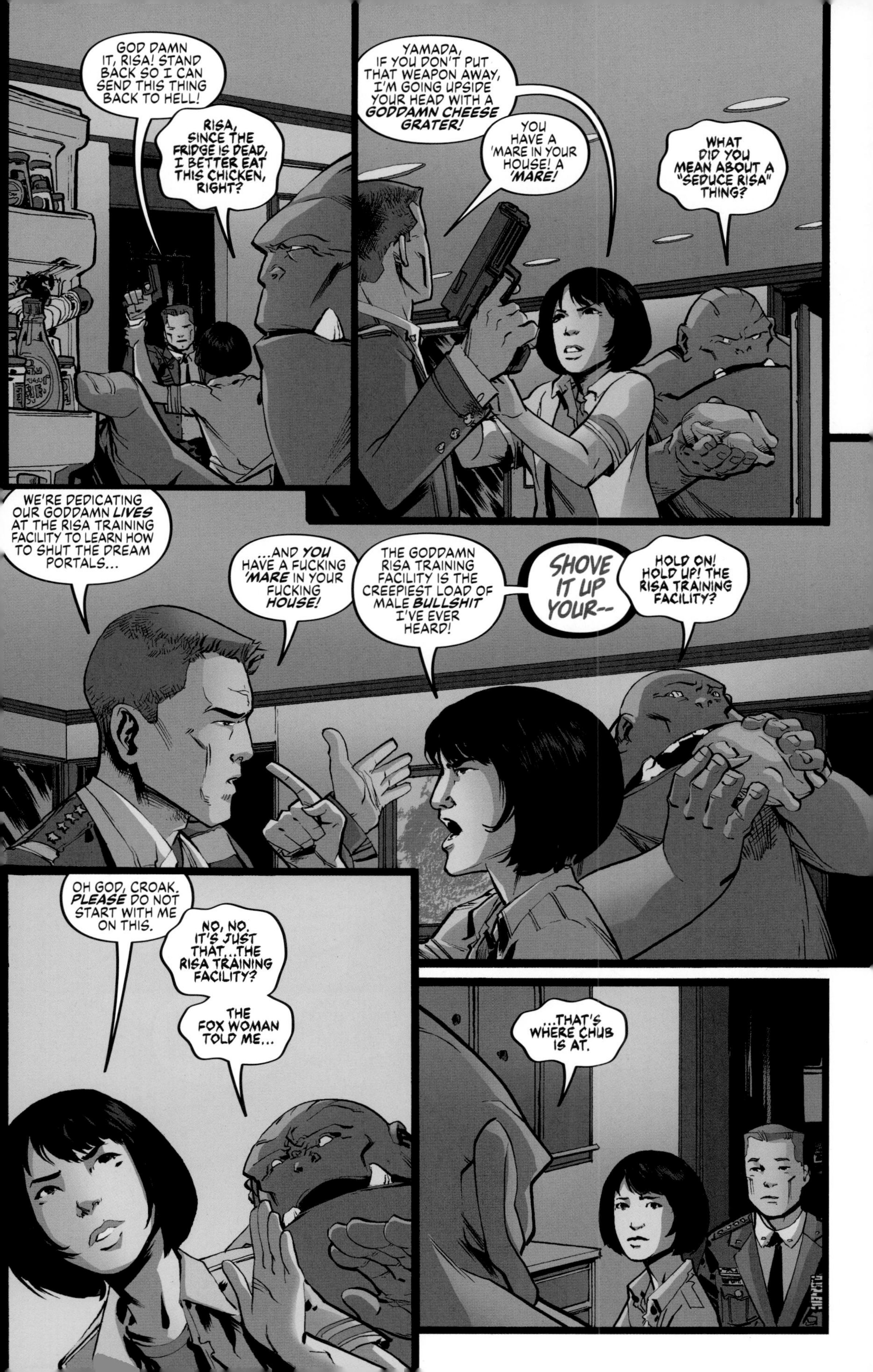
GOD DAMN IT, RISA! STAND BACK SO I CAN SEND THIS THING BACK TO HELL!
RISA, SINCE THE FRIDGE IS DEAD, I BETTER EAT THIS CHICKEN, RIGHT?
YAMADA, IF YOU DON'T PUT THAT WEAPON AWAY, I'M GOING UPSIDE YOUR HEAD WITH A GODDAMN CHEESE GRATER!
YOU HAVE A 'MARE IN YOUR HOUSE! A 'MARE!
WHAT DID YOU MEAN ABOUT A "SEDUCE RISA" THING?
WE'RE DEDICATING OUR GODDAMN LIVES AT THE RISA TRAINING FACILITY TO LEARN HOW TO SHUT THE DREAM PORTALS...
...AND YOU HAVE A FUCKING 'MARE IN YOUR FUCKING HOUSE!
THE GODDAMN RISA TRAINING FACILITY IS THE CREEPIEST LOAD OF MALE BULLSHIT I'VE EVER HEARD!
SHOVE IT UP YOUR--
HOLD ON! HOLD UP! THE RISA TRAINING FACILITY?
OH GOD, CROAK. PLEASE DO NOT START WITH ME ON THIS.
NO, NO. IT'S JUST THAT...THE RISA TRAINING FACILITY?
THE FOX WOMAN TOLD ME...
...THAT'S WHERE CHUB IS AT.

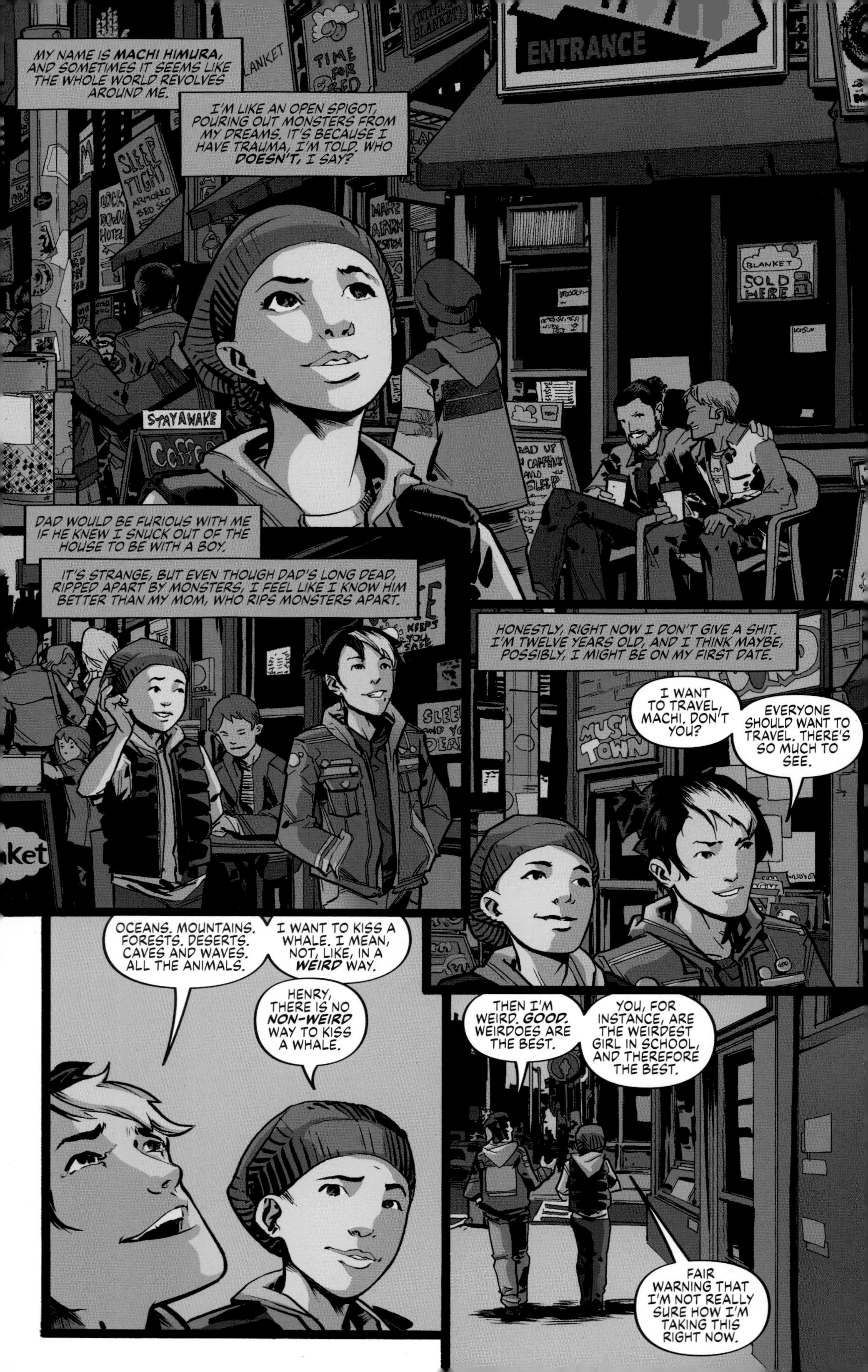
MY NAME IS **MACHI HIMURA**, AND SOMETIMES IT SEEMS LIKE THE WHOLE WORLD REVOLVES AROUND ME.
I'M LIKE AN OPEN SPIGOT, POURING OUT MONSTERS FROM MY DREAMS. IT'S BECAUSE I HAVE TRAUMA, I'M TOLD. WHO **DOESN'T**, I SAY?
ENTRANCE
TIME FOR BED
SLEEP TIGHT ARMORED BED SETS
LOCK DOWN HOTEL
STAYAWAKE
BLANKET SOLD HERE
DAD WOULD BE FURIOUS WITH ME IF HE KNEW I SNUCK OUT OF THE HOUSE TO BE WITH A BOY.
IT'S STRANGE, BUT EVEN THOUGH DAD'S LONG DEAD, RIPPED APART BY MONSTERS, I FEEL LIKE I KNOW HIM BETTER THAN MY MOM, WHO RIPS MONSTERS APART.
HONESTLY, RIGHT NOW I DON'T GIVE A SHIT. I'M TWELVE YEARS OLD, AND I THINK MAYBE, POSSIBLY, I MIGHT BE ON MY FIRST DATE.
I WANT TO TRAVEL, MACHI. DON'T YOU?
EVERYONE SHOULD WANT TO TRAVEL. THERE'S SO MUCH TO SEE.
OCEANS. MOUNTAINS. FORESTS. DESERTS. CAVES AND WAVES. ALL THE ANIMALS.
I WANT TO KISS A WHALE. I MEAN, NOT, LIKE, IN A ***WEIRD*** WAY.
HENRY, THERE IS NO ***NON-WEIRD*** WAY TO KISS A WHALE.
THEN I'M WEIRD. ***GOOD.*** WEIRDOES ARE THE BEST.
YOU, FOR INSTANCE, ARE THE WEIRDEST GIRL IN SCHOOL, AND THEREFORE THE BEST.
FAIR WARNING THAT I'M NOT REALLY SURE HOW I'M TAKING THIS RIGHT NOW.

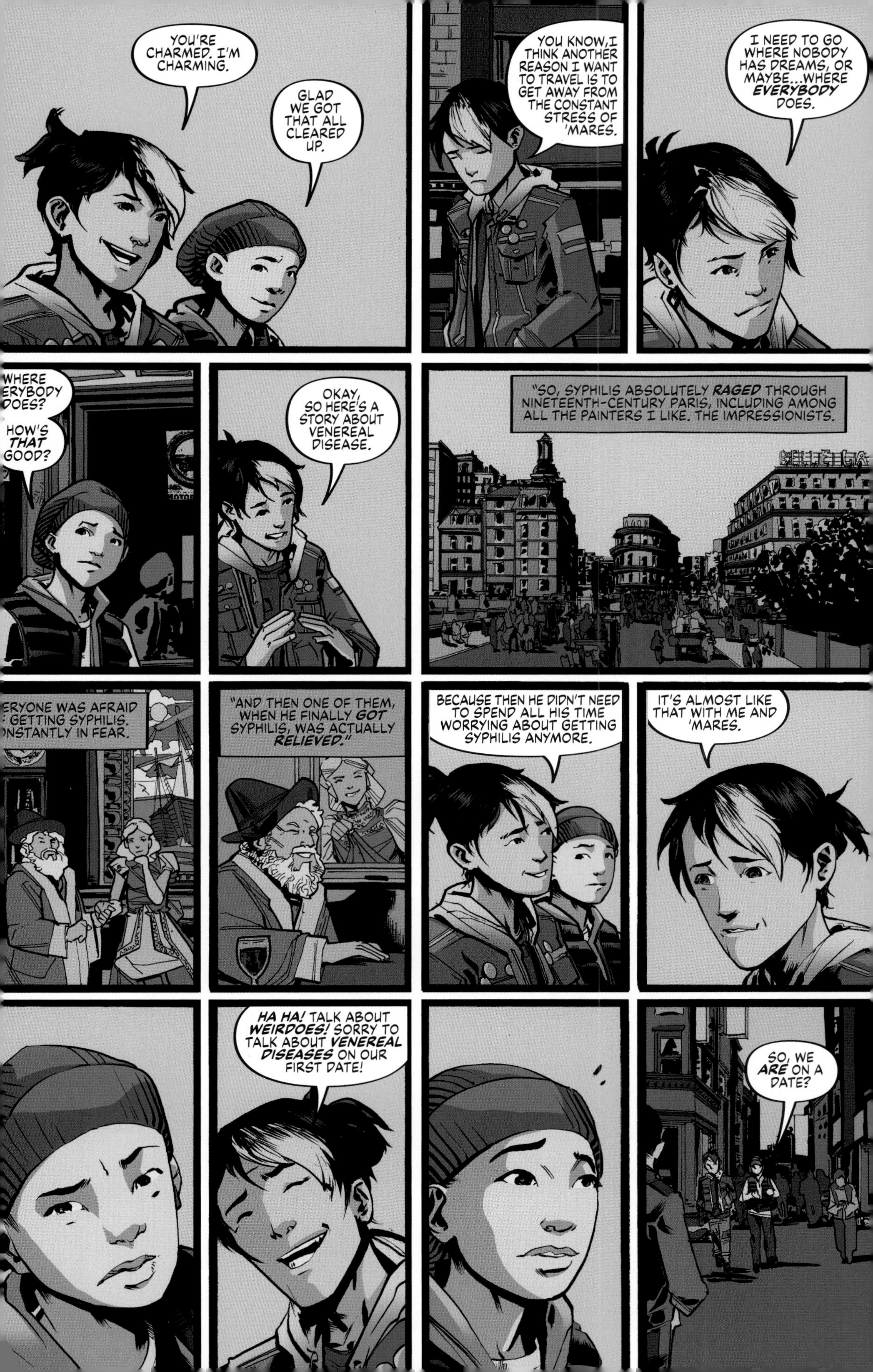
YOU'RE CHARMED. I'M CHARMING.
GLAD WE GOT THAT ALL CLEARED UP.
YOU KNOW, I THINK ANOTHER REASON I WANT TO TRAVEL IS TO GET AWAY FROM THE CONSTANT STRESS OF 'MARES.
I NEED TO GO WHERE NOBODY HAS DREAMS, OR MAYBE...WHERE EVERYBODY DOES.
WHERE ERYBODY DOES?
HOW'S THAT GOOD?
OKAY, SO HERE'S A STORY ABOUT VENEREAL DISEASE.
"SO, SYPHILIS ABSOLUTELY RAGED THROUGH NINETEENTH-CENTURY PARIS, INCLUDING AMONG ALL THE PAINTERS I LIKE. THE IMPRESSIONISTS.
ERYONE WAS AFRAID GETTING SYPHILIS. ONSTANTLY IN FEAR.
"AND THEN ONE OF THEM, WHEN HE FINALLY GOT SYPHILIS, WAS ACTUALLY RELIEVED."
BECAUSE THEN HE DIDN'T NEED TO SPEND ALL HIS TIME WORRYING ABOUT GETTING SYPHILIS ANYMORE.
IT'S ALMOST LIKE THAT WITH ME AND 'MARES.
HA HA! TALK ABOUT WEIRDOES! SORRY TO TALK ABOUT VENEREAL DISEASES ON OUR FIRST DATE!
SO, WE ARE ON A DATE?

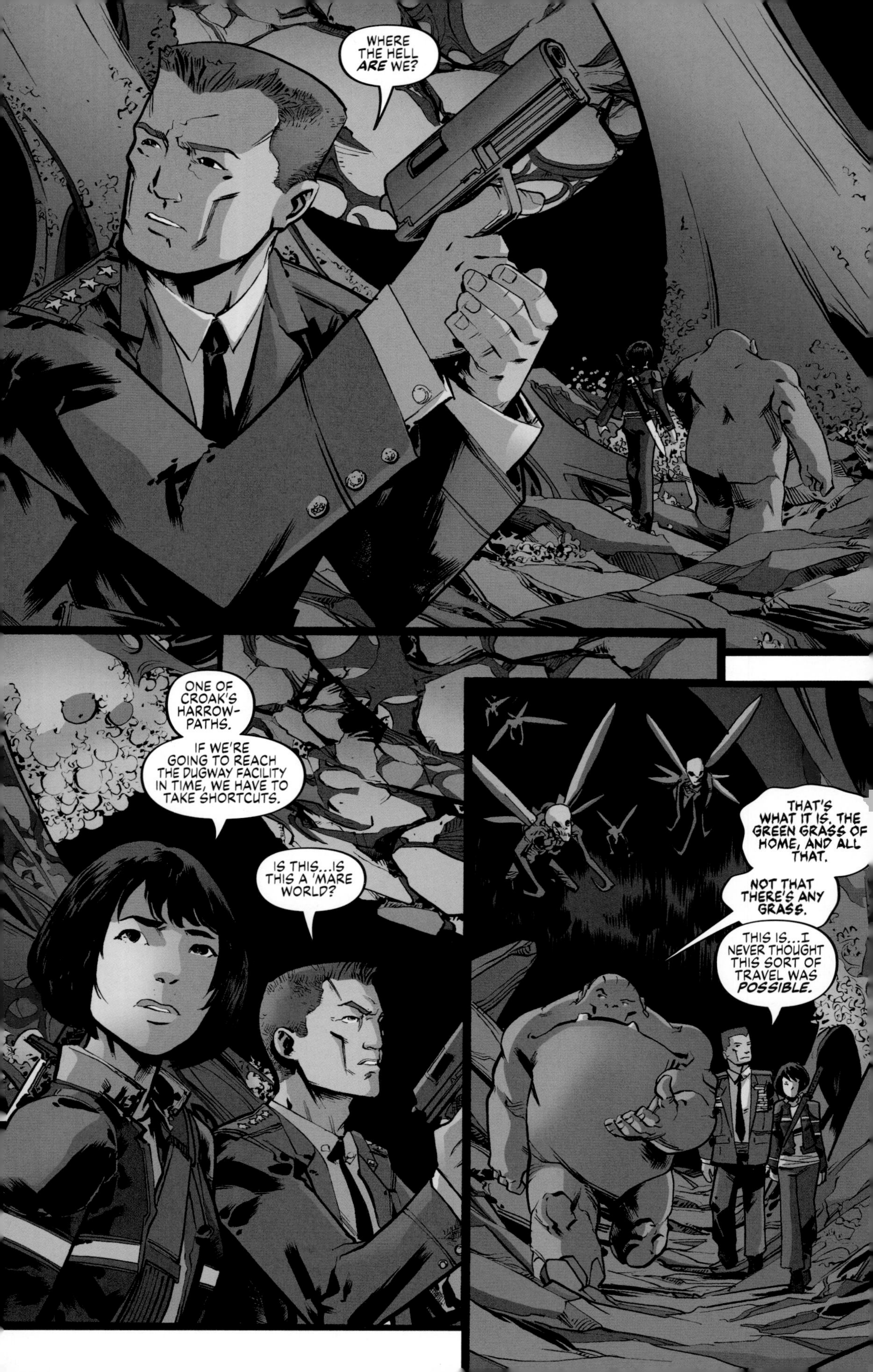
WHERE THE HELL *ARE* WE?
ONE OF CROAK'S HARROW-PATHS.
IF WE'RE GOING TO REACH THE DUGWAY FACILITY IN TIME, WE HAVE TO TAKE SHORTCUTS.
IS THIS...IS THIS A 'MARE WORLD?
THAT'S WHAT IT IS. THE GREEN GRASS OF HOME, AND ALL THAT.
NOT THAT THERE'S ANY GRASS.
THIS IS...I NEVER THOUGHT THIS SORT OF TRAVEL WAS *POSSIBLE.*

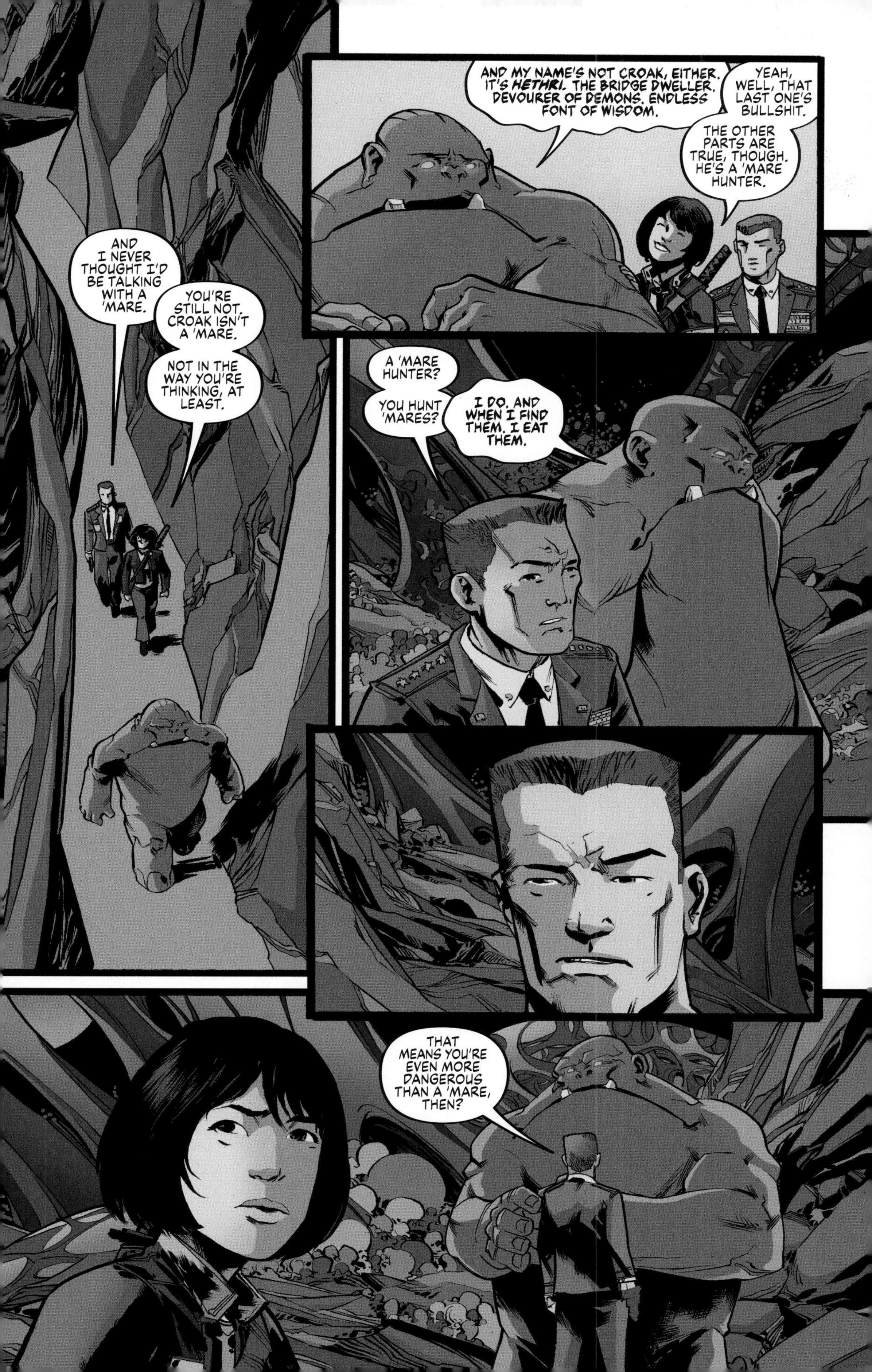
AND I NEVER THOUGHT I'D BE TALKING WITH A 'MARE.
YOU'RE STILL NOT. CROAK ISN'T A 'MARE.
NOT IN THE WAY YOU'RE THINKING, AT LEAST.
AND MY NAME'S NOT CROAK, EITHER. IT'S HETHRI. THE BRIDGE DWELLER. DEVOURER OF DEMONS. ENDLESS FONT OF WISDOM.
YEAH, WELL, THAT LAST ONE'S BULLSHIT.
THE OTHER PARTS ARE TRUE, THOUGH. HE'S A 'MARE HUNTER.
A 'MARE HUNTER?
YOU HUNT 'MARES?
I DO. AND WHEN I FIND THEM, I EAT THEM.
THAT MEANS YOU'RE EVEN MORE DANGEROUS THAN A 'MARE, THEN?

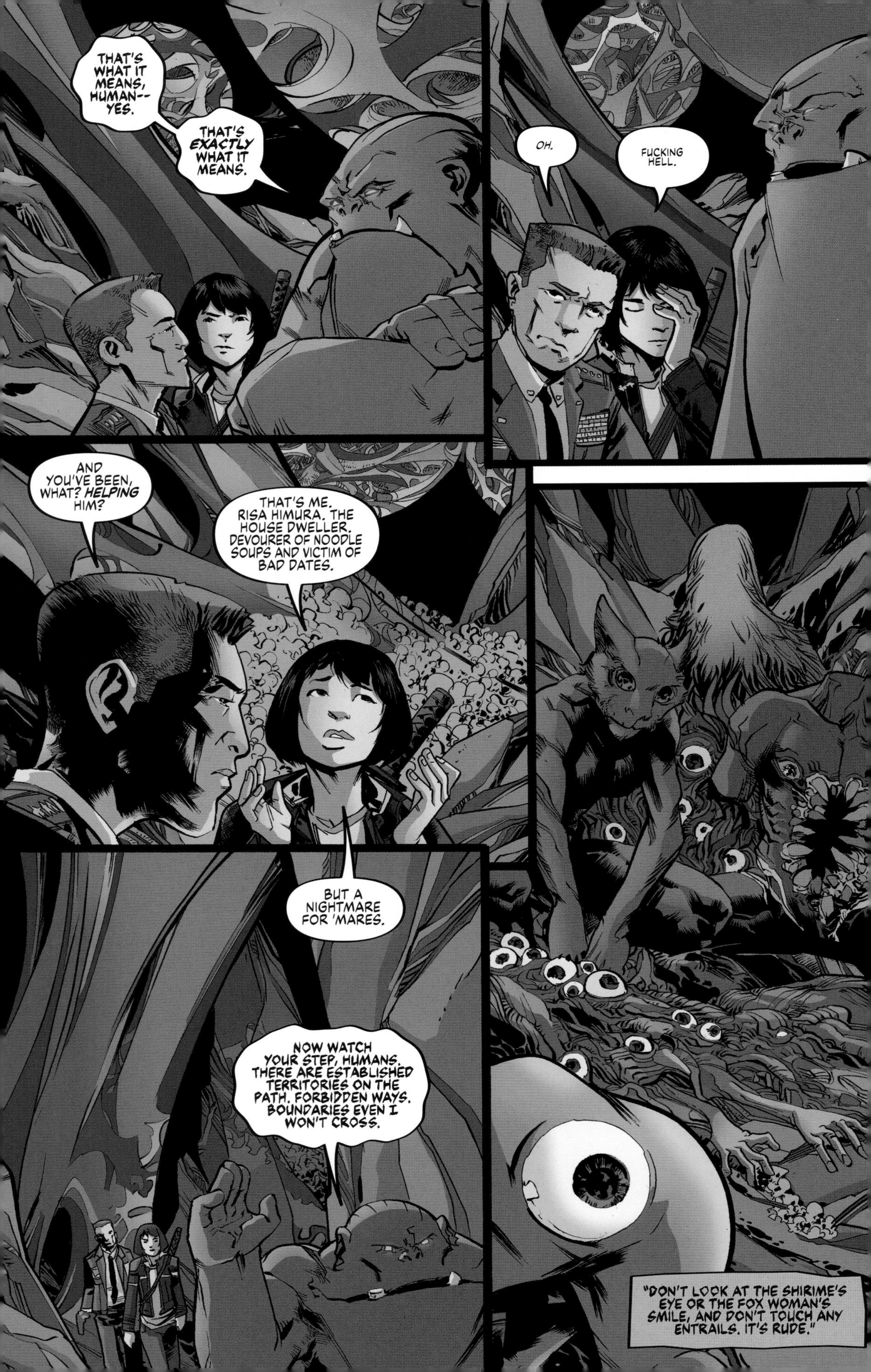
THAT'S WHAT IT MEANS, HUMAN-- YES.
THAT'S *EXACTLY* WHAT IT MEANS.
OH.
FUCKING HELL.
AND YOU'VE BEEN, WHAT? *HELPING* HIM?
THAT'S ME. RISA HIMURA. THE HOUSE DWELLER. DEVOURER OF NOODLE SOUPS AND VICTIM OF BAD DATES.
BUT A NIGHTMARE FOR 'MARES.
NOW WATCH YOUR STEP, HUMANS. THERE ARE ESTABLISHED TERRITORIES ON THE PATH. FORBIDDEN WAYS. BOUNDARIES EVEN I WON'T CROSS.
"DON'T LOOK AT THE SHIRIME'S EYE OR THE FOX WOMAN'S SMILE, AND DON'T TOUCH ANY ENTRAILS. IT'S RUDE."

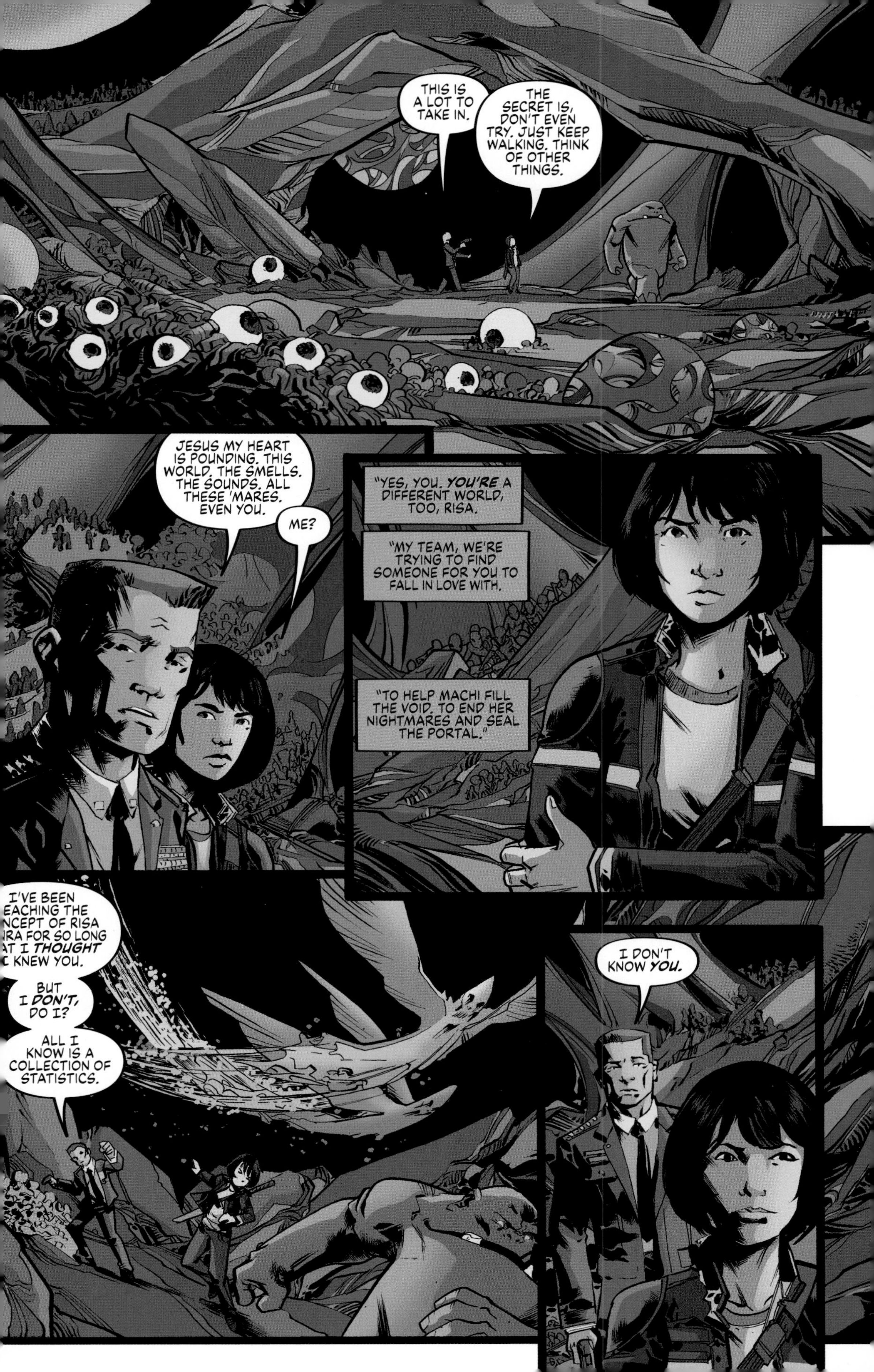
THIS IS A LOT TO TAKE IN.
THE SECRET IS, DON'T EVEN TRY. JUST KEEP WALKING. THINK OF OTHER THINGS.
JESUS MY HEART IS POUNDING. THIS WORLD. THE SMELLS. THE SOUNDS. ALL THESE 'MARES. EVEN YOU.
ME?
"YES, YOU. YOU'RE A DIFFERENT WORLD, TOO, RISA.
"MY TEAM, WE'RE TRYING TO FIND SOMEONE FOR YOU TO FALL IN LOVE WITH.
"TO HELP MACHI FILL THE VOID. TO END HER NIGHTMARES AND SEAL THE PORTAL."
BUT I DON'T, DO I?
ALL I KNOW IS A COLLECTION OF STATISTICS.
I DON'T KNOW YOU.

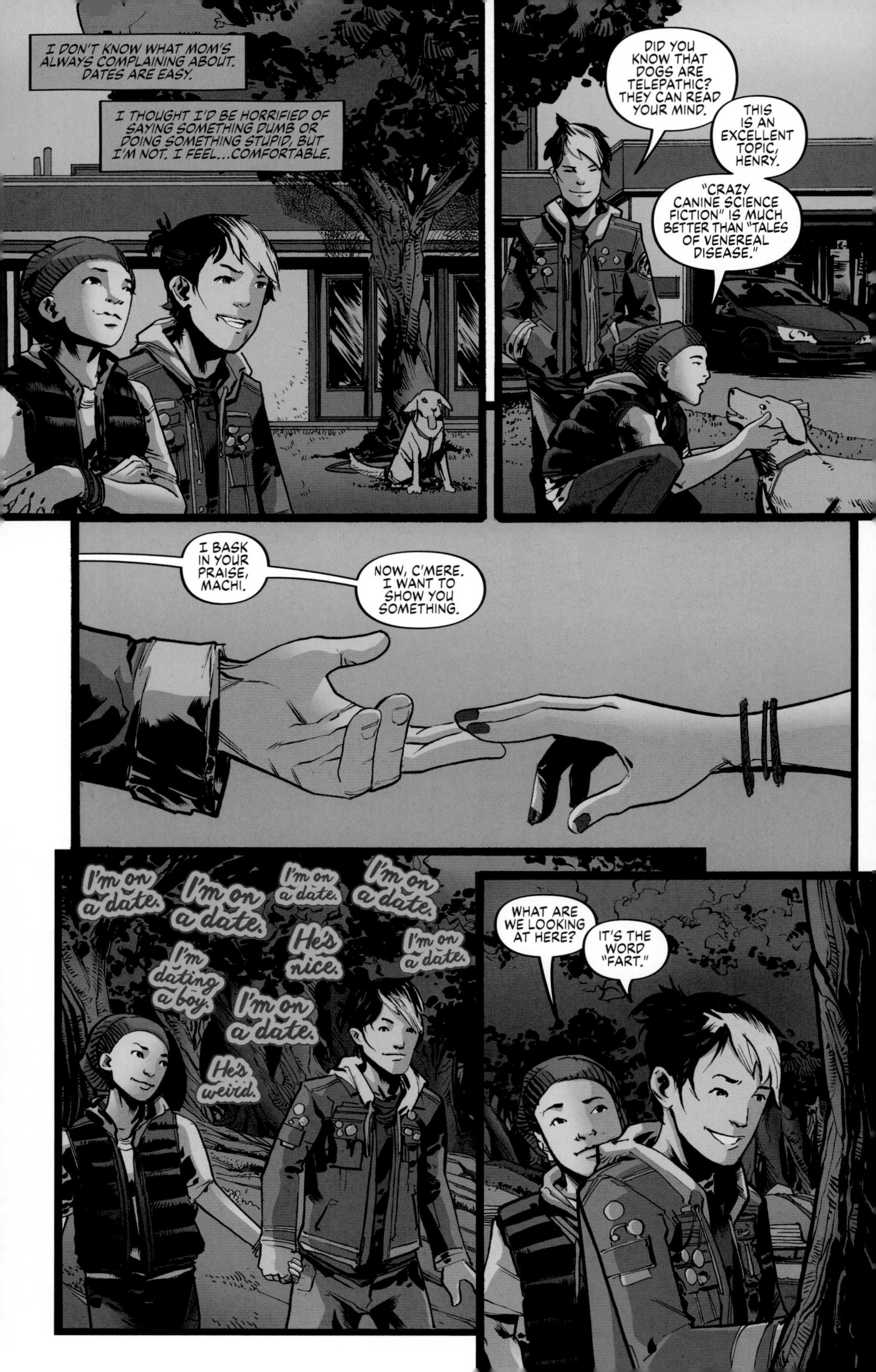
I DON'T KNOW WHAT MOM'S ALWAYS COMPLAINING ABOUT. DATES ARE EASY.
I THOUGHT I'D BE HORRIFIED OF SAYING SOMETHING DUMB OR DOING SOMETHING STUPID, BUT I'M NOT. I FEEL...COMFORTABLE.
DID YOU KNOW THAT DOGS ARE TELEPATHIC? THEY CAN READ YOUR MIND.
THIS IS AN EXCELLENT TOPIC, HENRY.
"CRAZY CANINE SCIENCE FICTION" IS MUCH BETTER THAN "TALES OF VENEREAL DISEASE."
I BASK IN YOUR PRAISE, MACHI.
NOW, C'MERE. I WANT TO SHOW YOU SOMETHING.
I'm on a date.
I'm on a date.
I'm on a date.
I'm on a date.
He's nice.
I'm on a date.
I'm dating a boy.
I'm on a date.
He's weird.
WHAT ARE WE LOOKING AT HERE?
IT'S THE WORD "FART."

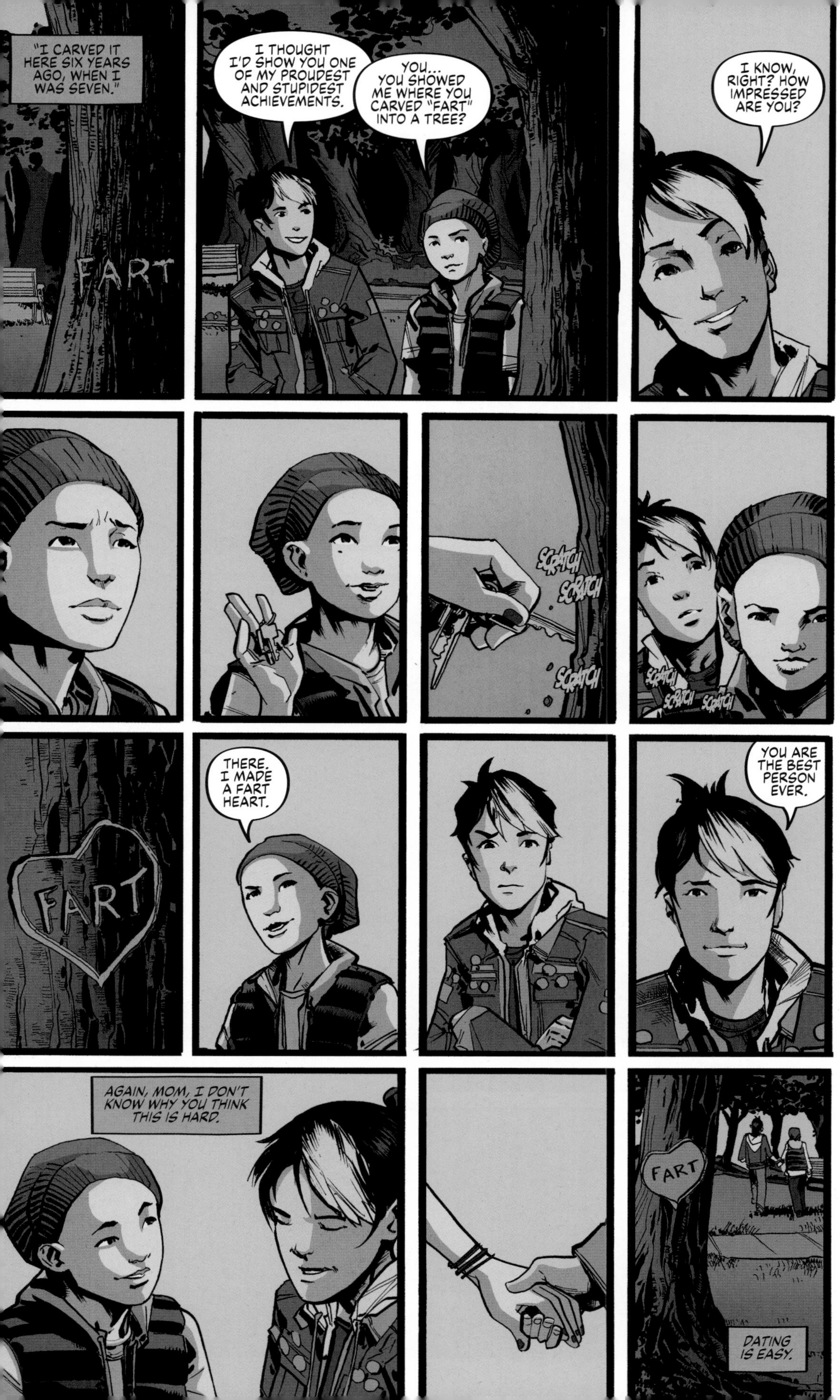
"I CARVED IT HERE SIX YEARS AGO, WHEN I WAS SEVEN."
FART
I THOUGHT I'D SHOW YOU ONE OF MY PROUDEST AND STUPIDEST ACHIEVEMENTS.
YOU... YOU SHOWED ME WHERE YOU CARVED "FART" INTO A TREE?
I KNOW, RIGHT? HOW IMPRESSED ARE YOU?
SCRATCH
SCRATCH
SCRATCH
SCRATCH
SCRATCH
SCRATCH
FART
THERE. I MADE A FART HEART.
YOU ARE THE BEST PERSON EVER.
AGAIN, MOM, I DON'T KNOW WHY YOU THINK THIS IS HARD.
FART
DATING IS EASY.

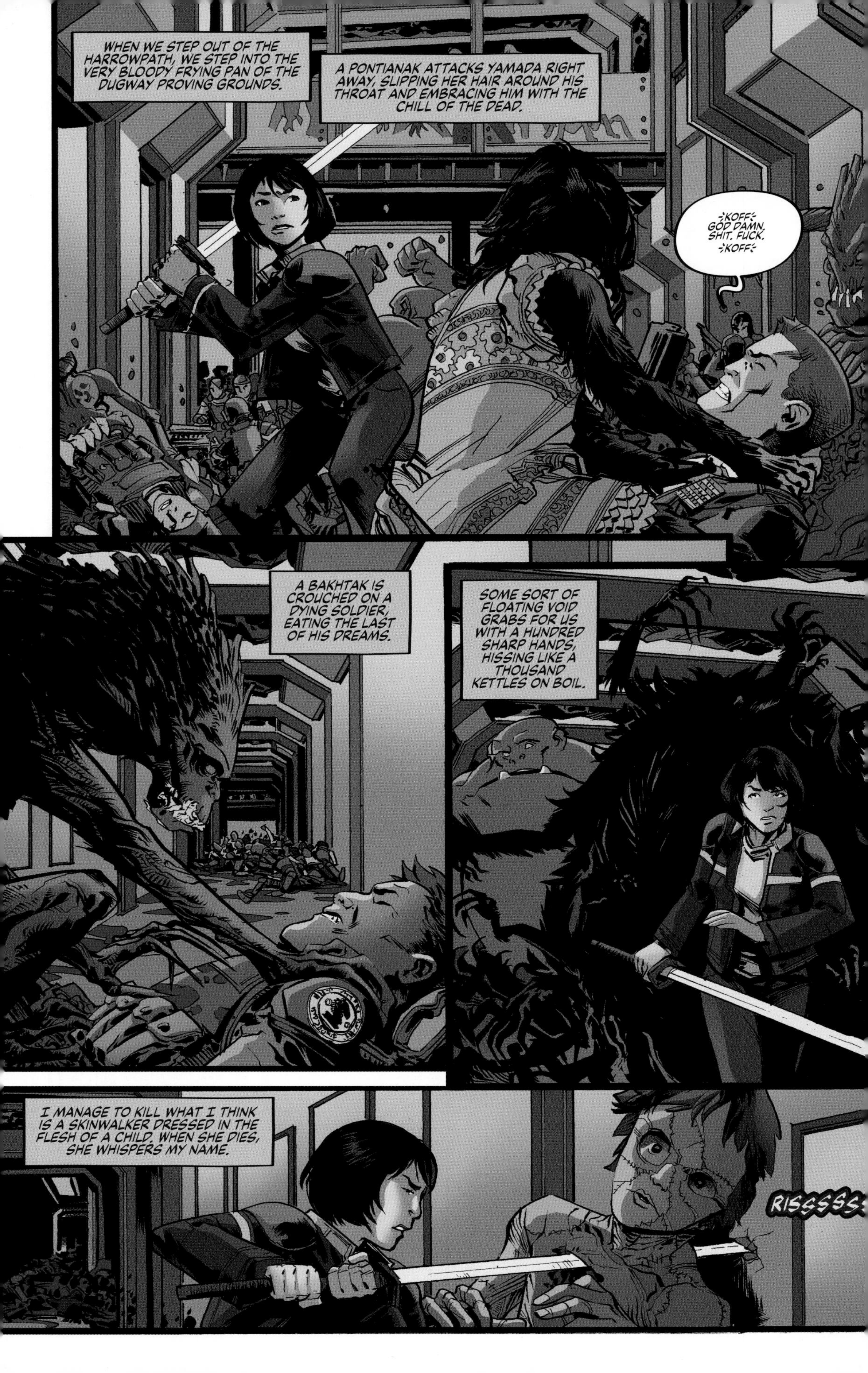
WHEN WE STEP OUT OF THE HARROWPATH, WE STEP INTO THE VERY BLOODY FRYING PAN OF THE DUGWAY PROVING GROUNDS.
A PONTIANAK ATTACKS YAMADA RIGHT AWAY, SLIPPING HER HAIR AROUND HIS THROAT AND EMBRACING HIM WITH THE CHILL OF THE DEAD.
-KOFF- GOD DAMN. SHIT. FUCK. -KOFF-
A BAKHTAK IS CROUCHED ON A DYING SOLDIER, EATING THE LAST OF HIS DREAMS.
SOME SORT OF FLOATING VOID GRABS FOR US WITH A HUNDRED SHARP HANDS, HISSING LIKE A THOUSAND KETTLES ON BOIL.
I MANAGE TO KILL WHAT I THINK IS A SKINWALKER DRESSED IN THE FLESH OF A CHILD. WHEN SHE DIES, SHE WHISPERS MY NAME.
RISSSSS

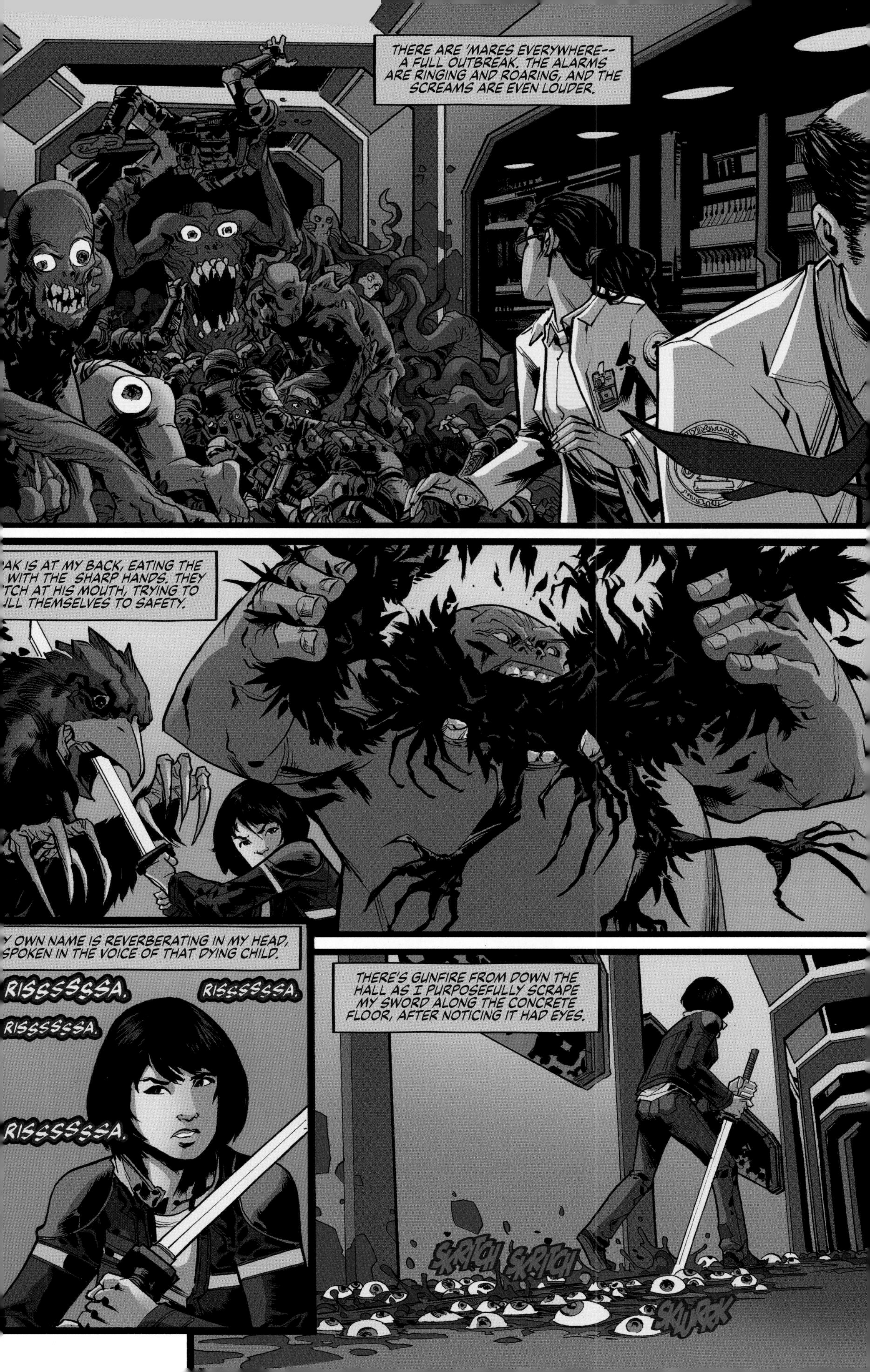

THERE ARE 'MARES EVERYWHERE-- A FULL OUTBREAK. THE ALARMS ARE RINGING AND ROARING, AND THE SCREAMS ARE EVEN LOUDER.
AK IS AT MY BACK, EATING THE WITH THE SHARP HANDS. THEY TCH AT HIS MOUTH, TRYING TO LL THEMSELVES TO SAFETY.
Y OWN NAME IS REVERBERATING IN MY HEAD, SPOKEN IN THE VOICE OF THAT DYING CHILD.
RISSSSSSA.
RISSSSSSA.
RISSSSSSA.
RISSSSSSA.
THERE'S GUNFIRE FROM DOWN THE HALL AS I PURPOSEFULLY SCRAPE MY SWORD ALONG THE CONCRETE FLOOR, AFTER NOTICING IT HAD EYES.
SKRITCH SKRITCH
SKLURRK

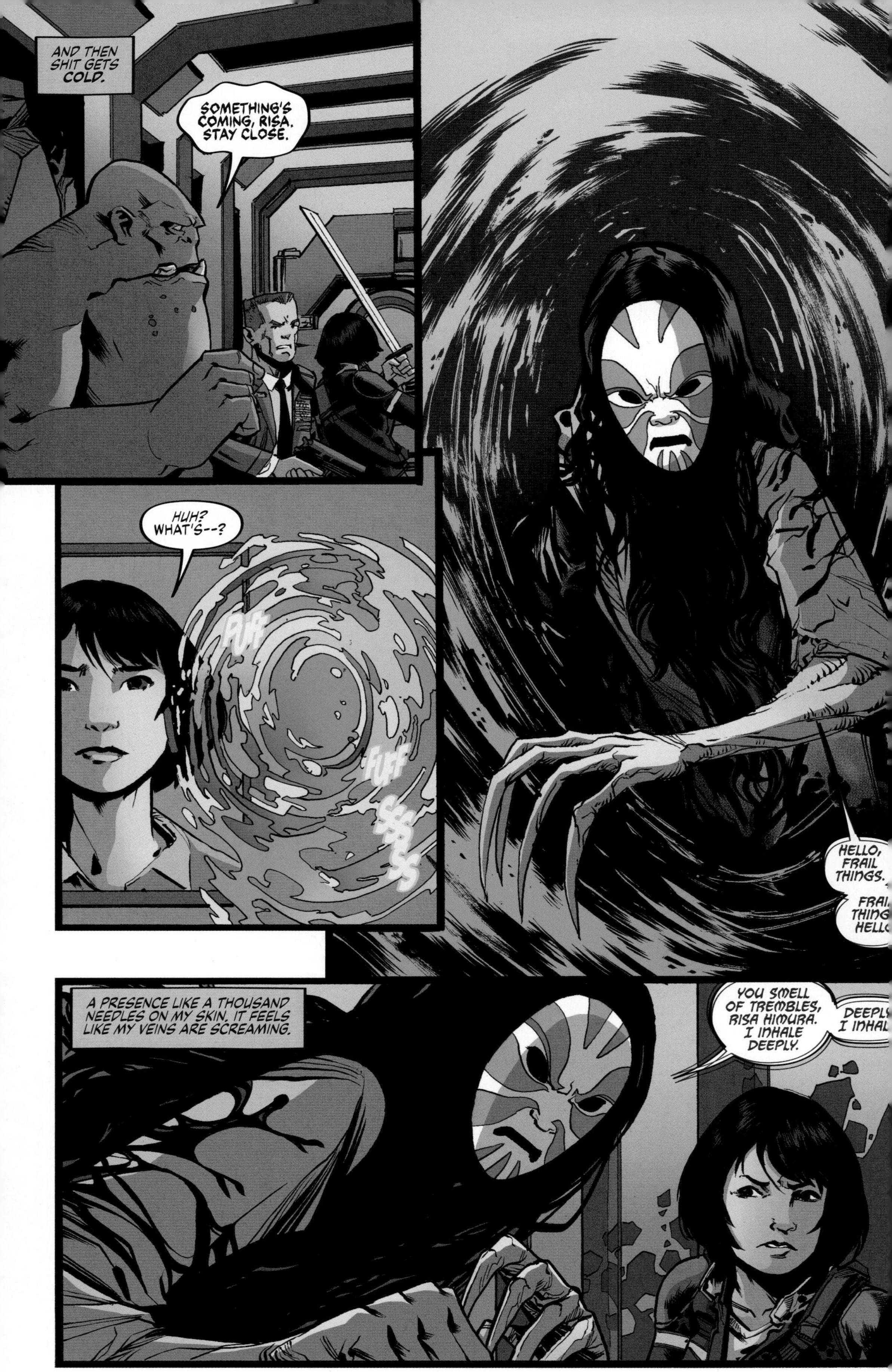
AND THEN SHIT GETS COLD.
SOMETHING'S COMING, RISA. STAY CLOSE.
HUH? WHAT'S--?
FUFF
FUFF
SSSSSS
HELLO, FRAIL THINGS.
A PRESENCE LIKE A THOUSAND NEEDLES ON MY SKIN. IT FEELS LIKE MY VEINS ARE SCREAMING.
YOU SMELL OF TREMBLES, RISA HIMURA. I INHALE DEEPLY.

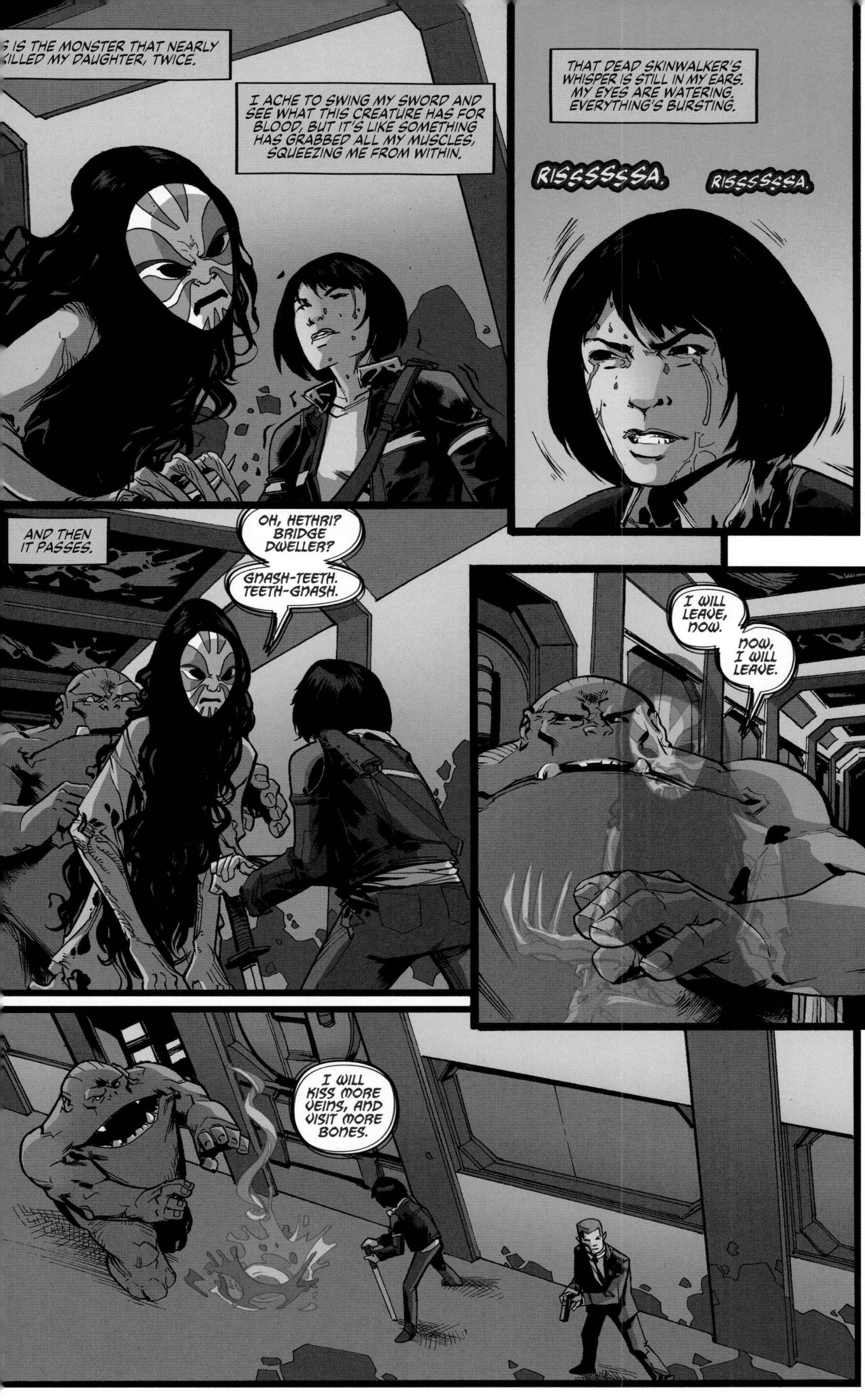
S IS THE MONSTER THAT NEARLY KILLED MY DAUGHTER, TWICE.
I ACHE TO SWING MY SWORD AND SEE WHAT THIS CREATURE HAS FOR BLOOD, BUT IT'S LIKE SOMETHING HAS GRABBED ALL MY MUSCLES, SQUEEZING ME FROM WITHIN.
THAT DEAD SKINWALKER'S WHISPER IS STILL IN MY EARS. MY EYES ARE WATERING. EVERYTHING'S BURSTING.
RISSSSSSA.
RISSSSSSA.
AND THEN IT PASSES.
OH, HETHRI? BRIDGE DWELLER?
GNASH-TEETH. TEETH-GNASH.
I WILL LEAVE, NOW.
NOW, I WILL LEAVE.
I WILL KISS MORE VEINS, AND VISIT MORE BONES.

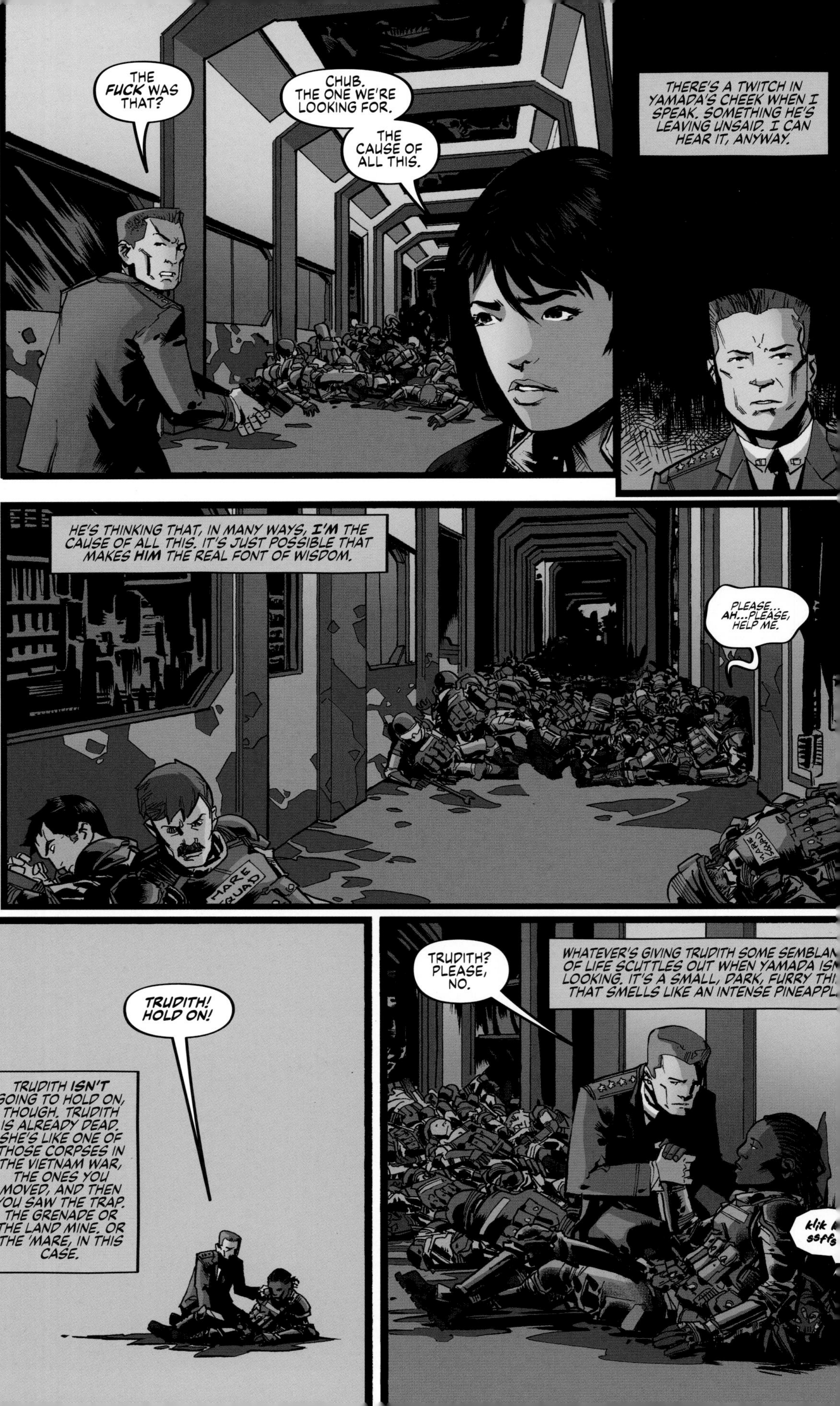

THE *FUCK* WAS THAT?
CHUB. THE ONE WE'RE LOOKING FOR.
THE CAUSE OF ALL THIS.
THERE'S A TWITCH IN YAMADA'S CHEEK WHEN I SPEAK. SOMETHING HE'S LEAVING UNSAID. I CAN HEAR IT, ANYWAY.
*HE'S THINKING THAT, IN MANY WAYS, **I'M** THE CAUSE OF ALL THIS. IT'S JUST POSSIBLE THAT MAKES **HIM** THE REAL FONT OF WISDOM.*
*PLEASE... **AH**...PLEASE, HELP ME.*
MARE GUAD
TRUDITH! HOLD ON!
*TRUDITH **ISN'T** GOING TO HOLD ON, THOUGH. TRUDITH IS ALREADY DEAD. SHE'S LIKE ONE OF THOSE CORPSES IN THE VIETNAM WAR, THE ONES YOU MOVED, AND THEN YOU SAW THE TRAP. THE GRENADE OR THE LAND MINE. OR THE 'MARE, IN THIS CASE.*
TRUDITH? PLEASE, NO.
WHATEVER'S GIVING TRUDITH SOME SEMBLAN OF LIFE SCUTTLES OUT WHEN YAMADA ISN LOOKING. IT'S A SMALL, DARK, FURRY THI THAT SMELLS LIKE AN INTENSE PINEAPPL
klik
ssfs

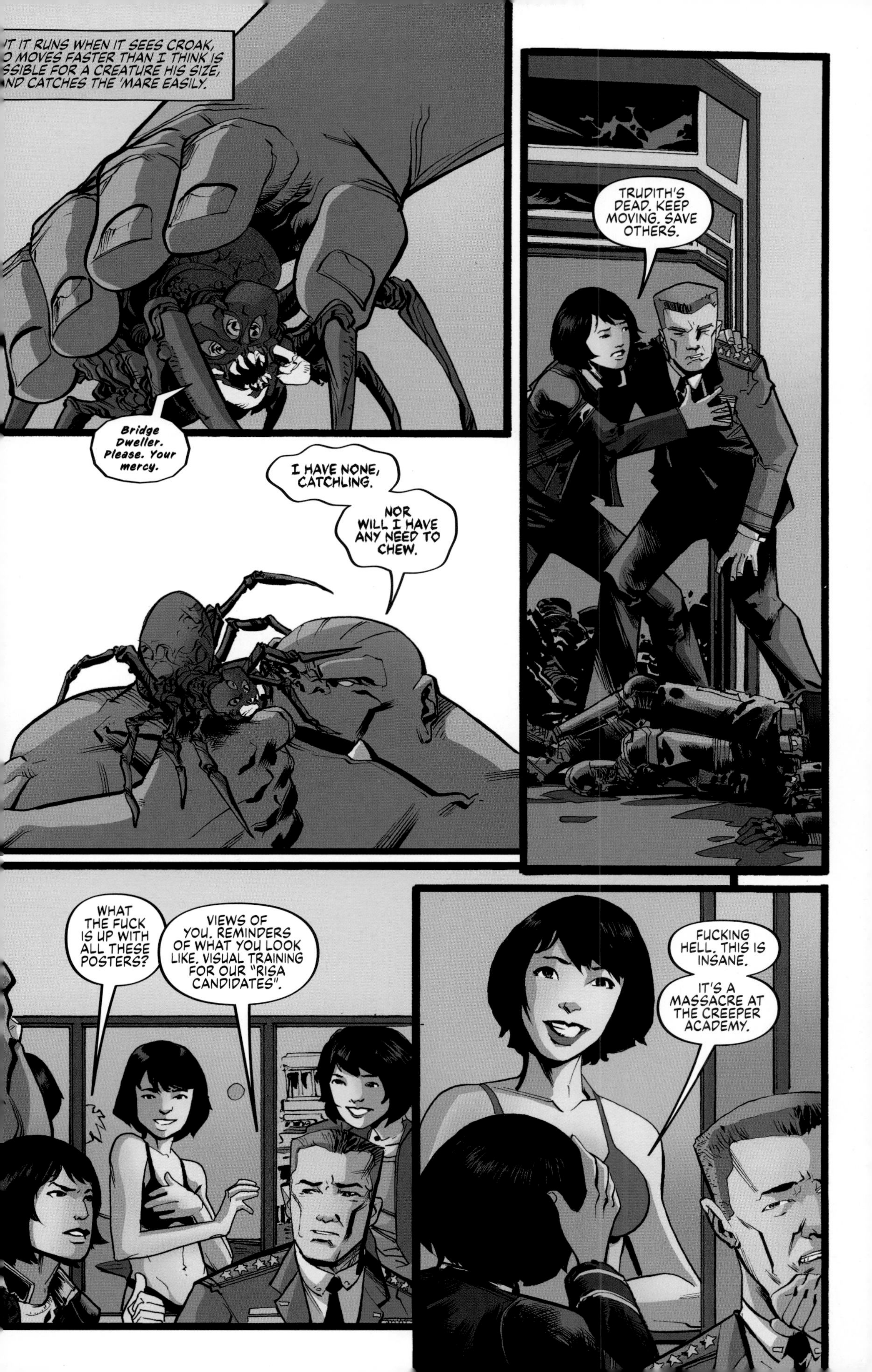
...T IT RUNS WHEN IT SEES CROAK, ...O MOVES FASTER THAN I THINK IS ...SSIBLE FOR A CREATURE HIS SIZE, ...ND CATCHES THE 'MARE EASILY.
Bridge Dweller. Please. Your mercy.
I HAVE NONE, CATCHLING.
NOR WILL I HAVE ANY NEED TO CHEW.
TRUDITH'S DEAD. KEEP MOVING. SAVE OTHERS.
WHAT THE FUCK IS UP WITH ALL THESE POSTERS?
VIEWS OF YOU. REMINDERS OF WHAT YOU LOOK LIKE. VISUAL TRAINING FOR OUR "RISA CANDIDATES".
FUCKING HELL. THIS IS INSANE.
IT'S A MASSACRE AT THE CREEPER ACADEMY.

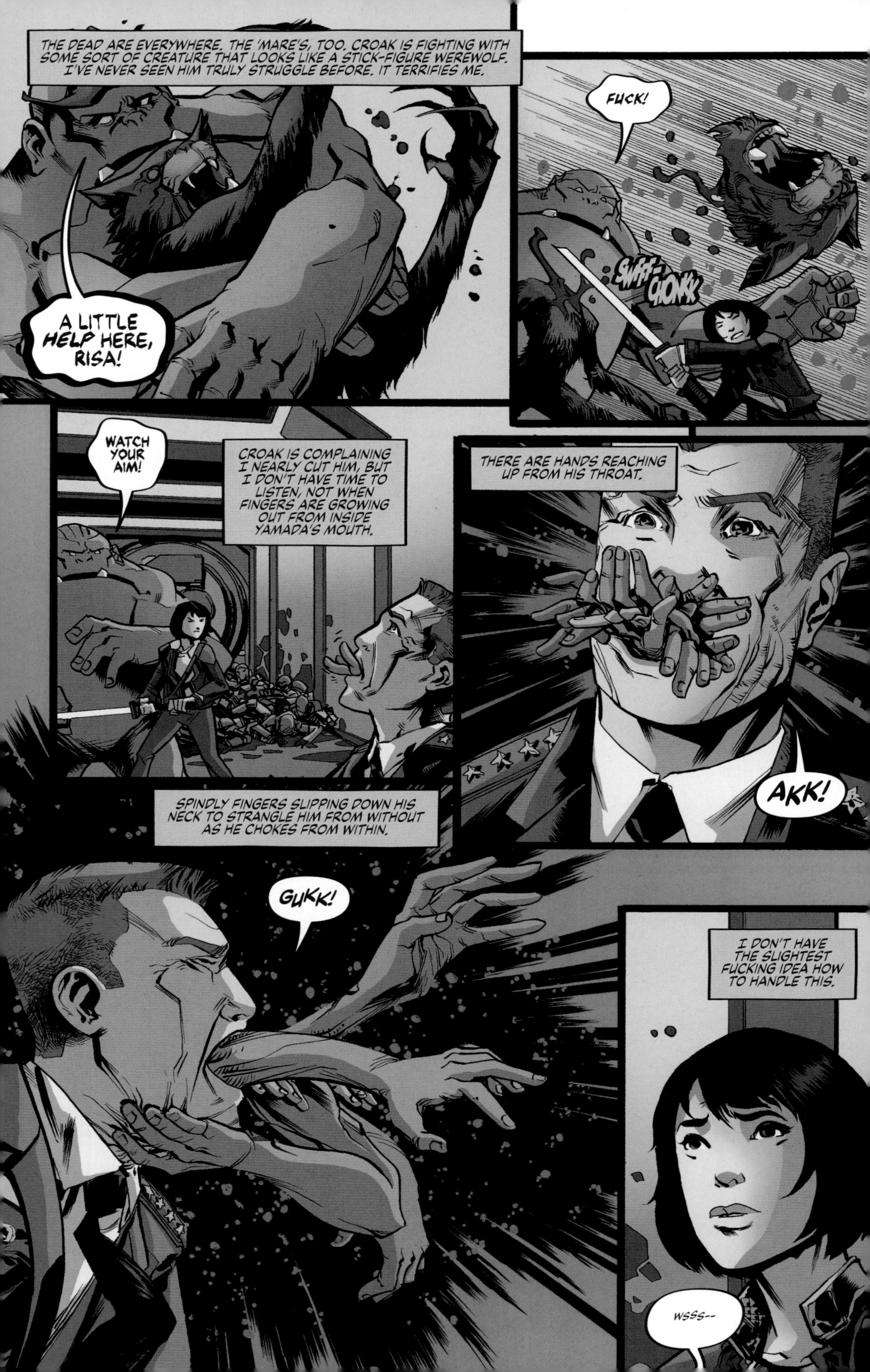
THE DEAD ARE EVERYWHERE. THE 'MARE'S, TOO. CROAK IS FIGHTING WITH SOME SORT OF CREATURE THAT LOOKS LIKE A STICK-FIGURE WEREWOLF. I'VE NEVER SEEN HIM TRULY STRUGGLE BEFORE. IT TERRIFIES ME.
A LITTLE HELP HERE, RISA!
FUCK!
SWIFF-CHONKK
WATCH YOUR AIM!
CROAK IS COMPLAINING I NEARLY CUT HIM, BUT I DON'T HAVE TIME TO LISTEN, NOT WHEN FINGERS ARE GROWING OUT FROM INSIDE YAMADA'S MOUTH.
THERE ARE HANDS REACHING UP FROM HIS THROAT.
AKK!
SPINDLY FINGERS SLIPPING DOWN HIS NECK TO STRANGLE HIM FROM WITHOUT AS HE CHOKES FROM WITHIN.
GUKK!
I DON'T HAVE THE SLIGHTEST FUCKING IDEA HOW TO HANDLE THIS.
WSSS--

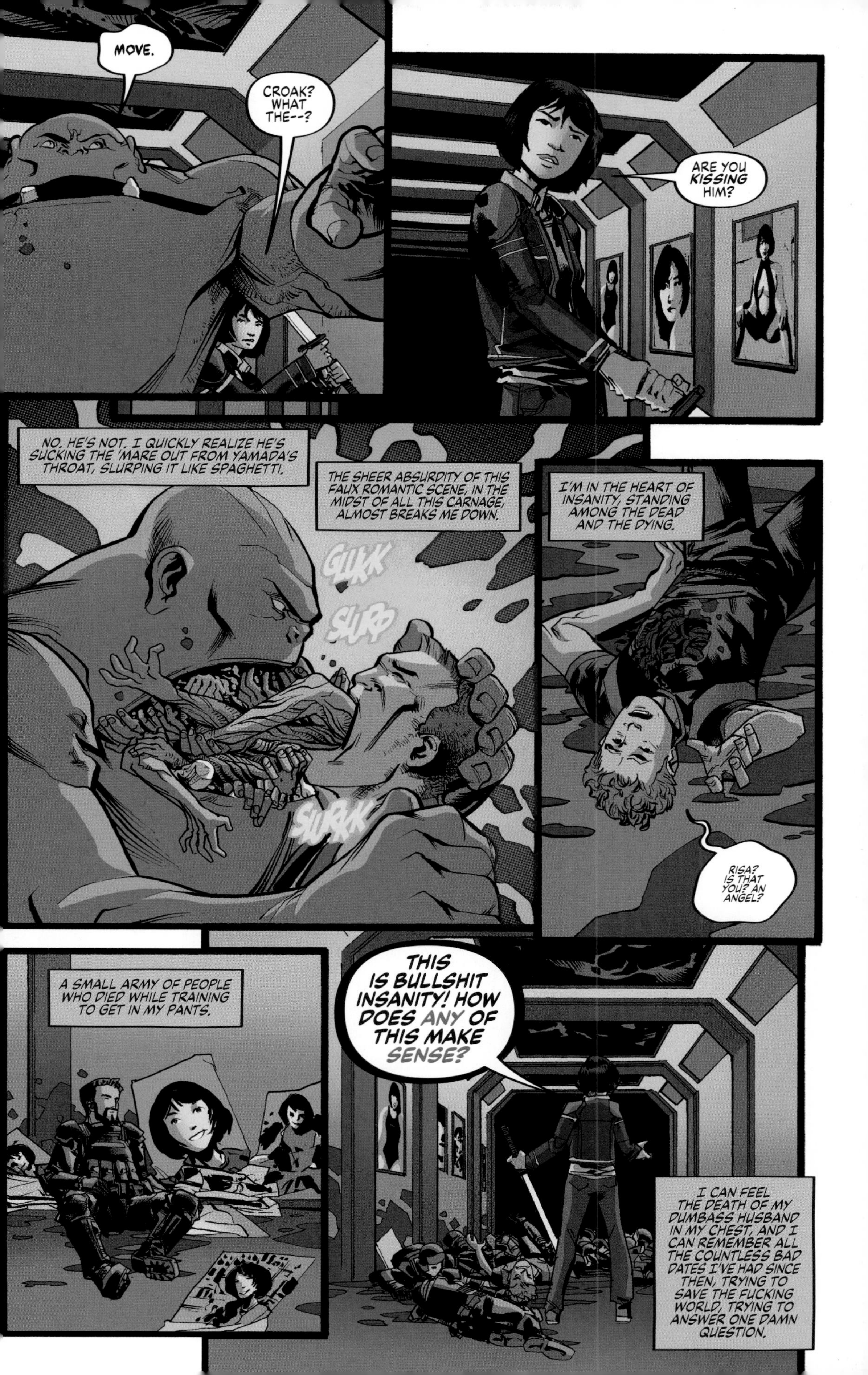
MOVE.
CROAK? WHAT THE--?
ARE YOU KISSING HIM?
NO. HE'S NOT. I QUICKLY REALIZE HE'S SUCKING THE 'MARE OUT FROM YAMADA'S THROAT, SLURPING IT LIKE SPAGHETTI.
THE SHEER ABSURDITY OF THIS FAUX ROMANTIC SCENE, IN THE MIDST OF ALL THIS CARNAGE, ALMOST BREAKS ME DOWN.
GLUKK
SLURP
SLURKK
I'M IN THE HEART OF INSANITY, STANDING AMONG THE DEAD AND THE DYING.
RISA? IS THAT YOU? AN ANGEL?
A SMALL ARMY OF PEOPLE WHO DIED WHILE TRAINING TO GET IN MY PANTS.
THIS IS BULLSHIT INSANITY! HOW DOES ANY OF THIS MAKE SENSE?
I CAN FEEL THE DEATH OF MY DUMBASS HUSBAND IN MY CHEST, AND I CAN REMEMBER ALL THE COUNTLESS BAD DATES I'VE HAD SINCE THEN, TRYING TO SAVE THE FUCKING WORLD, TRYING TO ANSWER ONE DAMN QUESTION.

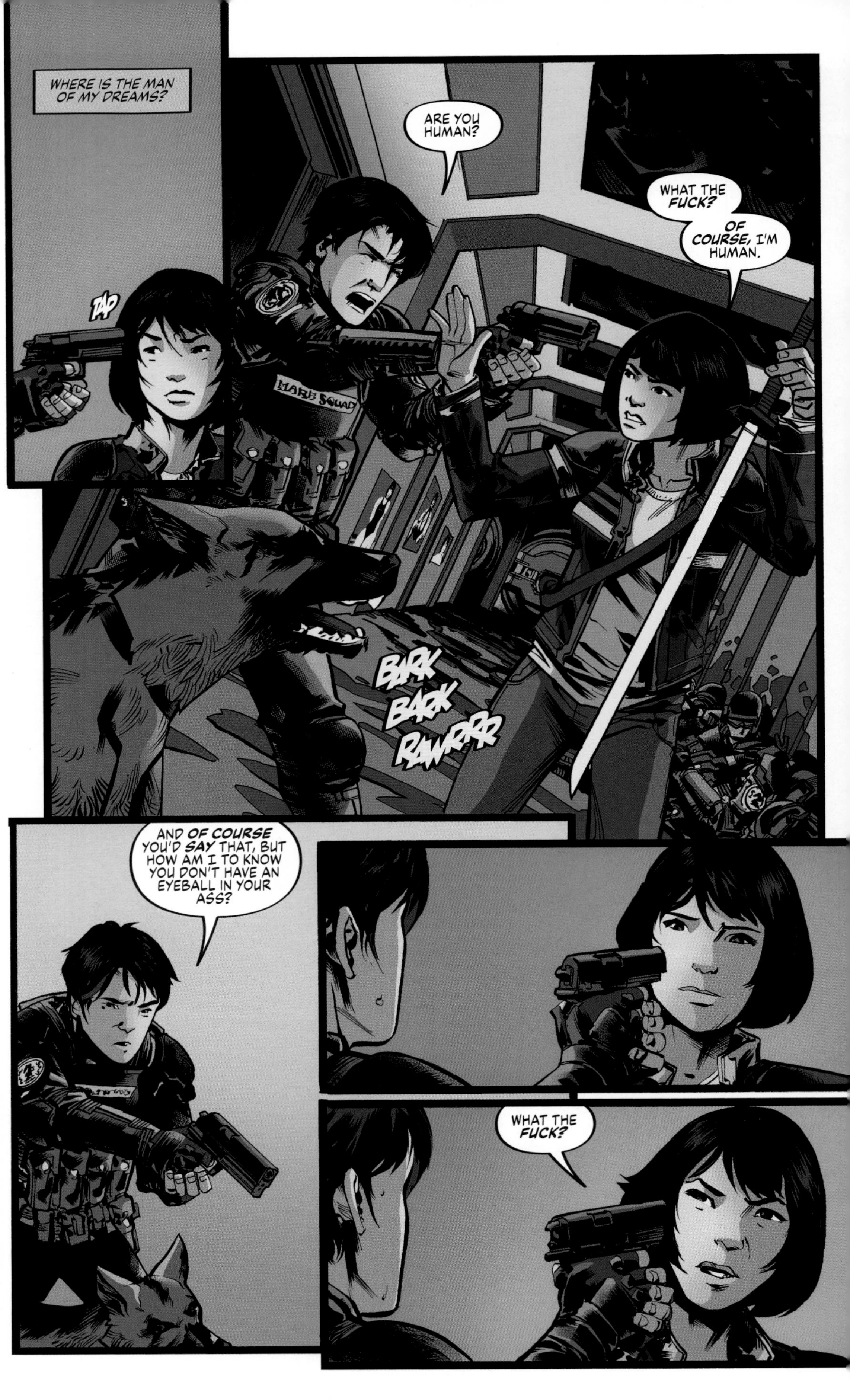
WHERE IS THE MAN OF MY DREAMS?
TAP
ARE YOU HUMAN?
WHAT THE FUCK?
OF COURSE, I'M HUMAN.
MARS SQUAD
BARK
BARK
RAWRRR
AND OF COURSE YOU'D SAY THAT, BUT HOW AM I TO KNOW YOU DON'T HAVE AN EYEBALL IN YOUR ASS?
WHAT THE FUCK?

5

THE MAN OF MY DREAMS

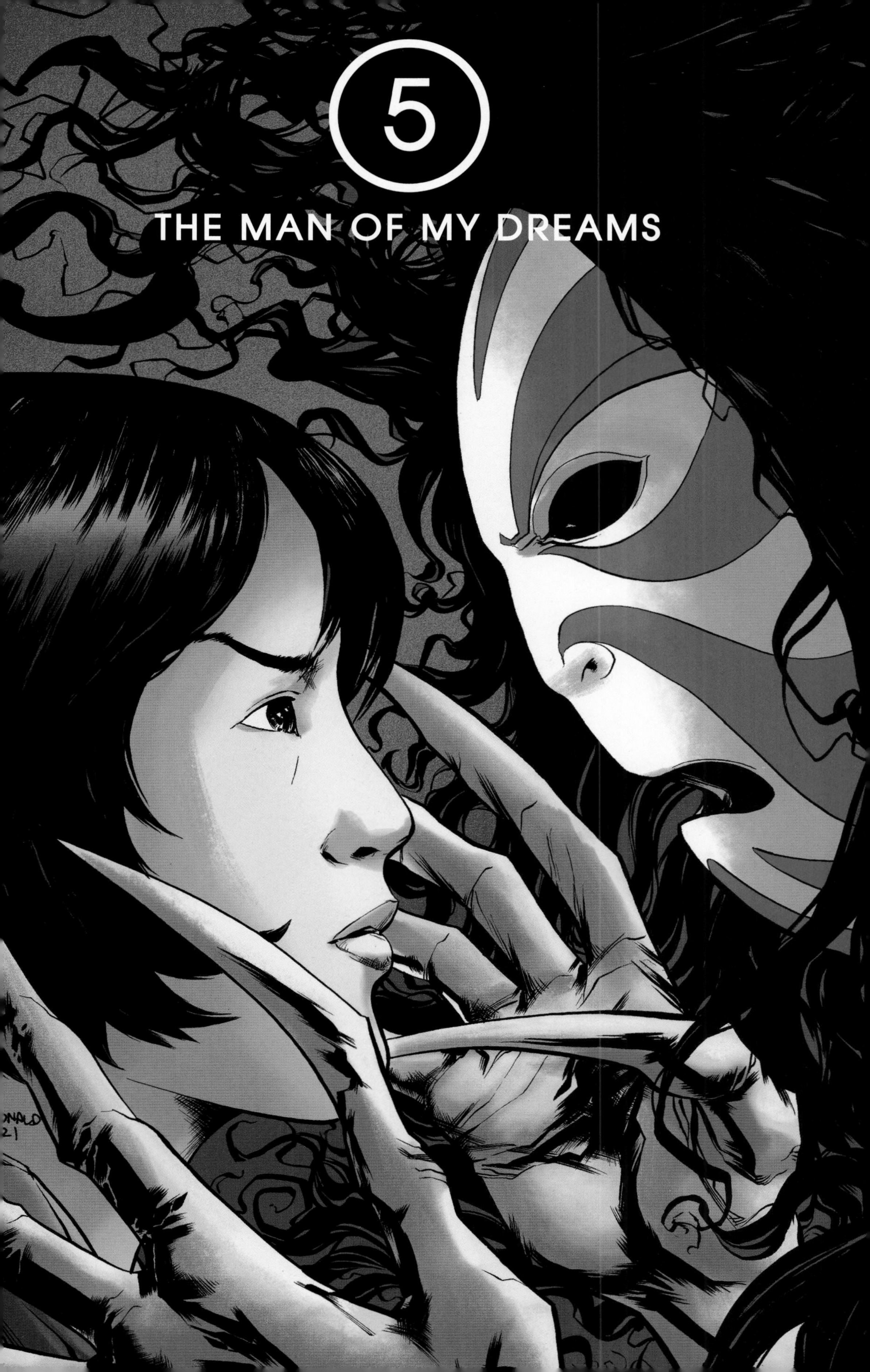

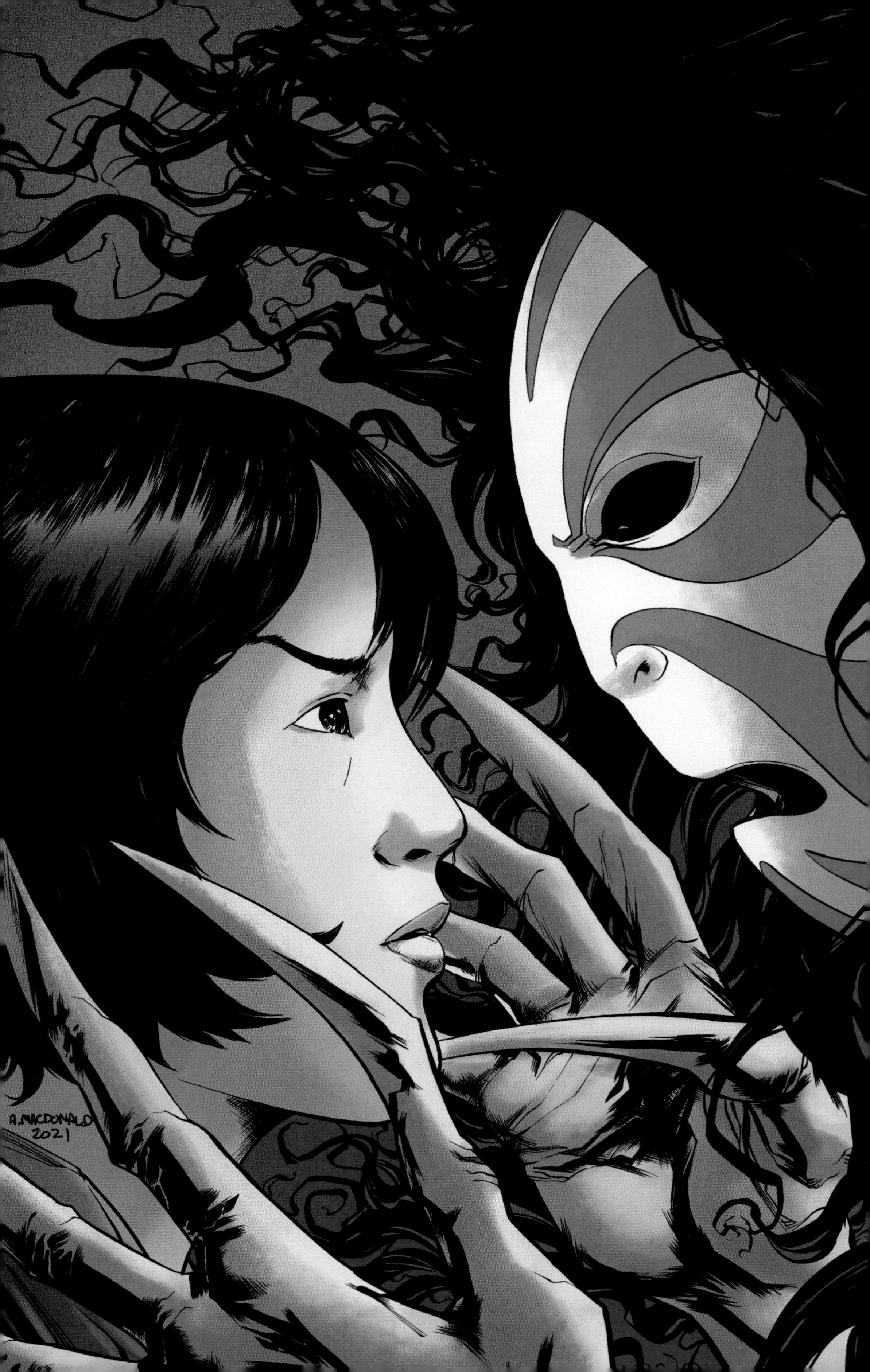
A. MACDONALD
2021

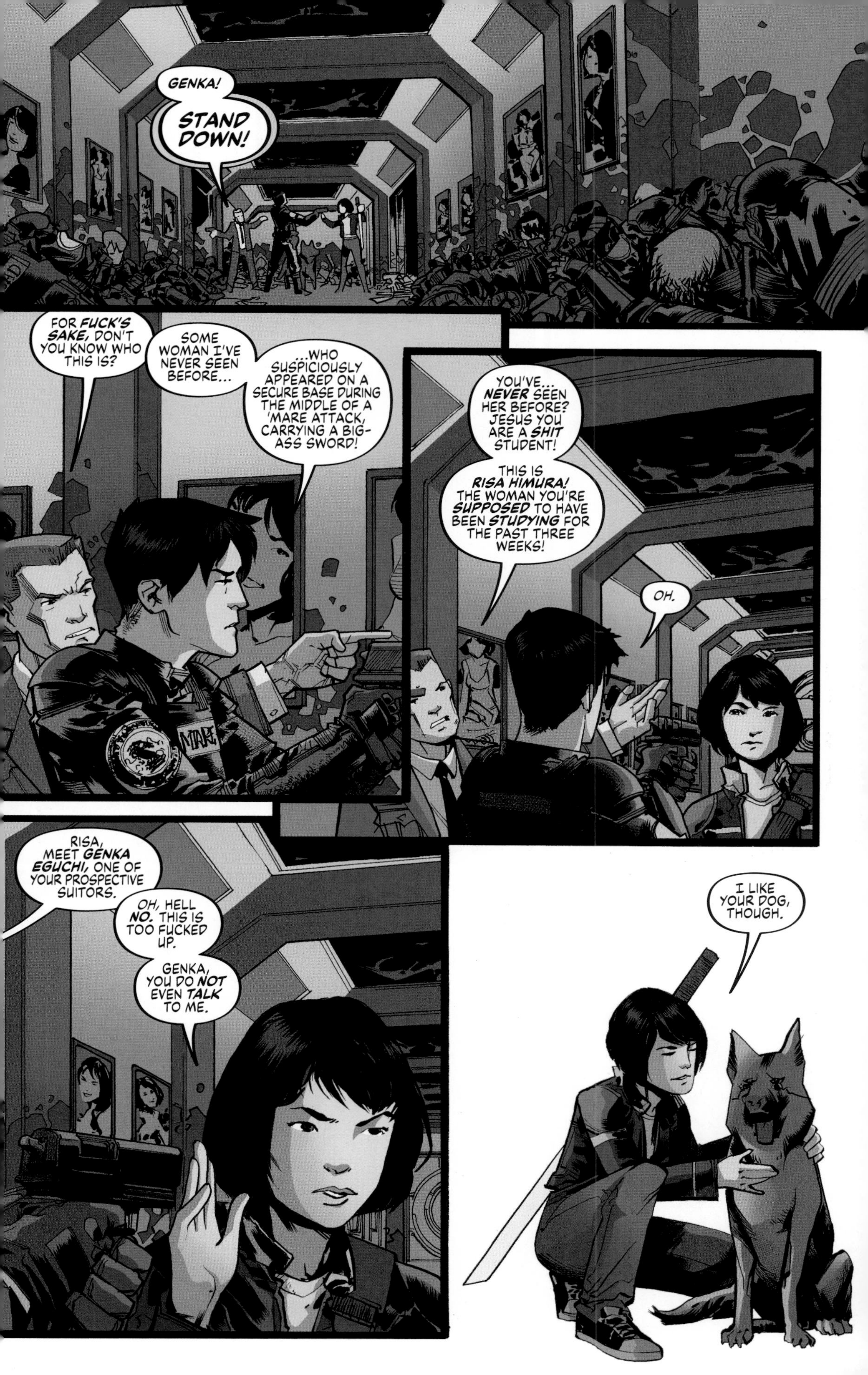
GENKA!
STAND DOWN!
FOR FUCK'S SAKE, DON'T YOU KNOW WHO THIS IS?
SOME WOMAN I'VE NEVER SEEN BEFORE...
...WHO SUSPICIOUSLY APPEARED ON A SECURE BASE DURING THE MIDDLE OF A 'MARE ATTACK, CARRYING A BIG-ASS SWORD!
YOU'VE... NEVER SEEN HER BEFORE? JESUS YOU ARE A SHIT STUDENT!
THIS IS RISA HIMURA! THE WOMAN YOU'RE SUPPOSED TO HAVE BEEN STUDYING FOR THE PAST THREE WEEKS!
OH.
RISA, MEET GENKA EGUCHI, ONE OF YOUR PROSPECTIVE SUITORS.
OH, HELL NO. THIS IS TOO FUCKED UP.
GENKA, YOU DO NOT EVEN TALK TO ME.
I LIKE YOUR DOG, THOUGH.

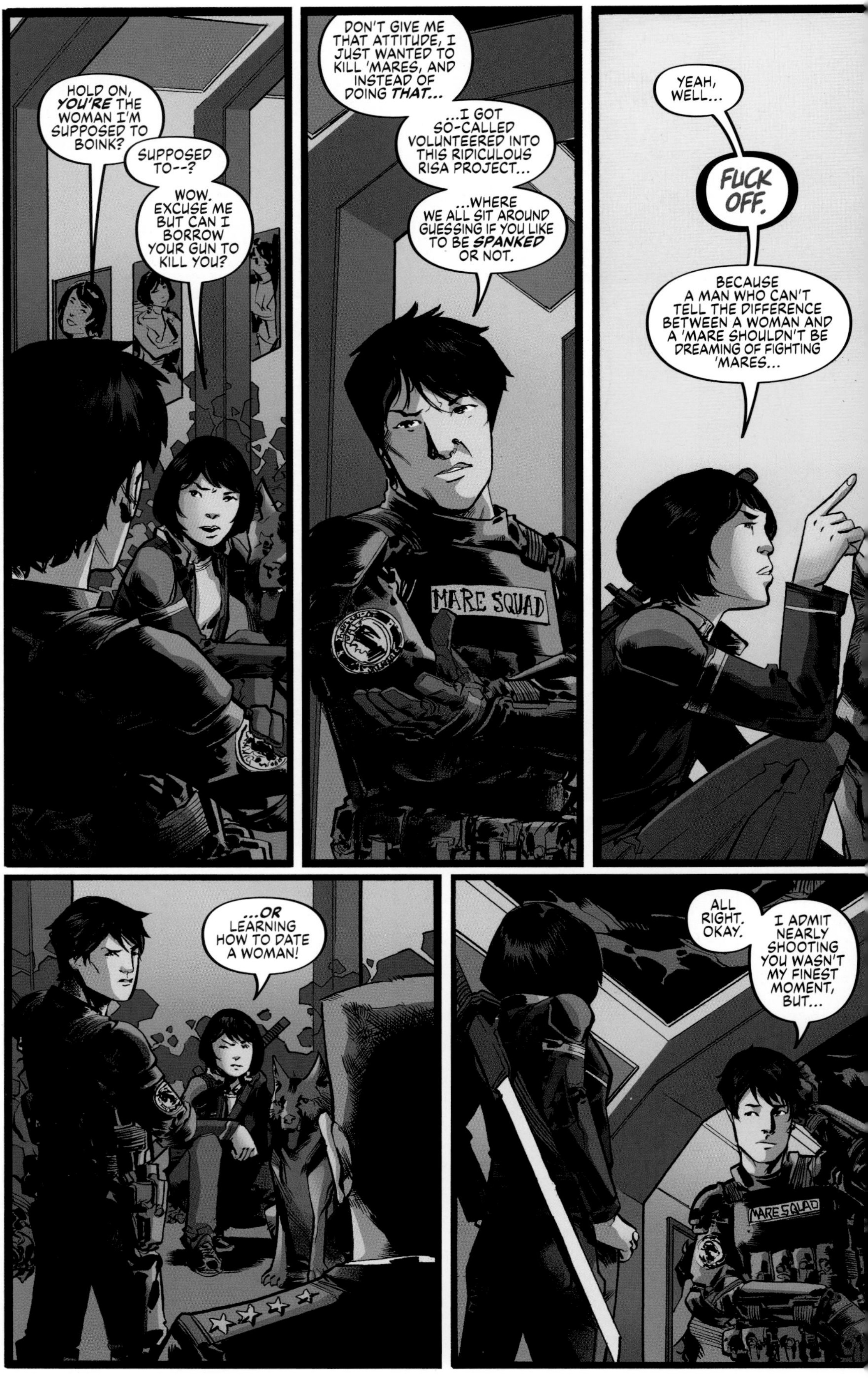
HOLD ON, YOU'RE THE WOMAN I'M SUPPOSED TO BOINK?
SUPPOSED TO--?
WOW. EXCUSE ME BUT CAN I BORROW YOUR GUN TO KILL YOU?
DON'T GIVE ME THAT ATTITUDE, I JUST WANTED TO KILL 'MARES, AND INSTEAD OF DOING THAT...
...I GOT SO-CALLED VOLUNTEERED INTO THIS RIDICULOUS RISA PROJECT...
...WHERE WE ALL SIT AROUND GUESSING IF YOU LIKE TO BE SPANKED OR NOT.
MARE SQUAD
YEAH, WELL...
FUCK OFF.
BECAUSE A MAN WHO CAN'T TELL THE DIFFERENCE BETWEEN A WOMAN AND A 'MARE SHOULDN'T BE DREAMING OF FIGHTING 'MARES...
...OR LEARNING HOW TO DATE A WOMAN!
ALL RIGHT. OKAY.
I ADMIT NEARLY SHOOTING YOU WASN'T MY FINEST MOMENT, BUT...
MARE SQUAD

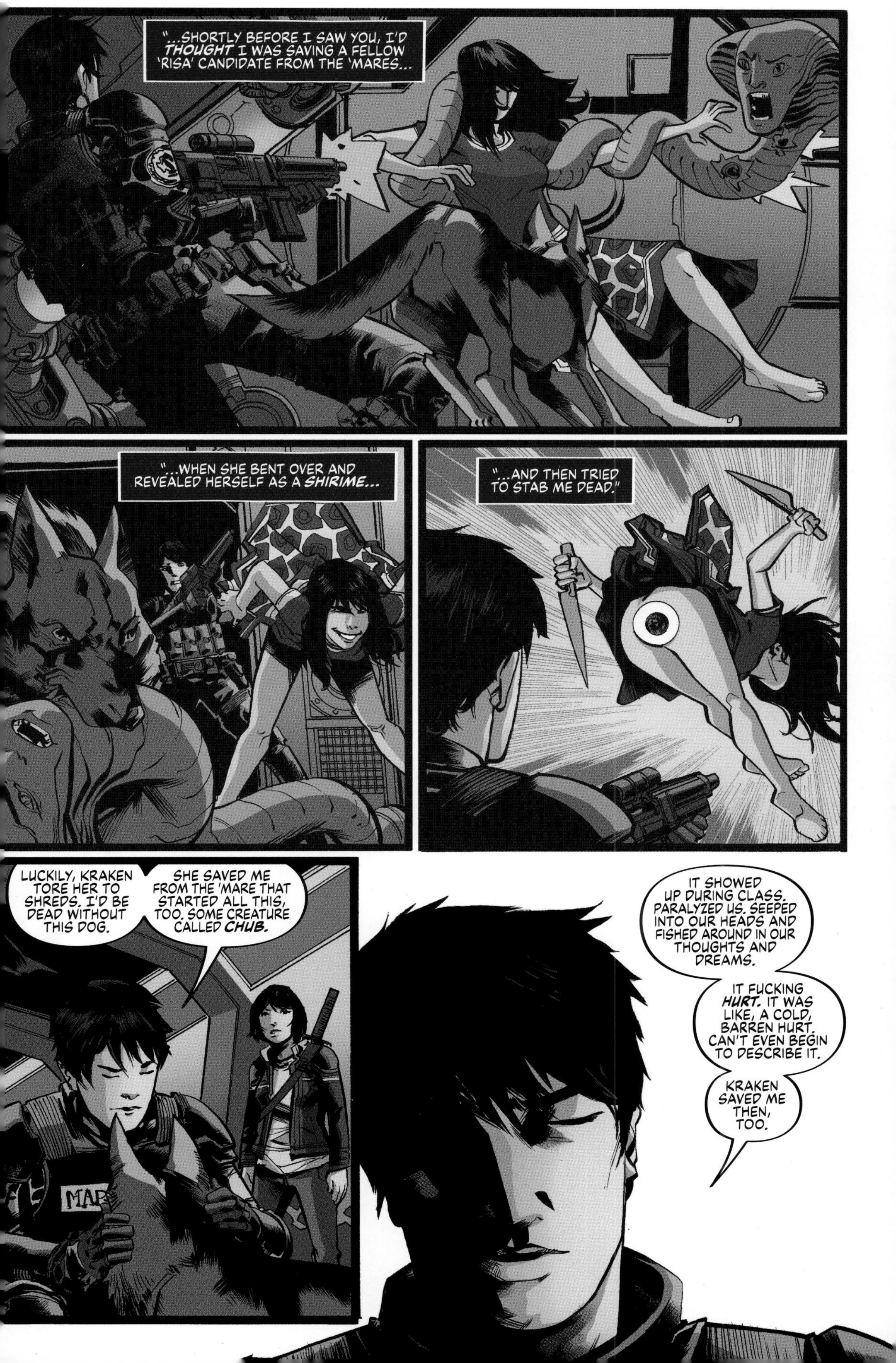
"...SHORTLY BEFORE I SAW YOU, I'D THOUGHT I WAS SAVING A FELLOW 'RISA' CANDIDATE FROM THE 'MARES...
"...WHEN SHE BENT OVER AND REVEALED HERSELF AS A SHIRIME...
"...AND THEN TRIED TO STAB ME DEAD."
LUCKILY, KRAKEN TORE HER TO SHREDS. I'D BE DEAD WITHOUT THIS DOG.
SHE SAVED ME FROM THE 'MARE THAT STARTED ALL THIS, TOO. SOME CREATURE CALLED CHUB.
IT SHOWED UP DURING CLASS. PARALYZED US. SEEPED INTO OUR HEADS AND FISHED AROUND IN OUR THOUGHTS AND DREAMS.
IT FUCKING HURT. IT WAS LIKE, A COLD, BARREN HURT. CAN'T EVEN BEGIN TO DESCRIBE IT.
KRAKEN SAVED ME THEN, TOO.
MAR

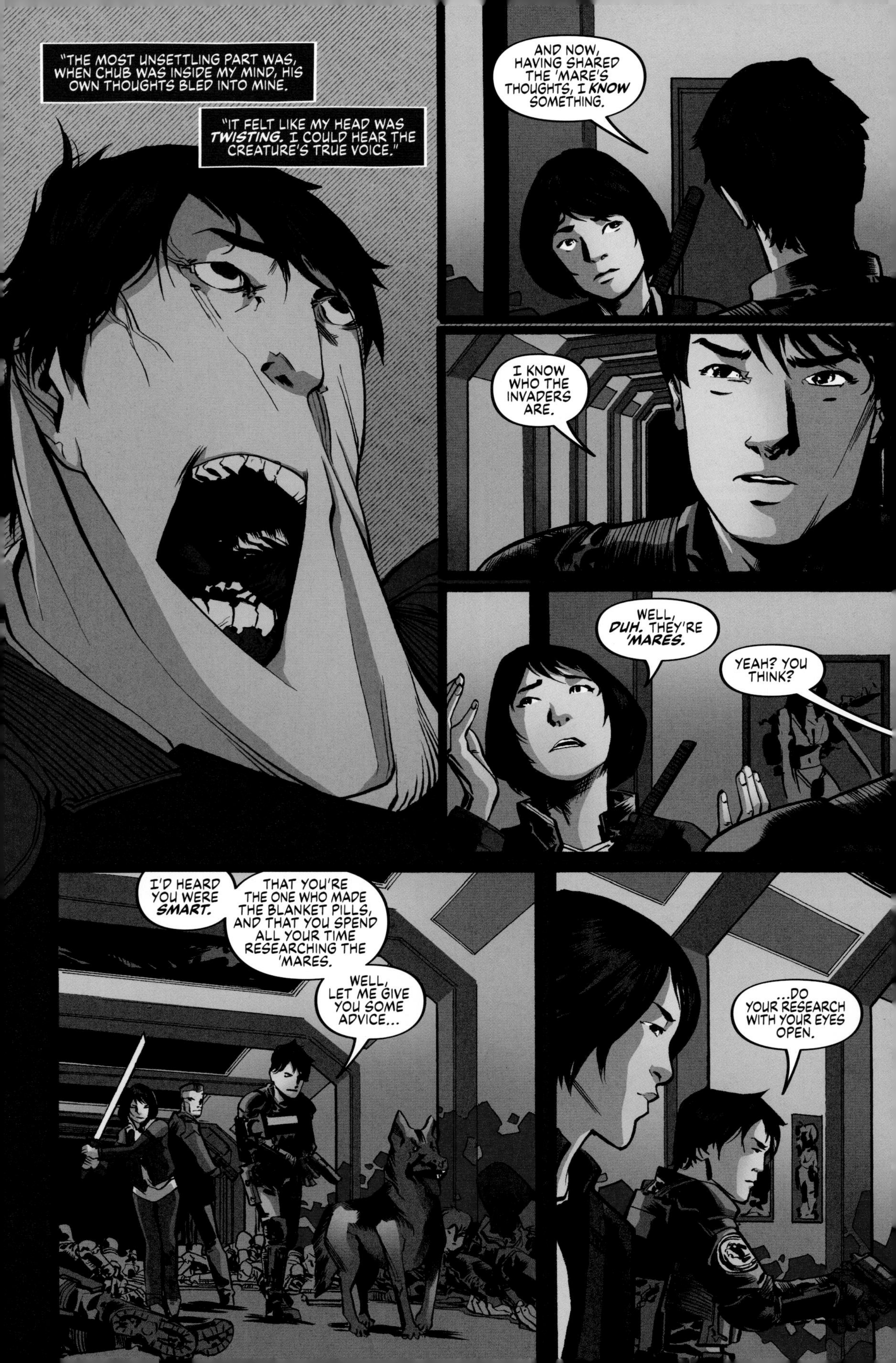
"THE MOST UNSETTLING PART WAS, WHEN CHUB WAS INSIDE MY MIND, HIS OWN THOUGHTS BLED INTO MINE.
"IT FELT LIKE MY HEAD WAS *TWISTING.* I COULD HEAR THE CREATURE'S TRUE VOICE."
AND NOW, HAVING SHARED THE 'MARE'S THOUGHTS, I *KNOW* SOMETHING.
I KNOW WHO THE INVADERS ARE.
WELL, *DUH.* THEY'RE *'MARES.*
YEAH? YOU THINK?
I'D HEARD YOU WERE *SMART.*
THAT YOU'RE THE ONE WHO MADE THE BLANKET PILLS, AND THAT YOU SPEND ALL YOUR TIME RESEARCHING THE 'MARES.
WELL, LET ME GIVE YOU SOME ADVICE...
...DO YOUR RESEARCH WITH YOUR EYES OPEN.

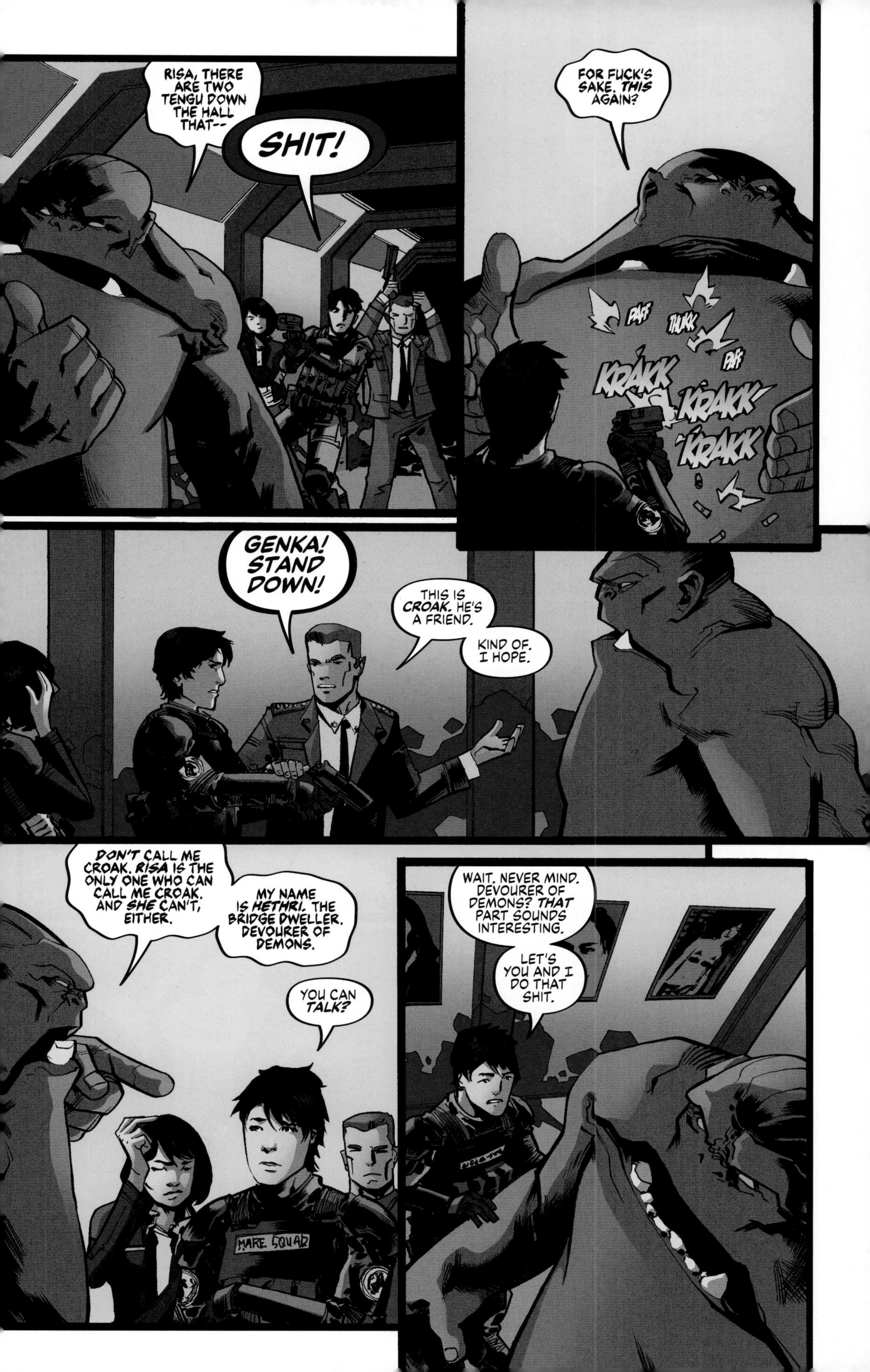

RISA, THERE ARE TWO TENGU DOWN THE HALL THAT--
SHIT!
FOR FUCK'S SAKE. THIS AGAIN?
PAFF
THUKK
PAFF
KRAKK
KRAKK!
KRAKK
GENKA! STAND DOWN!
THIS IS CROAK. HE'S A FRIEND.
KIND OF. I HOPE.
DON'T CALL ME CROAK. RISA IS THE ONLY ONE WHO CAN CALL ME CROAK. AND SHE CAN'T, EITHER.
MY NAME IS HETHRI. THE BRIDGE DWELLER. DEVOURER OF DEMONS.
YOU CAN TALK?
WAIT. NEVER MIND. DEVOURER OF DEMONS? THAT PART SOUNDS INTERESTING.
LET'S YOU AND I DO THAT SHIT.
MARE. SQUAD

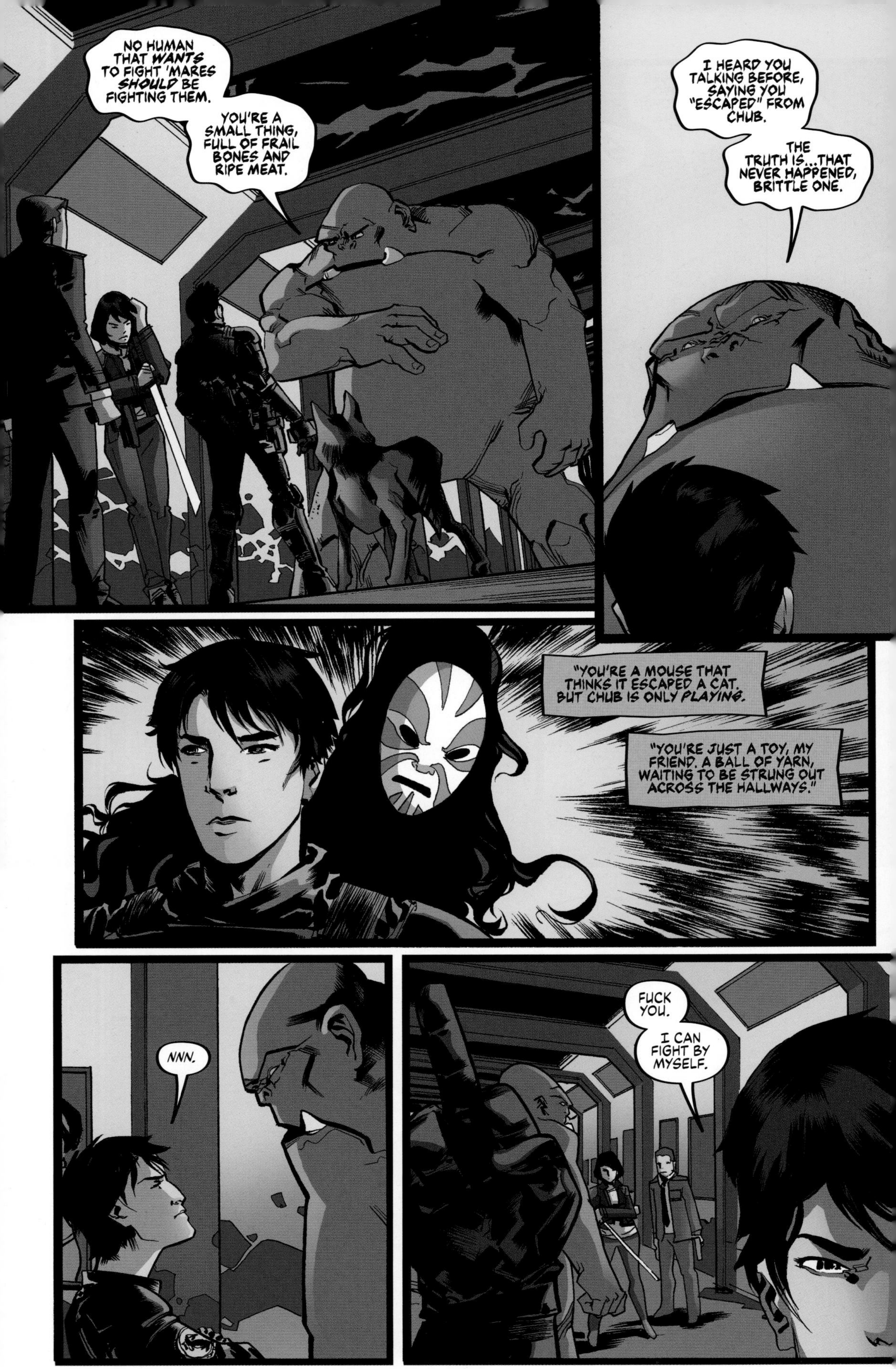
NO HUMAN THAT WANTS TO FIGHT 'MARES SHOULD BE FIGHTING THEM.
YOU'RE A SMALL THING, FULL OF FRAIL BONES AND RIPE MEAT.
I HEARD YOU TALKING BEFORE, SAYING YOU "ESCAPED" FROM CHUB.
THE TRUTH IS...THAT NEVER HAPPENED, BRITTLE ONE.
"YOU'RE A MOUSE THAT THINKS IT ESCAPED A CAT. BUT CHUB IS ONLY PLAYING.
"YOU'RE JUST A TOY, MY FRIEND. A BALL OF YARN, WAITING TO BE STRUNG OUT ACROSS THE HALLWAYS."
NNN.
FUCK YOU.
I CAN FIGHT BY MYSELF.

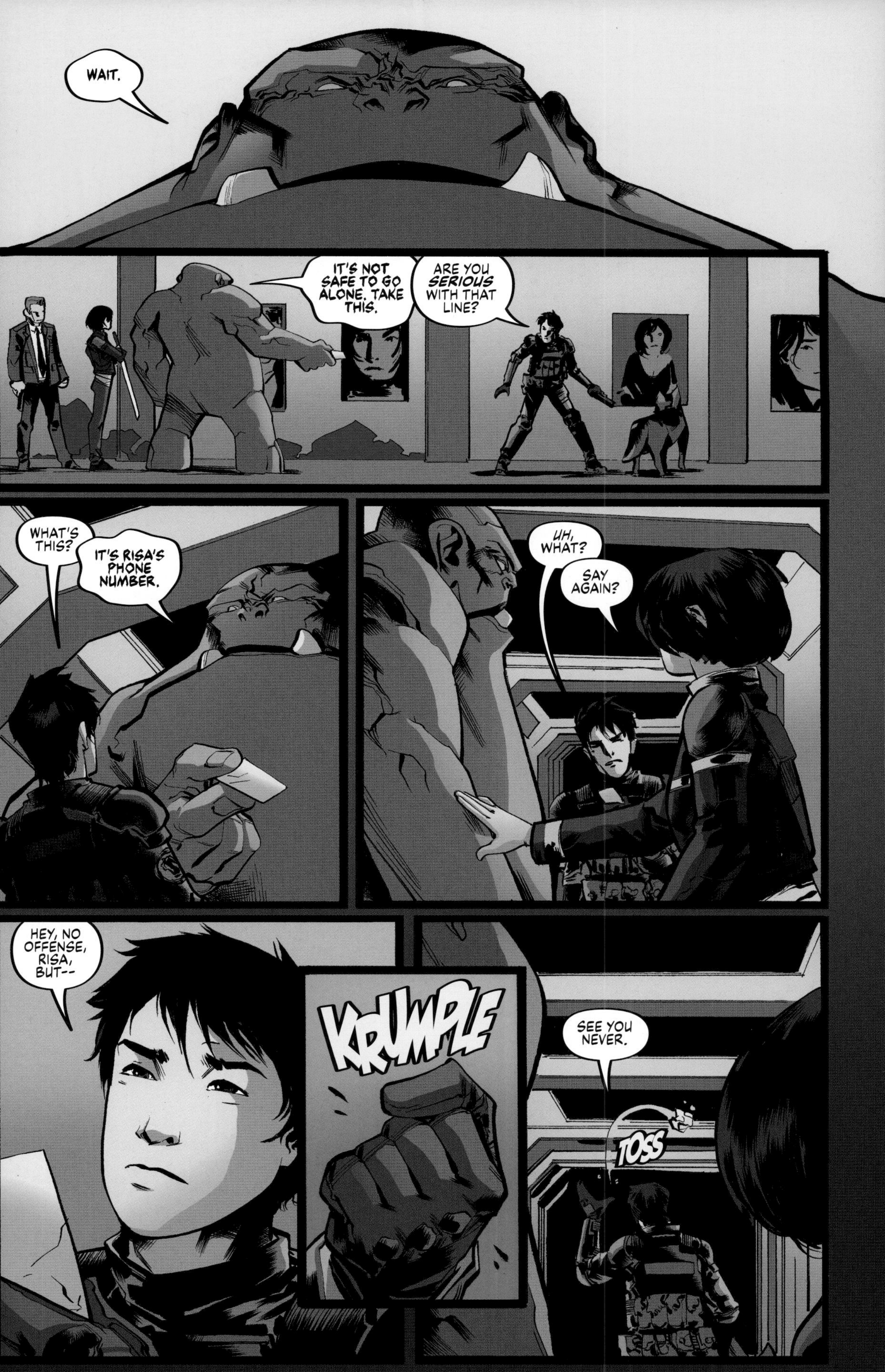
WAIT.
IT'S NOT SAFE TO GO ALONE. TAKE THIS.
ARE YOU *SERIOUS* WITH THAT LINE?
WHAT'S THIS?
IT'S RISA'S PHONE NUMBER.
UH, WHAT?
SAY AGAIN?
HEY, NO OFFENSE, RISA, BUT--
KRUMPLE
SEE YOU NEVER.
TOSS

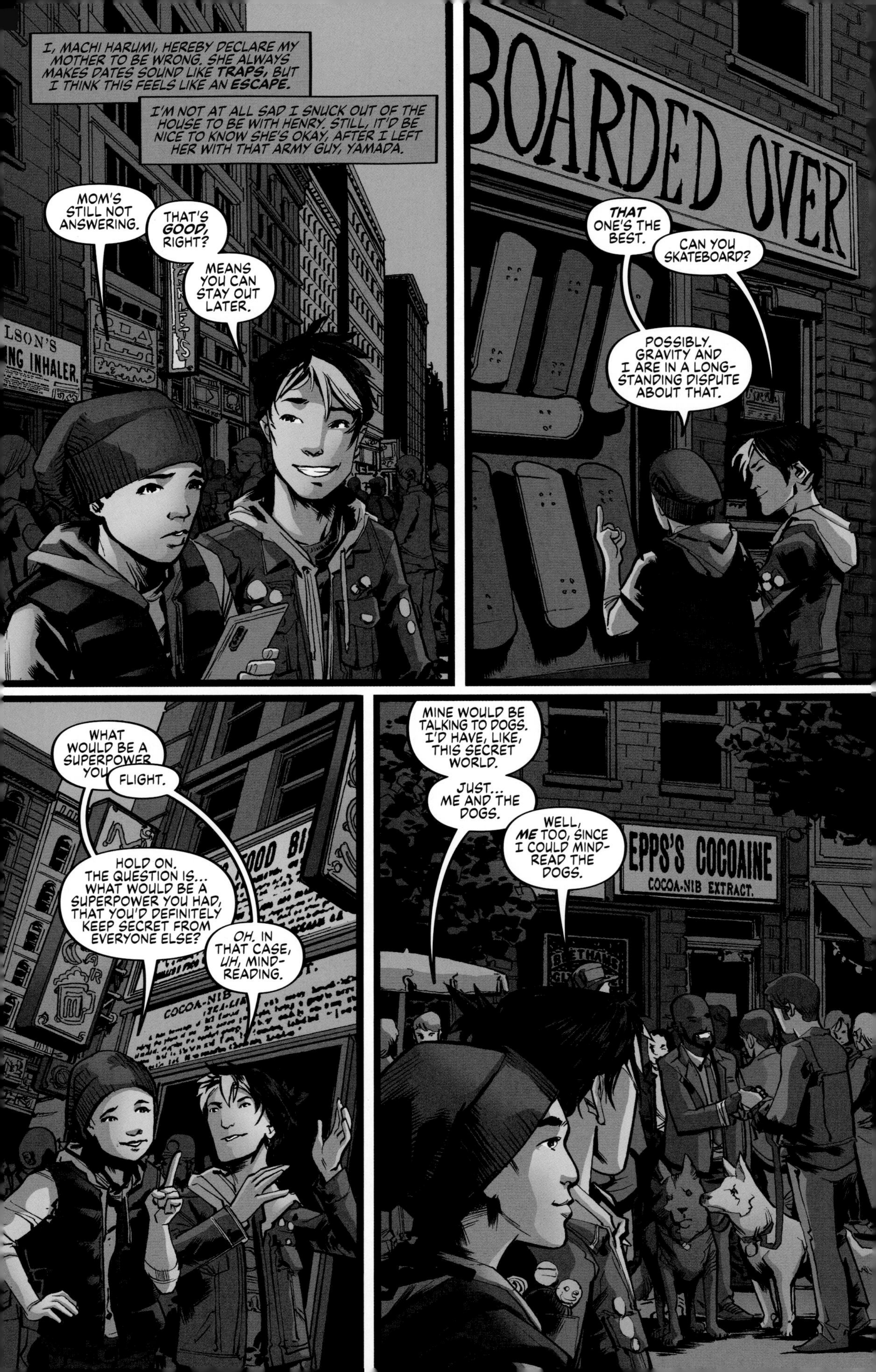
I, MACHI HARUMI, HEREBY DECLARE MY MOTHER TO BE WRONG. SHE ALWAYS MAKES DATES SOUND LIKE TRAPS, BUT I THINK THIS FEELS LIKE AN ESCAPE.
I'M NOT AT ALL SAD I SNUCK OUT OF THE HOUSE TO BE WITH HENRY. STILL, IT'D BE NICE TO KNOW SHE'S OKAY, AFTER I LEFT HER WITH THAT ARMY GUY, YAMADA.
MOM'S STILL NOT ANSWERING.
THAT'S GOOD, RIGHT?
MEANS YOU CAN STAY OUT LATER.
LSON'S
NG INHALER.
BOARDED OVER
THAT ONE'S THE BEST.
CAN YOU SKATEBOARD?
POSSIBLY. GRAVITY AND I ARE IN A LONG-STANDING DISPUTE ABOUT THAT.
WHAT WOULD BE A SUPERPOWER YOU
FLIGHT.
HOLD ON. THE QUESTION IS... WHAT WOULD BE A SUPERPOWER YOU HAD, THAT YOU'D DEFINITELY KEEP SECRET FROM EVERYONE ELSE?
OH. IN THAT CASE, UH, MIND-READING.
COCOA-NIB
MINE WOULD BE TALKING TO DOGS. I'D HAVE, LIKE, THIS SECRET WORLD.
JUST... ME AND THE DOGS.
WELL, ME TOO, SINCE I COULD MIND-READ THE DOGS.
EPPS'S COCOAINE
COCOA-NIB EXTRACT.

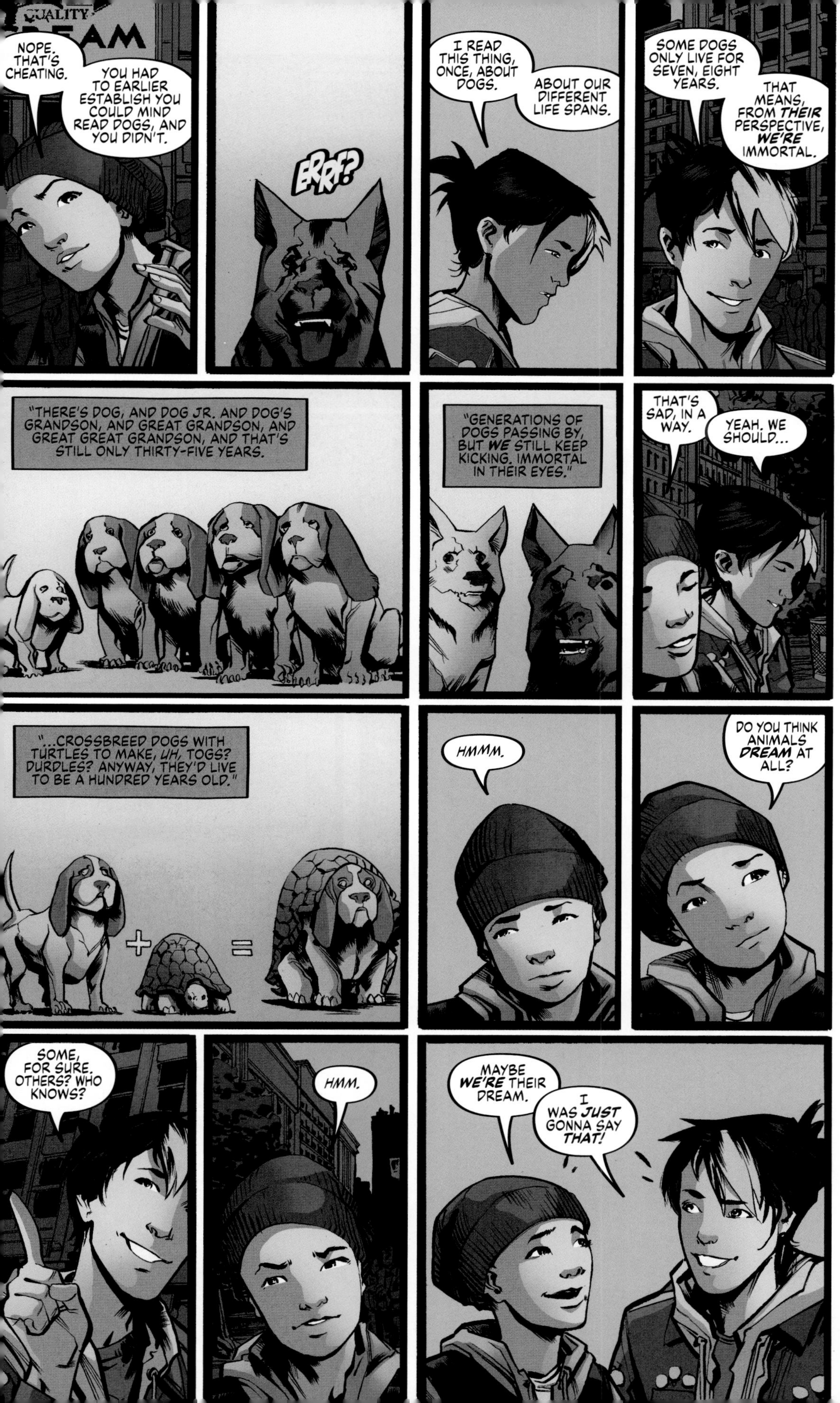
QUALITY
DREAM
NOPE. THAT'S CHEATING.
YOU HAD TO EARLIER ESTABLISH YOU COULD MIND READ DOGS, AND YOU DIDN'T.
ERRF?
I READ THIS THING, ONCE, ABOUT DOGS.
ABOUT OUR DIFFERENT LIFE SPANS.
SOME DOGS ONLY LIVE FOR SEVEN, EIGHT YEARS.
THAT MEANS, FROM THEIR PERSPECTIVE, WE'RE IMMORTAL.
"THERE'S DOG, AND DOG JR. AND DOG'S GRANDSON, AND GREAT GRANDSON, AND GREAT GREAT GRANDSON, AND THAT'S STILL ONLY THIRTY-FIVE YEARS.
"GENERATIONS OF DOGS PASSING BY, BUT WE STILL KEEP KICKING. IMMORTAL IN THEIR EYES."
THAT'S SAD, IN A WAY.
YEAH. WE SHOULD...
"...CROSSBREED DOGS WITH TURTLES TO MAKE, UH, TOGS? DURDLES? ANYWAY, THEY'D LIVE TO BE A HUNDRED YEARS OLD."
HMMM.
DO YOU THINK ANIMALS DREAM AT ALL?
SOME, FOR SURE. OTHERS? WHO KNOWS?
HMM.
MAYBE WE'RE THEIR DREAM.
I WAS JUST GONNA SAY THAT!

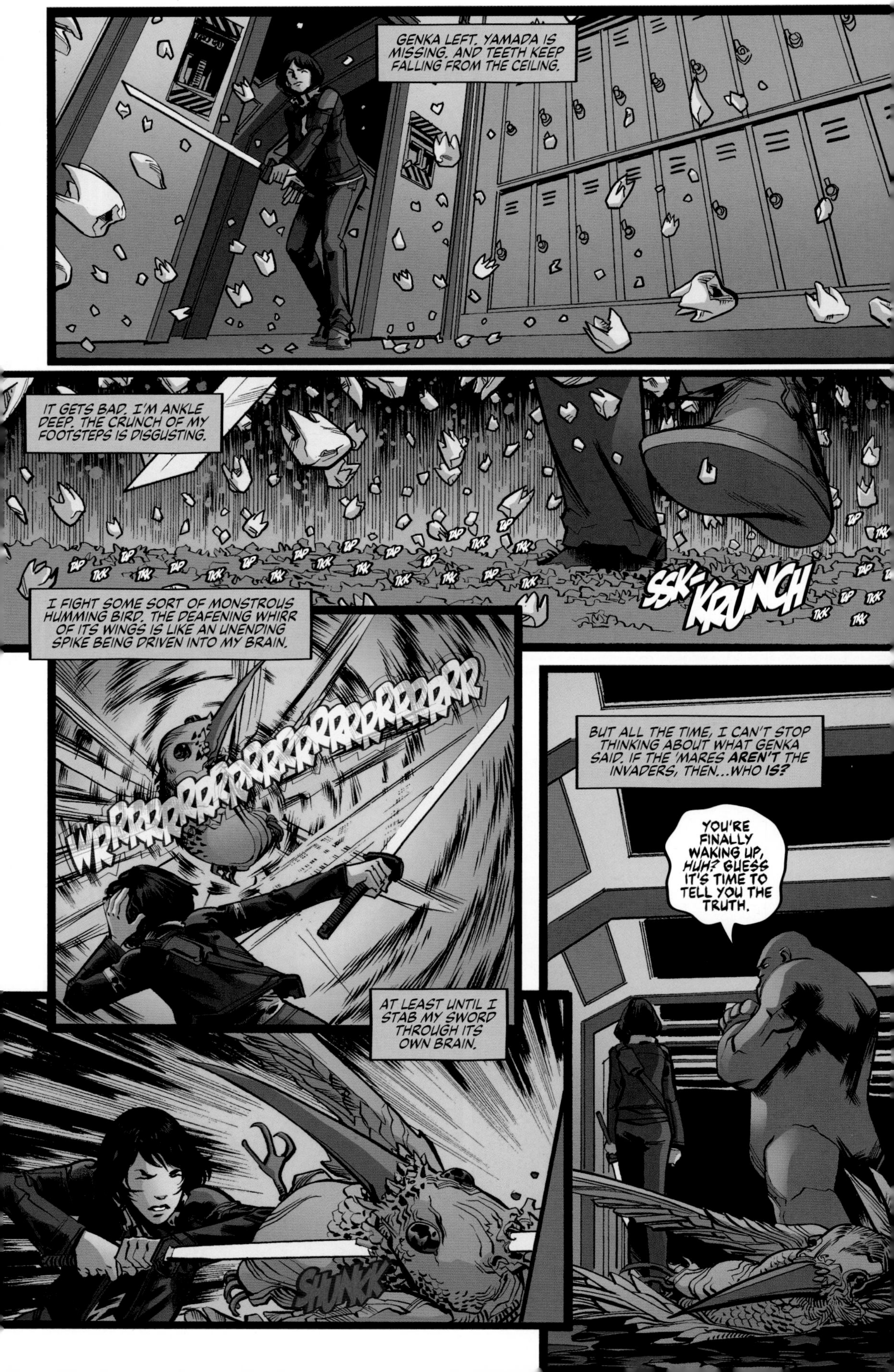
GENKA LEFT. YAMADA IS MISSING. AND TEETH KEEP FALLING FROM THE CEILING.
IT GETS BAD. I'M ANKLE DEEP. THE CRUNCH OF MY FOOTSTEPS IS DISGUSTING.
TAP TKK TAP TKK
SSK-KRUNCH
I FIGHT SOME SORT OF MONSTROUS HUMMING BIRD. THE DEAFENING WHIRR OF ITS WINGS IS LIKE AN UNENDING SPIKE BEING DRIVEN INTO MY BRAIN.
WRRRRRRRRRRRRRRRRRRRRRRRR
AT LEAST UNTIL I STAB MY SWORD THROUGH ITS OWN BRAIN.
SHUNKK
BUT ALL THE TIME, I CAN'T STOP THINKING ABOUT WHAT GENKA SAID. IF THE 'MARES AREN'T THE INVADERS, THEN...WHO IS?
YOU'RE FINALLY WAKING UP, HUH? GUESS IT'S TIME TO TELL YOU THE TRUTH.

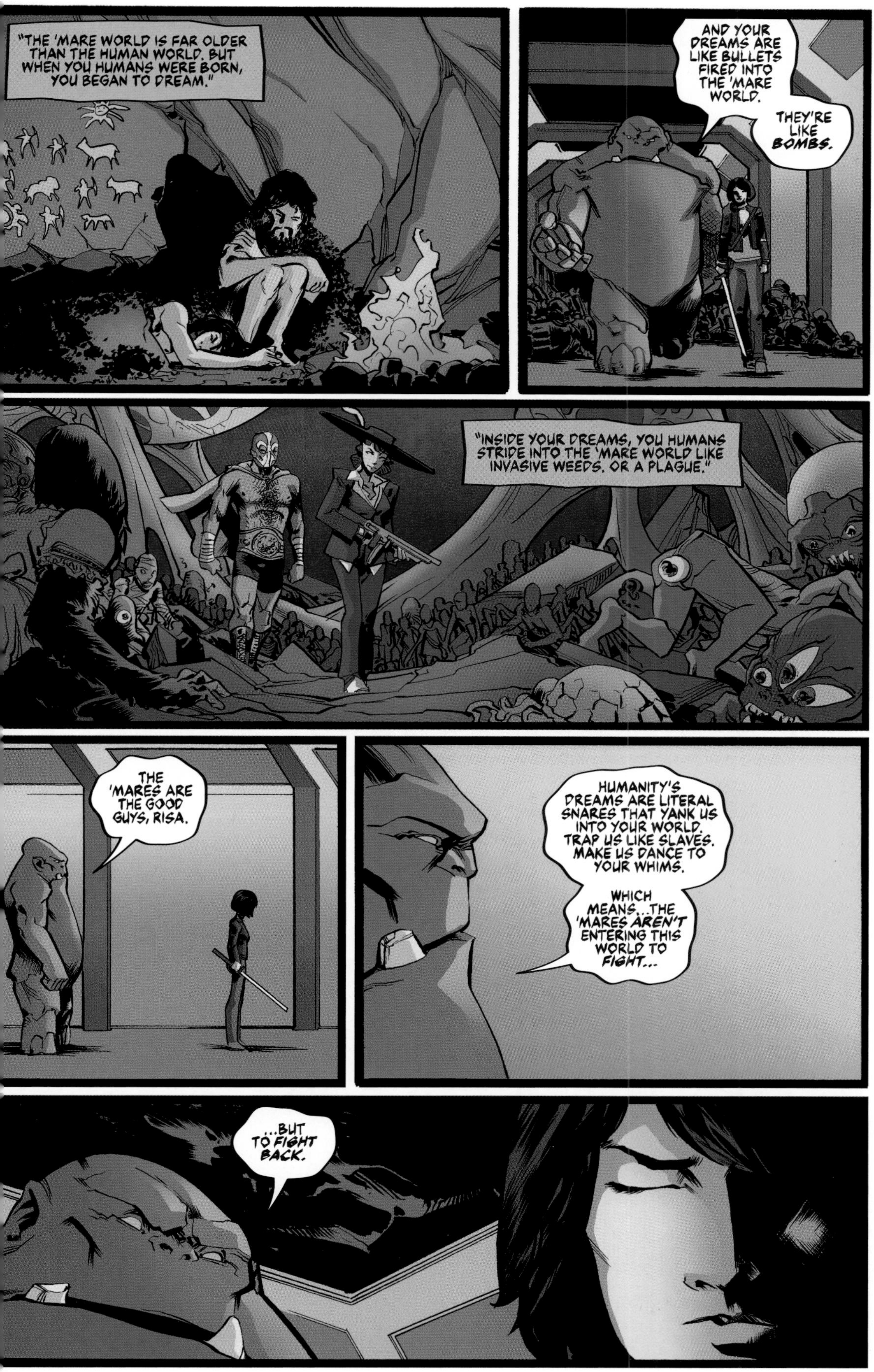
"THE 'MARE WORLD IS FAR OLDER THAN THE HUMAN WORLD. BUT WHEN YOU HUMANS WERE BORN, YOU BEGAN TO DREAM."
AND YOUR DREAMS ARE LIKE BULLETS FIRED INTO THE 'MARE WORLD.
THEY'RE LIKE BOMBS.
"INSIDE YOUR DREAMS, YOU HUMANS STRIDE INTO THE 'MARE WORLD LIKE INVASIVE WEEDS. OR A PLAGUE."
THE 'MARES ARE THE GOOD GUYS, RISA.
HUMANITY'S DREAMS ARE LITERAL SNARES THAT YANK US INTO YOUR WORLD. TRAP US LIKE SLAVES. MAKE US DANCE TO YOUR WHIMS.
WHICH MEANS...THE 'MARES AREN'T ENTERING THIS WORLD TO FIGHT...
...BUT TO FIGHT BACK.

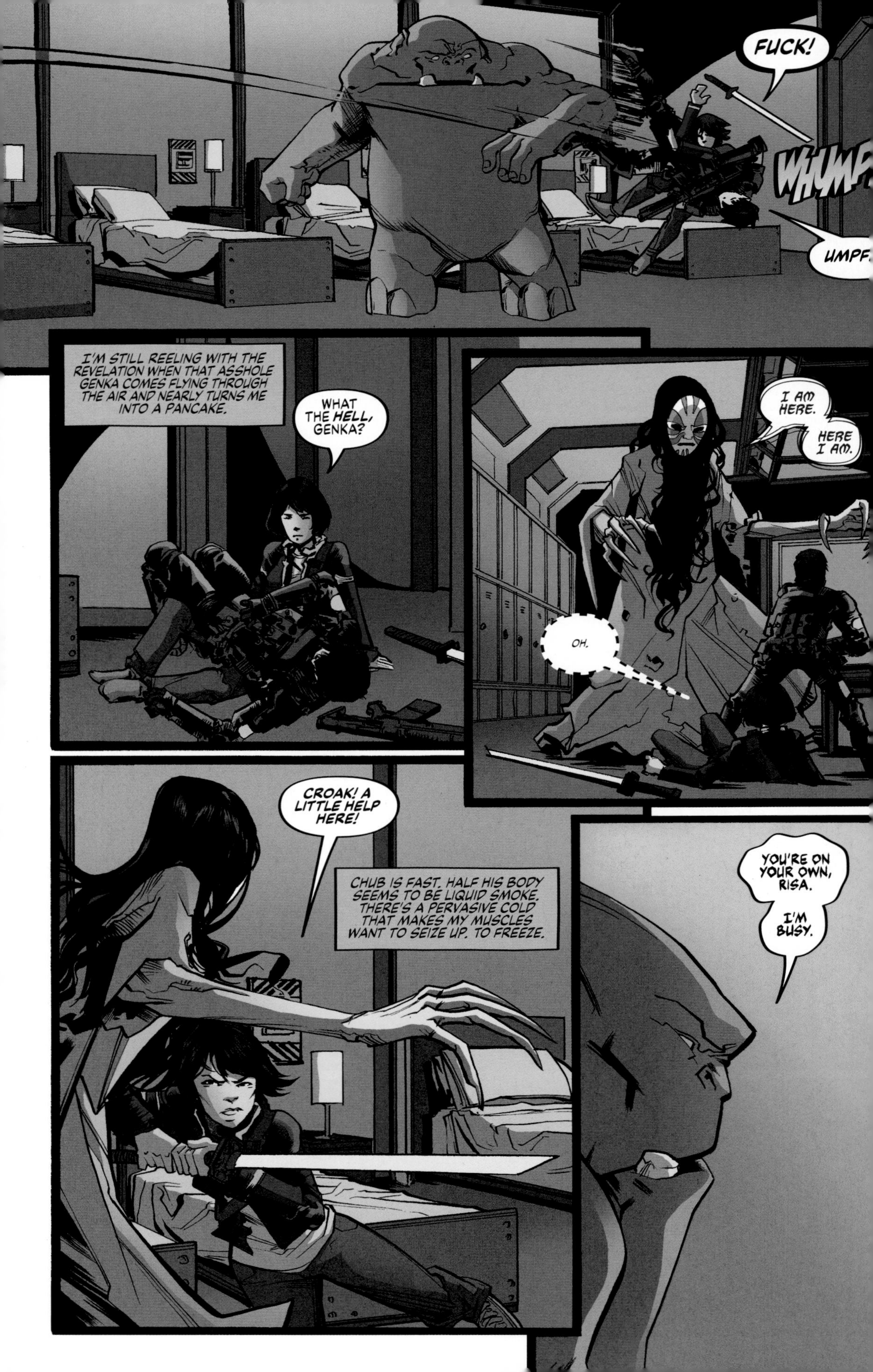
FUCK!
WHUMPF
UMPF.
I'M STILL REELING WITH THE REVELATION WHEN THAT ASSHOLE GENKA COMES FLYING THROUGH THE AIR AND NEARLY TURNS ME INTO A PANCAKE.
WHAT THE HELL, GENKA?
I AM HERE.
HERE I AM.
OH.
CROAK! A LITTLE HELP HERE!
CHUB IS FAST. HALF HIS BODY SEEMS TO BE LIQUID SMOKE. THERE'S A PERVASIVE COLD THAT MAKES MY MUSCLES WANT TO SEIZE UP. TO FREEZE.
YOU'RE ON YOUR OWN, RISA.
I'M BUSY.

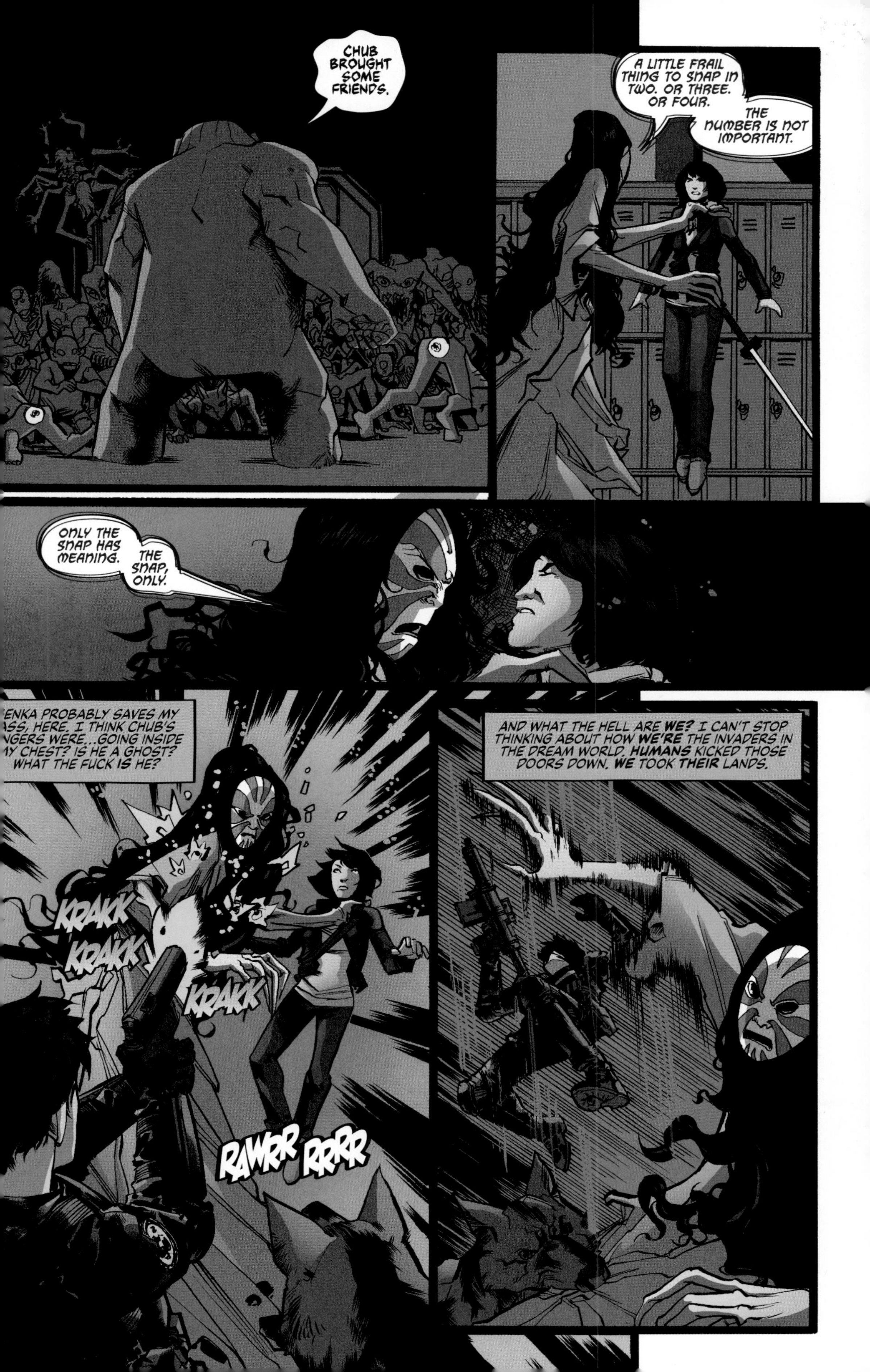

CHUB BROUGHT SOME FRIENDS.
A LITTLE FRAIL THING TO SNAP IN TWO. OR THREE. OR FOUR.
THE NUMBER IS NOT IMPORTANT.
ONLY THE SNAP HAS MEANING.
THE SNAP, ONLY.
FENKA PROBABLY SAVES MY ASS, HERE. I THINK CHUB'S FINGERS WERE...GOING INSIDE MY CHEST? IS HE A GHOST? WHAT THE FUCK IS HE?
KRAKK
KRAKK
KRAKK
RAWRR RRRR
AND WHAT THE HELL ARE WE? I CAN'T STOP THINKING ABOUT HOW WE'RE THE INVADERS IN THE DREAM WORLD. HUMANS KICKED THOSE DOORS DOWN. WE TOOK THEIR LANDS.

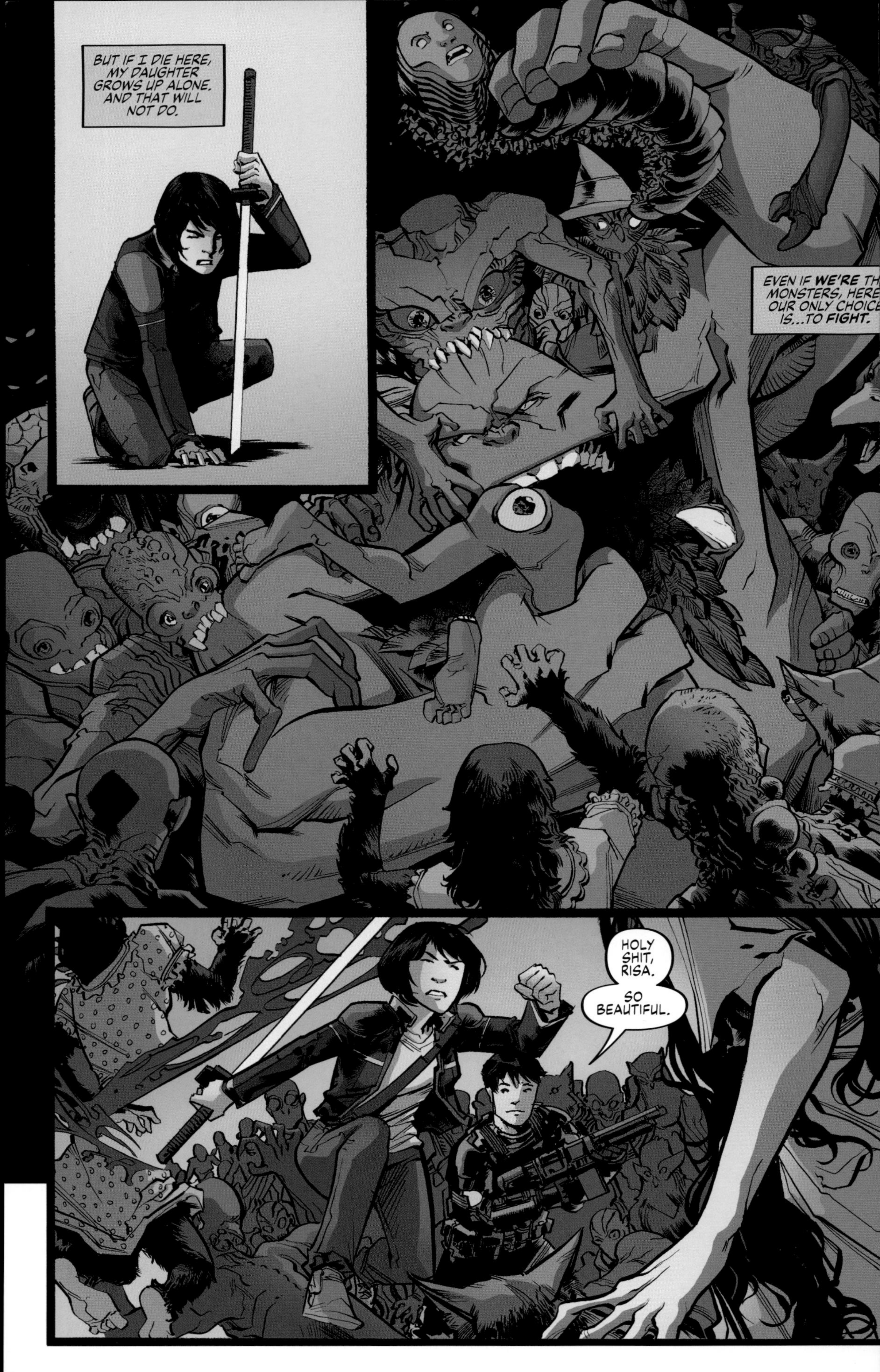
BUT IF I DIE HERE, MY DAUGHTER GROWS UP ALONE. AND THAT WILL NOT DO.
EVEN IF WE'RE TH MONSTERS, HERE OUR ONLY CHOICE IS...TO FIGHT.
HOLY SHIT, RISA.
SO BEAUTIFUL.

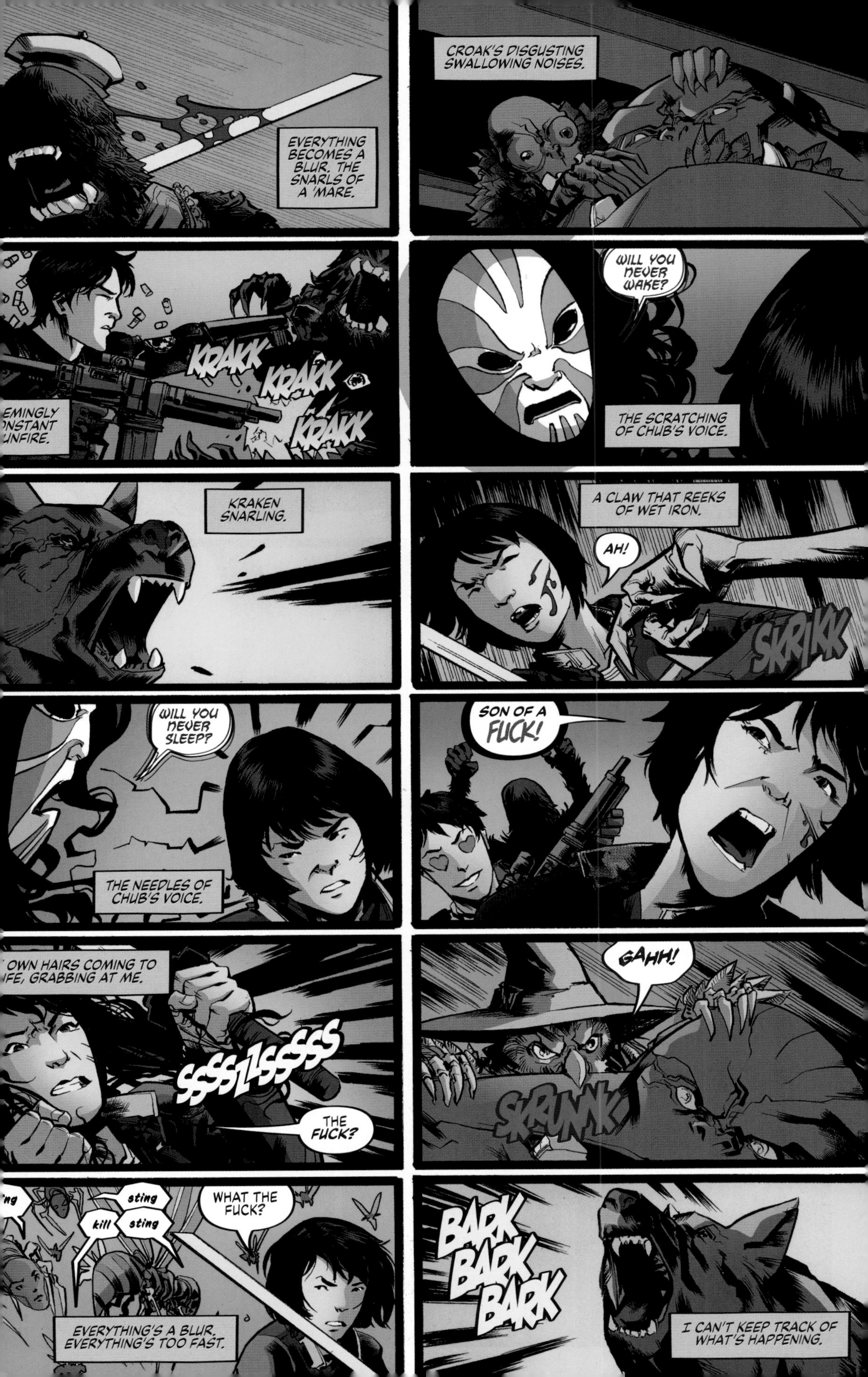

EVERYTHING BECOMES A BLUR. THE SNARLS OF A 'MARE.
CROAK'S DISGUSTING SWALLOWING NOISES.
KRAKK
KRAKK
KRAKK
EMINGLY ONSTANT UNFIRE.
WILL YOU NEVER WAKE?
THE SCRATCHING OF CHUB'S VOICE.
KRAKEN SNARLING.
A CLAW THAT REEKS OF WET IRON.
AH!
SKRIKK
WILL YOU NEVER SLEEP?
THE NEEDLES OF CHUB'S VOICE.
SON OF A FUCK!
OWN HAIRS COMING TO IFE, GRABBING AT ME.
SSSSZZSSSSS
THE FUCK?
GAHH!
SKRUNNK
sting
kill
sting
WHAT THE FUCK?
EVERYTHING'S A BLUR. EVERYTHING'S TOO FAST.
BARK
BARK
BARK
I CAN'T KEEP TRACK OF WHAT'S HAPPENING.

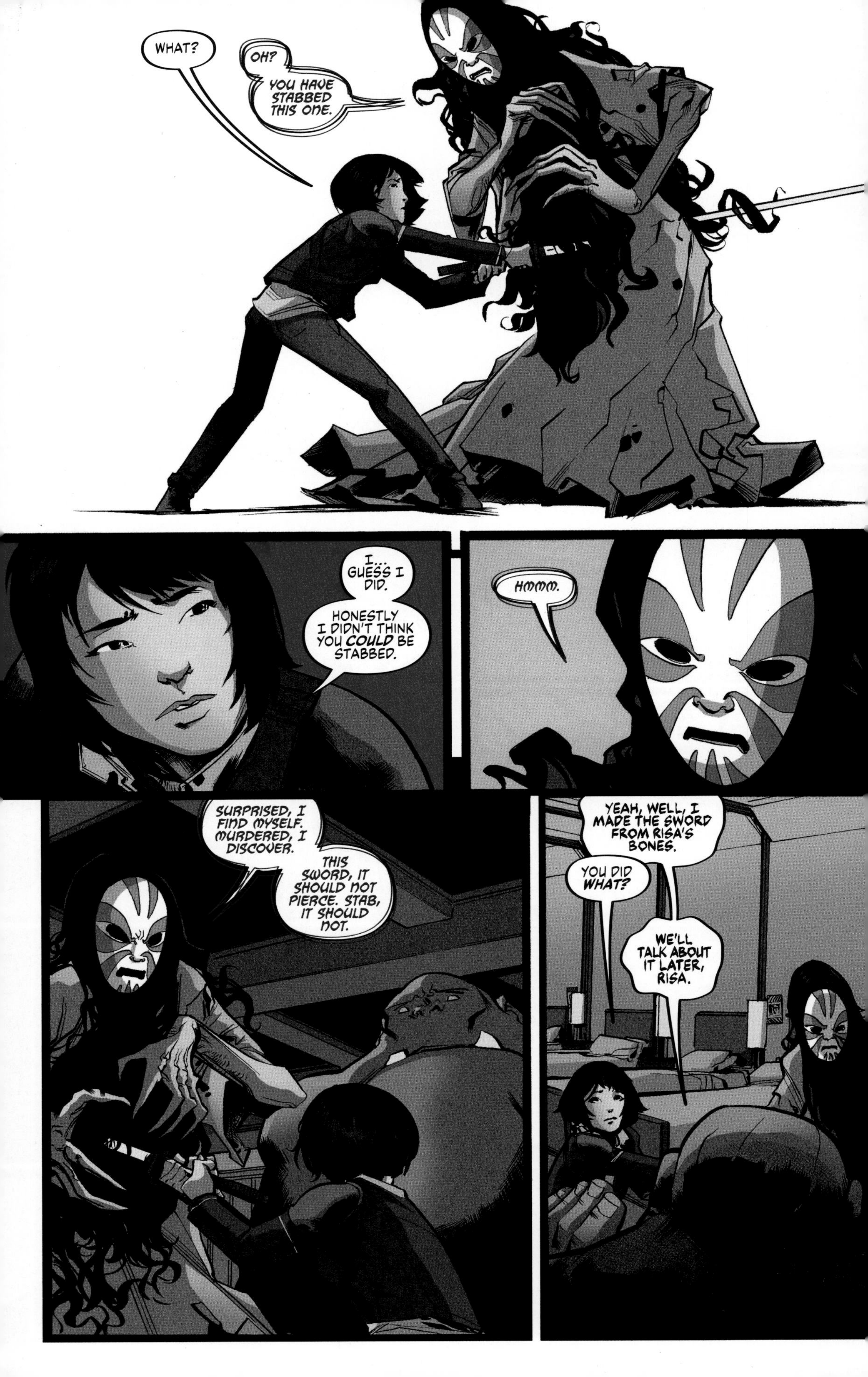
WHAT?
OH?
YOU HAVE STABBED THIS ONE.
I... GUESS I DID.
HONESTLY I DIDN'T THINK YOU *COULD* BE STABBED.
HMMM.
SURPRISED, I FIND MYSELF. MURDERED, I DISCOVER.
THIS SWORD, IT SHOULD NOT PIERCE. STAB, IT SHOULD NOT.
YEAH, WELL, I MADE THE SWORD FROM RISA'S BONES.
YOU DID *WHAT?*
WE'LL TALK ABOUT IT LATER, RISA.

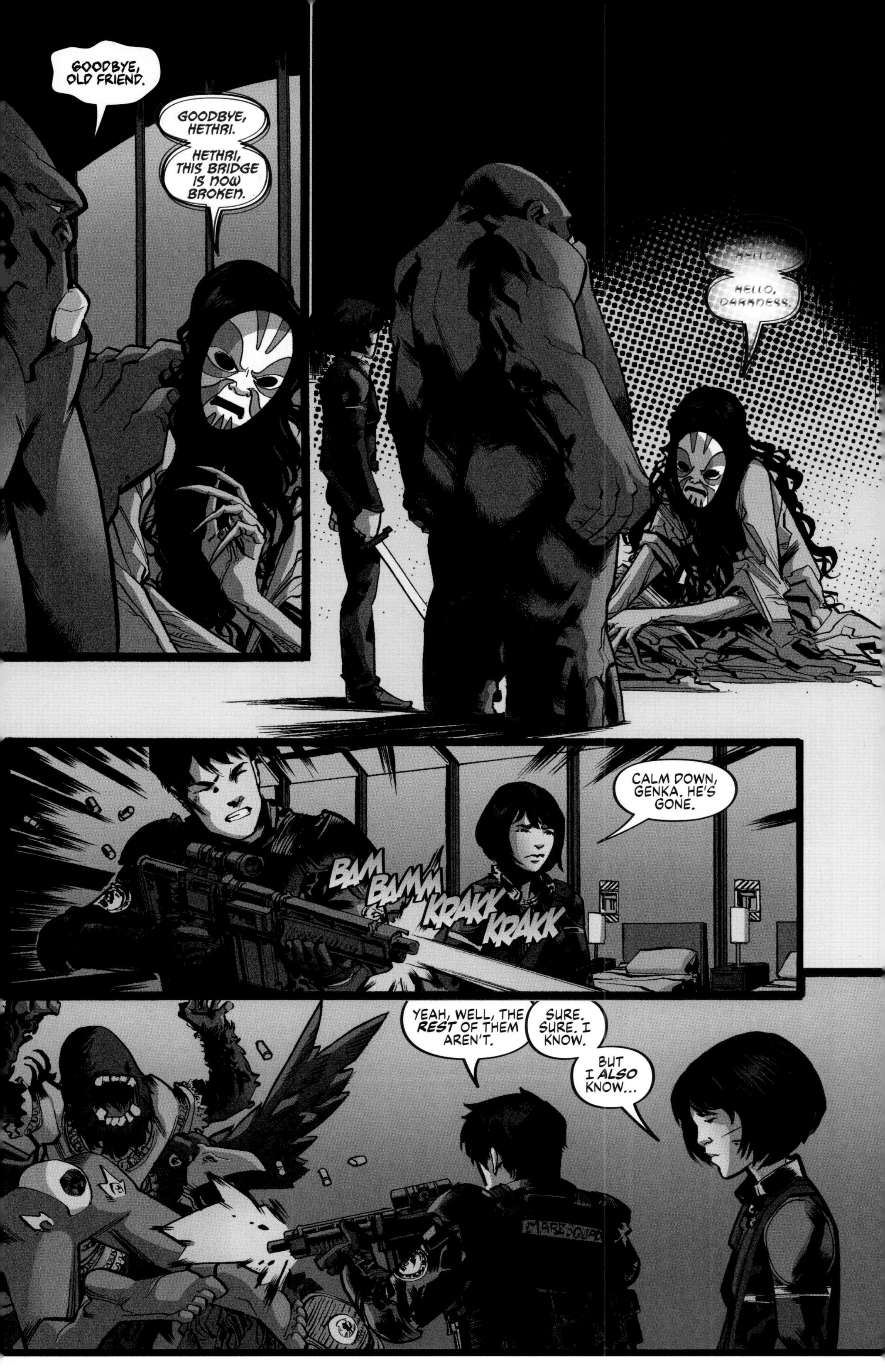
GOODBYE, OLD FRIEND.
GOODBYE, HETHRI.
HETHRI, THIS BRIDGE IS NOW BROKEN.
HELLO.
HELLO, DARKNESS.
CALM DOWN, GENKA. HE'S GONE.
BAM BAMM KRAKK KRAKK
YEAH, WELL, THE REST OF THEM AREN'T.
SURE. SURE. I KNOW.
BUT I ALSO KNOW...
MARE SQUAD

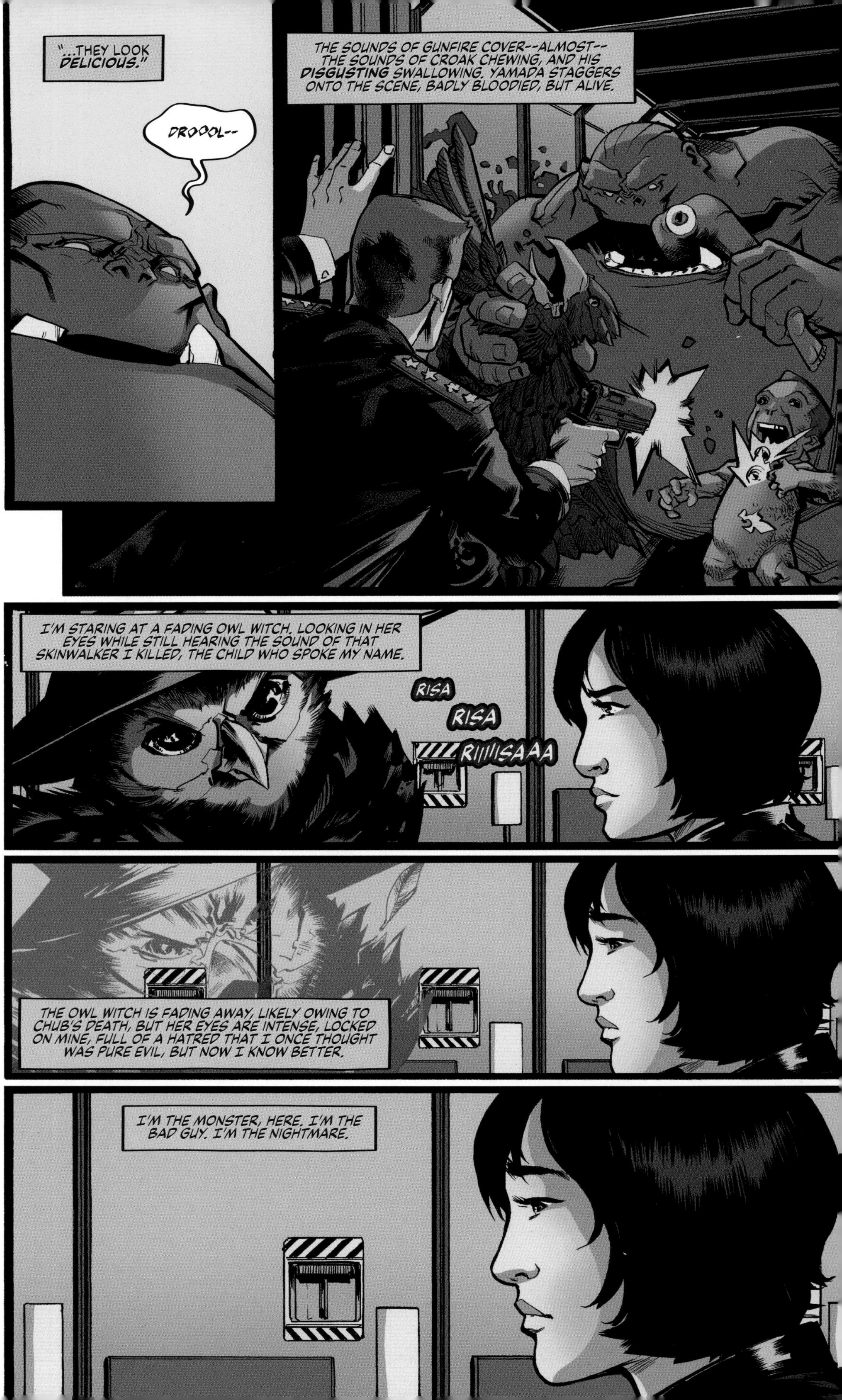
"...THEY LOOK DELICIOUS."
DROOOL--
THE SOUNDS OF GUNFIRE COVER--ALMOST-- THE SOUNDS OF CROAK CHEWING, AND HIS DISGUSTING SWALLOWING. YAMADA STAGGERS ONTO THE SCENE, BADLY BLOODIED, BUT ALIVE.
I'M STARING AT A FADING OWL WITCH. LOOKING IN HER EYES WHILE STILL HEARING THE SOUND OF THAT SKINWALKER I KILLED, THE CHILD WHO SPOKE MY NAME.
RISA
RISA
RIIIISAAA
THE OWL WITCH IS FADING AWAY, LIKELY OWING TO CHUB'S DEATH, BUT HER EYES ARE INTENSE, LOCKED ON MINE, FULL OF A HATRED THAT I ONCE THOUGHT WAS PURE EVIL, BUT NOW I KNOW BETTER.
I'M THE MONSTER, HERE. I'M THE BAD GUY. I'M THE NIGHTMARE.

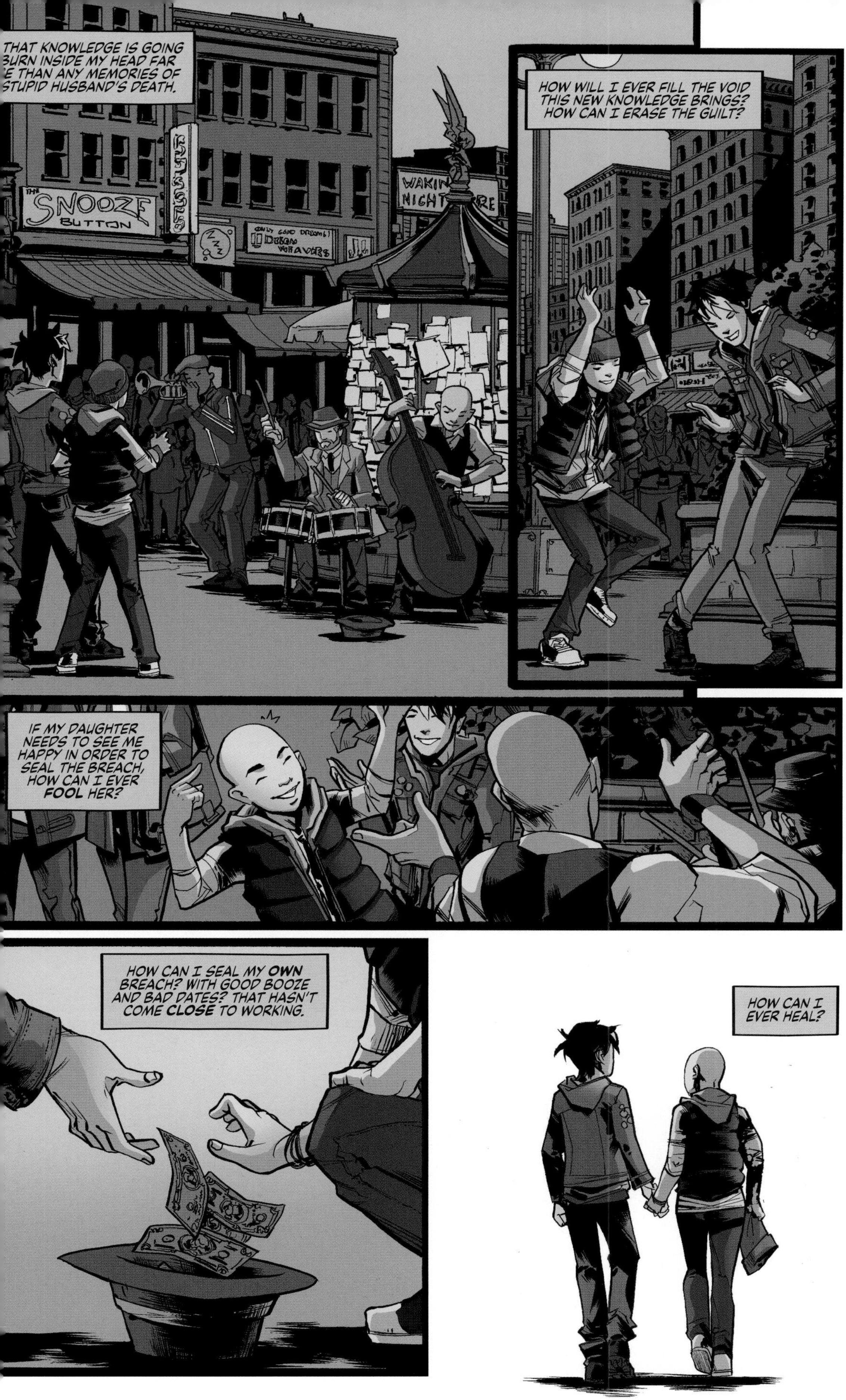
THAT KNOWLEDGE IS GOING
BURN INSIDE MY HEAD FAR
E THAN ANY MEMORIES OF
STUPID HUSBAND'S DEATH.
THE SNOOZE BUTTON
DREAM WEAVERS
HOW WILL I EVER FILL THE VOID THIS NEW KNOWLEDGE BRINGS? HOW CAN I ERASE THE GUILT?
IF MY DAUGHTER NEEDS TO SEE ME HAPPY IN ORDER TO SEAL THE BREACH, HOW CAN I EVER FOOL HER?
HOW CAN I SEAL MY OWN BREACH? WITH GOOD BOOZE AND BAD DATES? THAT HASN'T COME CLOSE TO WORKING.
HOW CAN I EVER HEAL?

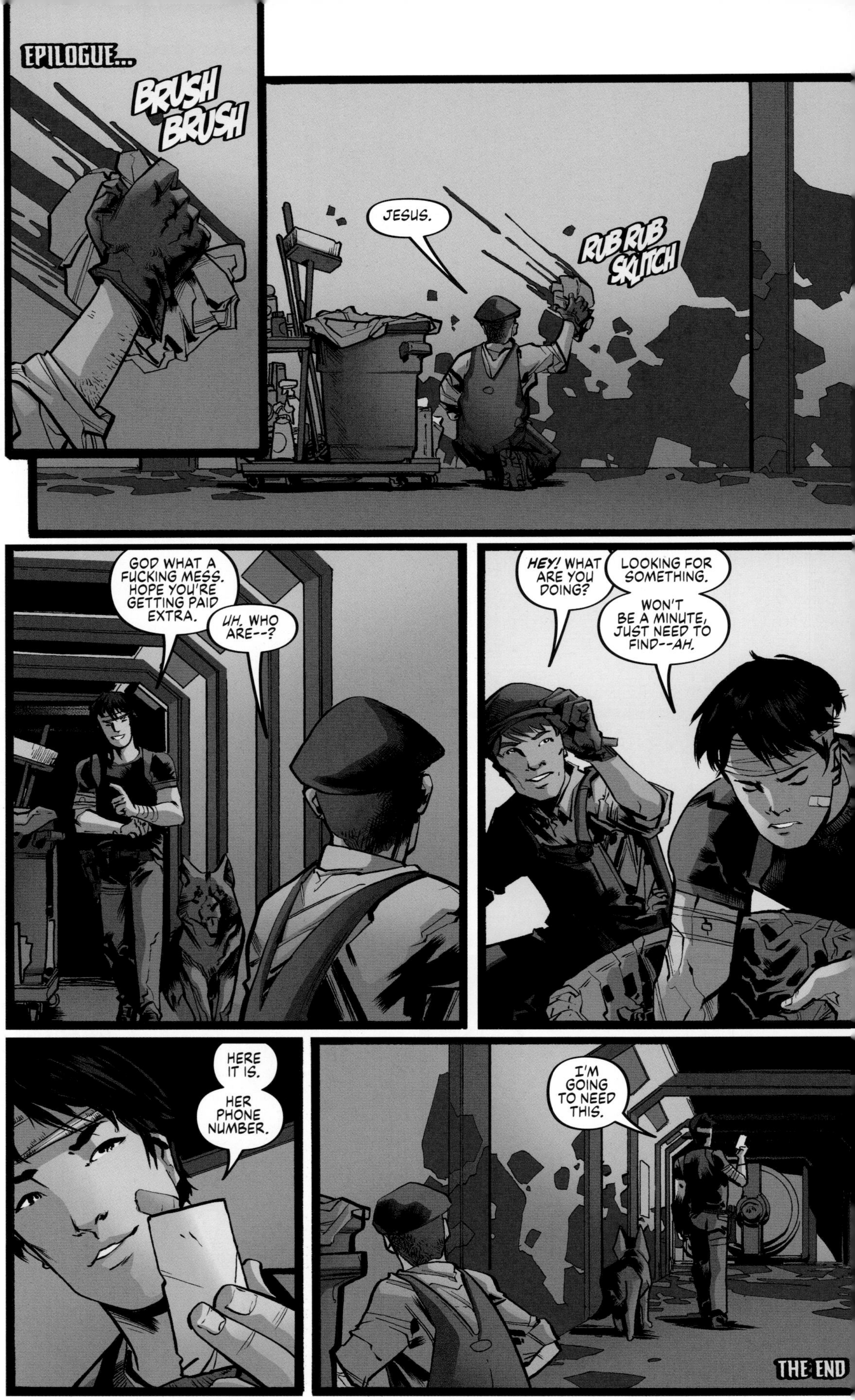
EPILOGUE...
BRUSH
BRUSH
JESUS.
RUB RUB
SKLITCH
GOD WHAT A FUCKING MESS. HOPE YOU'RE GETTING PAID EXTRA.
UH. WHO ARE--?
HEY! WHAT ARE YOU DOING?
LOOKING FOR SOMETHING.
WON'T BE A MINUTE, JUST NEED TO FIND--AH.
HERE IT IS.
HER PHONE NUMBER.
I'M GOING TO NEED THIS.
THE END

MONSTERS

COVER GALLERY & EXTRAS

Issue 1
JAMES HARREN
Incentive Cover

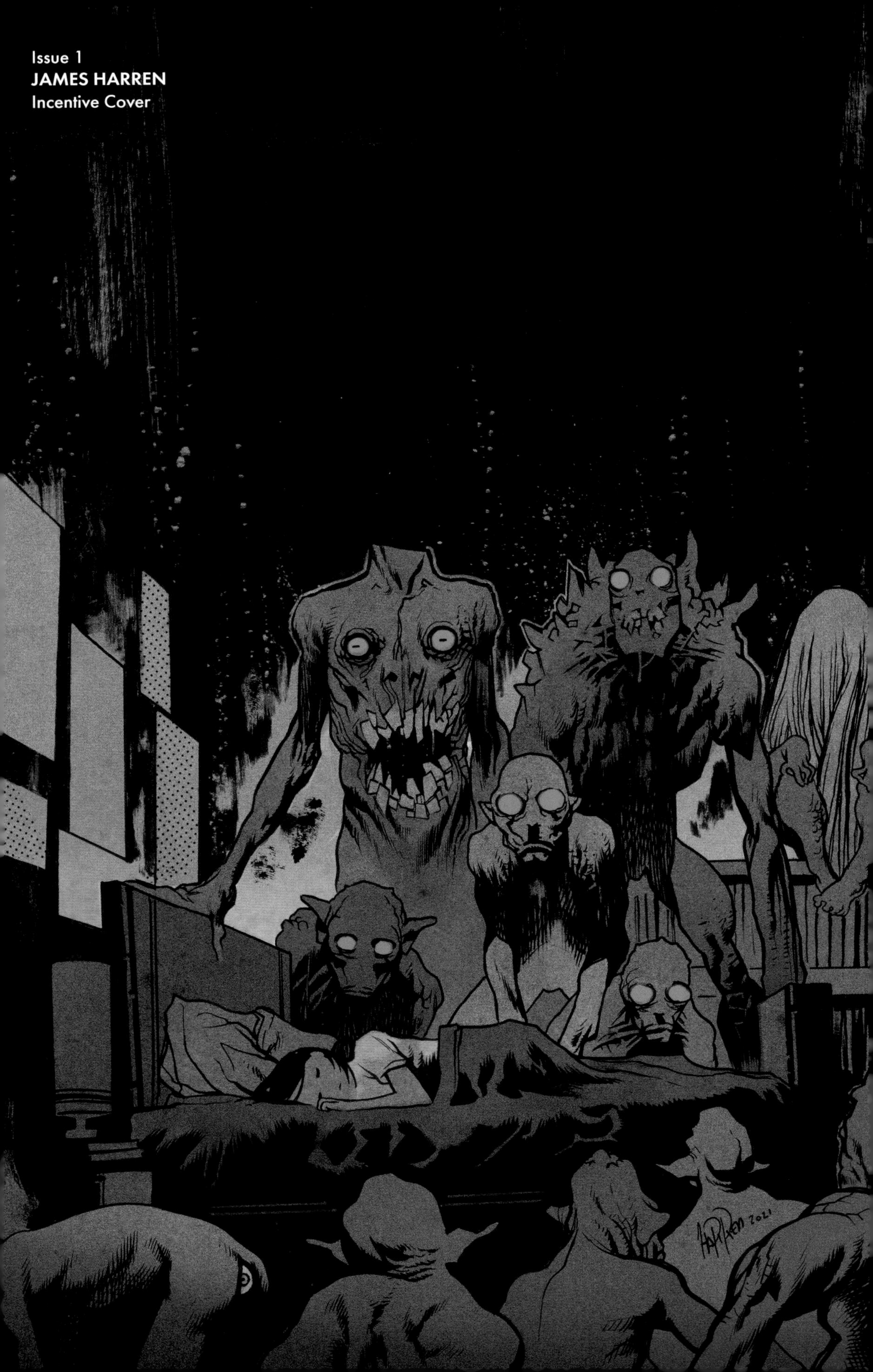

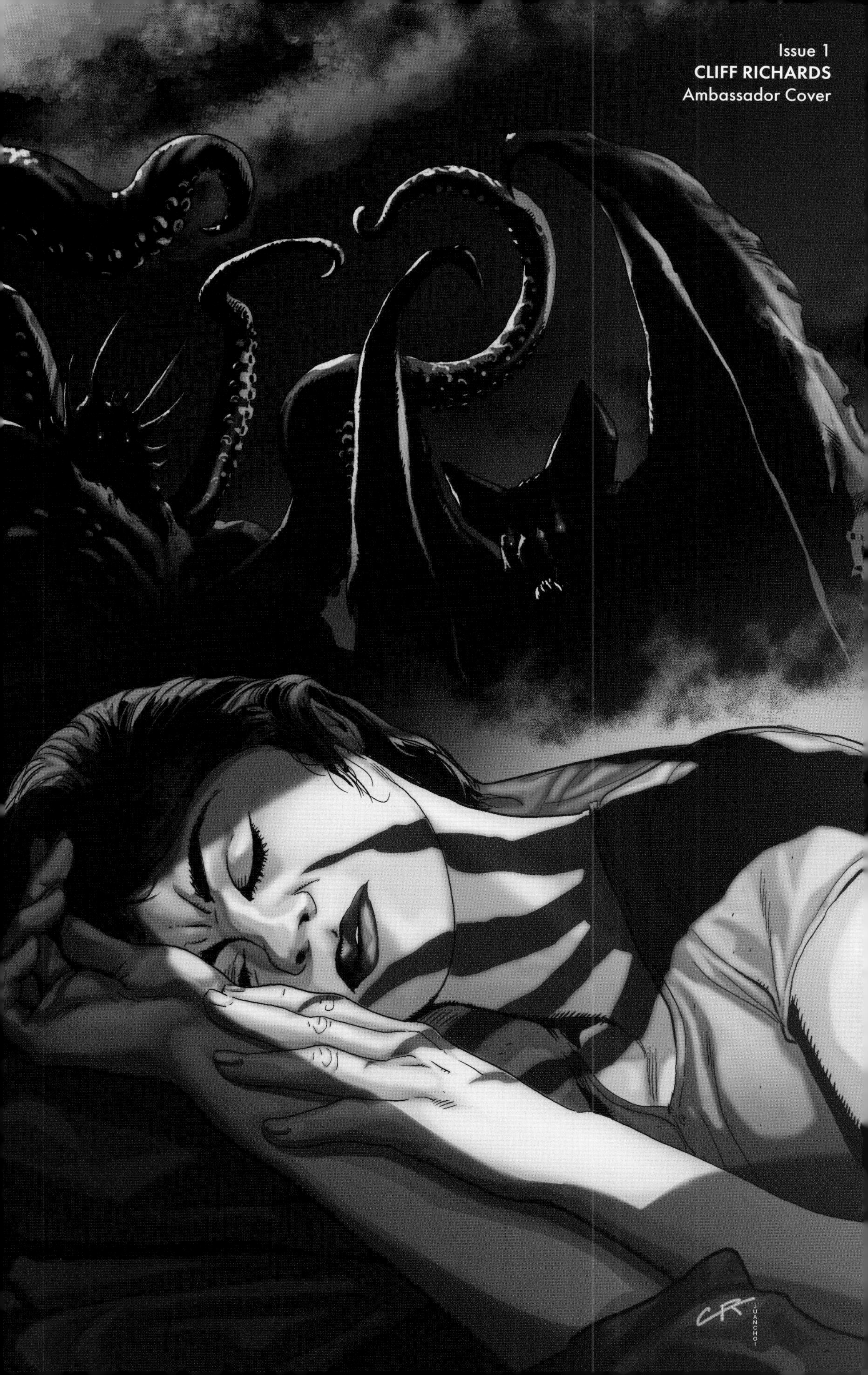

Issue 1
CLIFF RICHARDS
Ambassador Cover

Issue 1
MIKE ROOTH
Happy Hour Cover

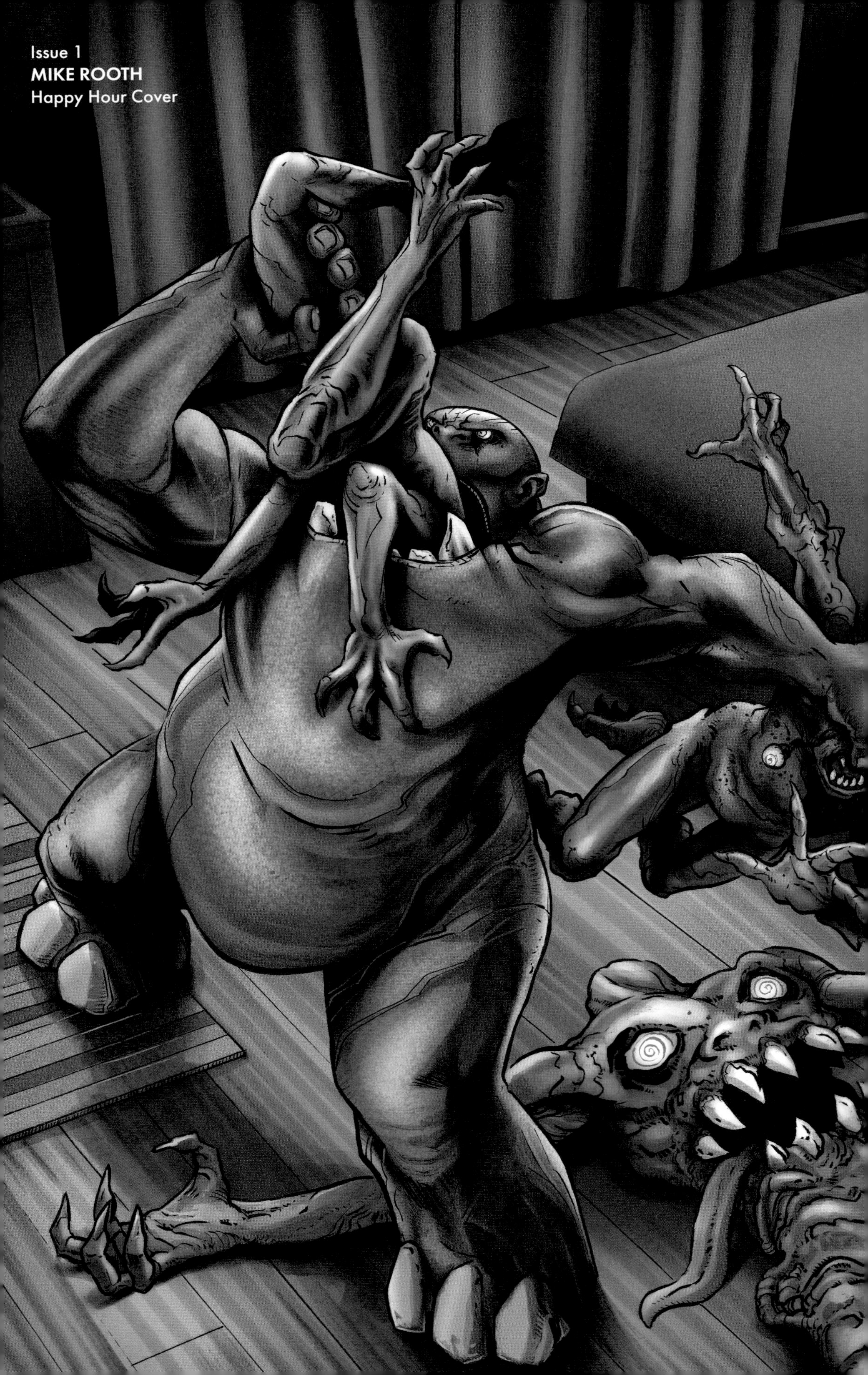

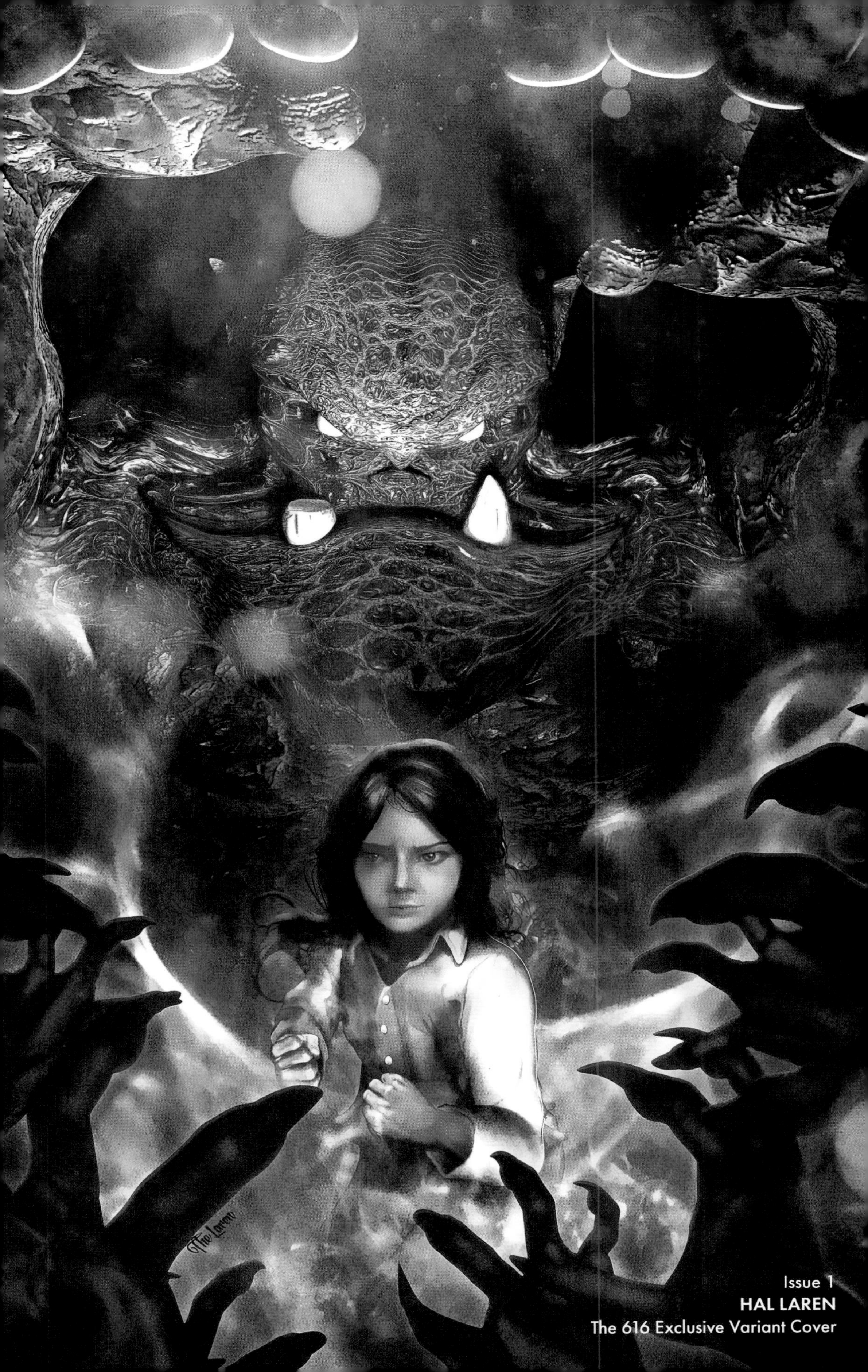

Issue 1
HAL LAREN
The 616 Exclusive Variant Cover

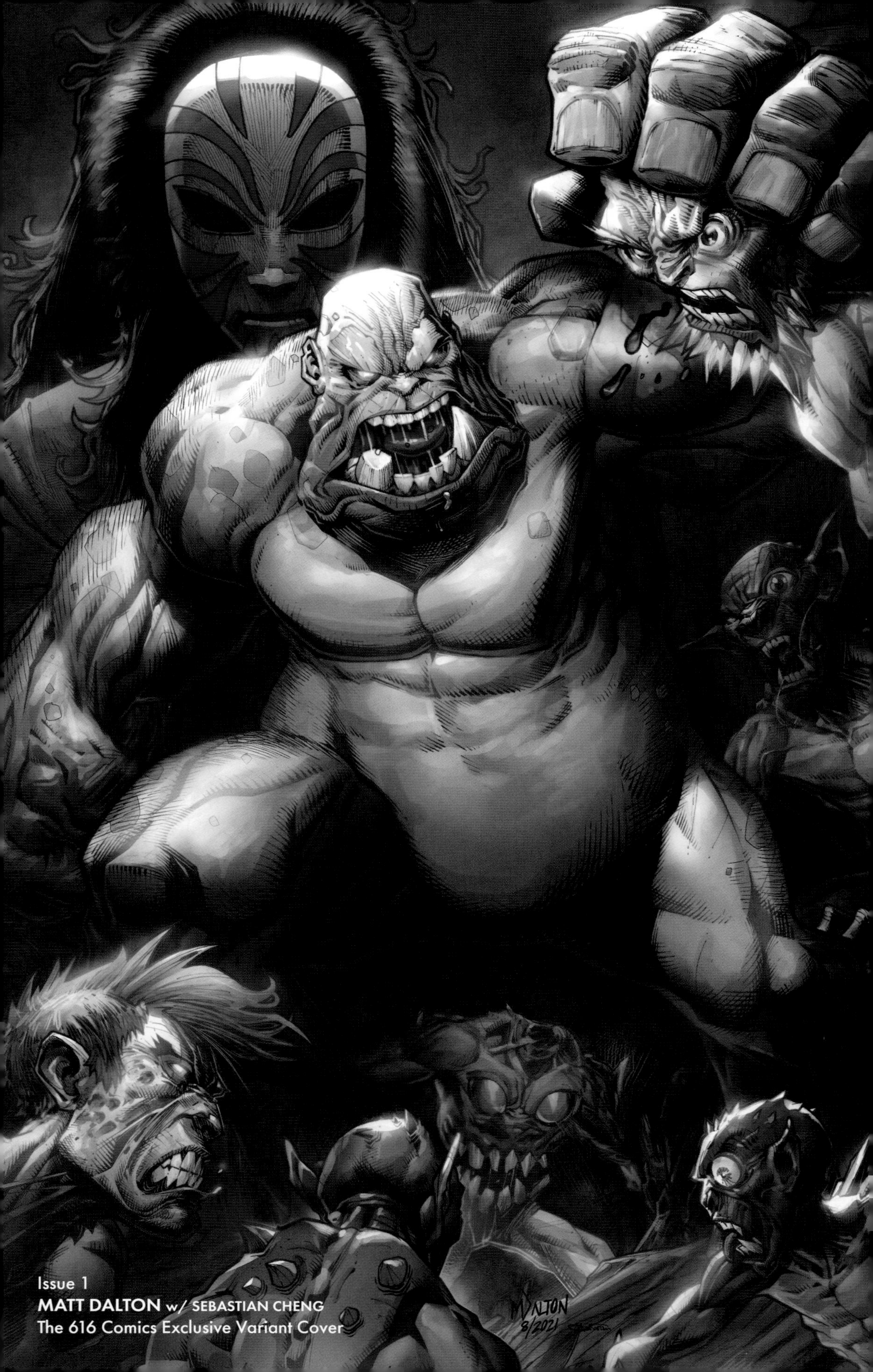

Issue 1
MATT DALTON w/ SEBASTIAN CHENG
The 616 Comics Exclusive Variant Cover

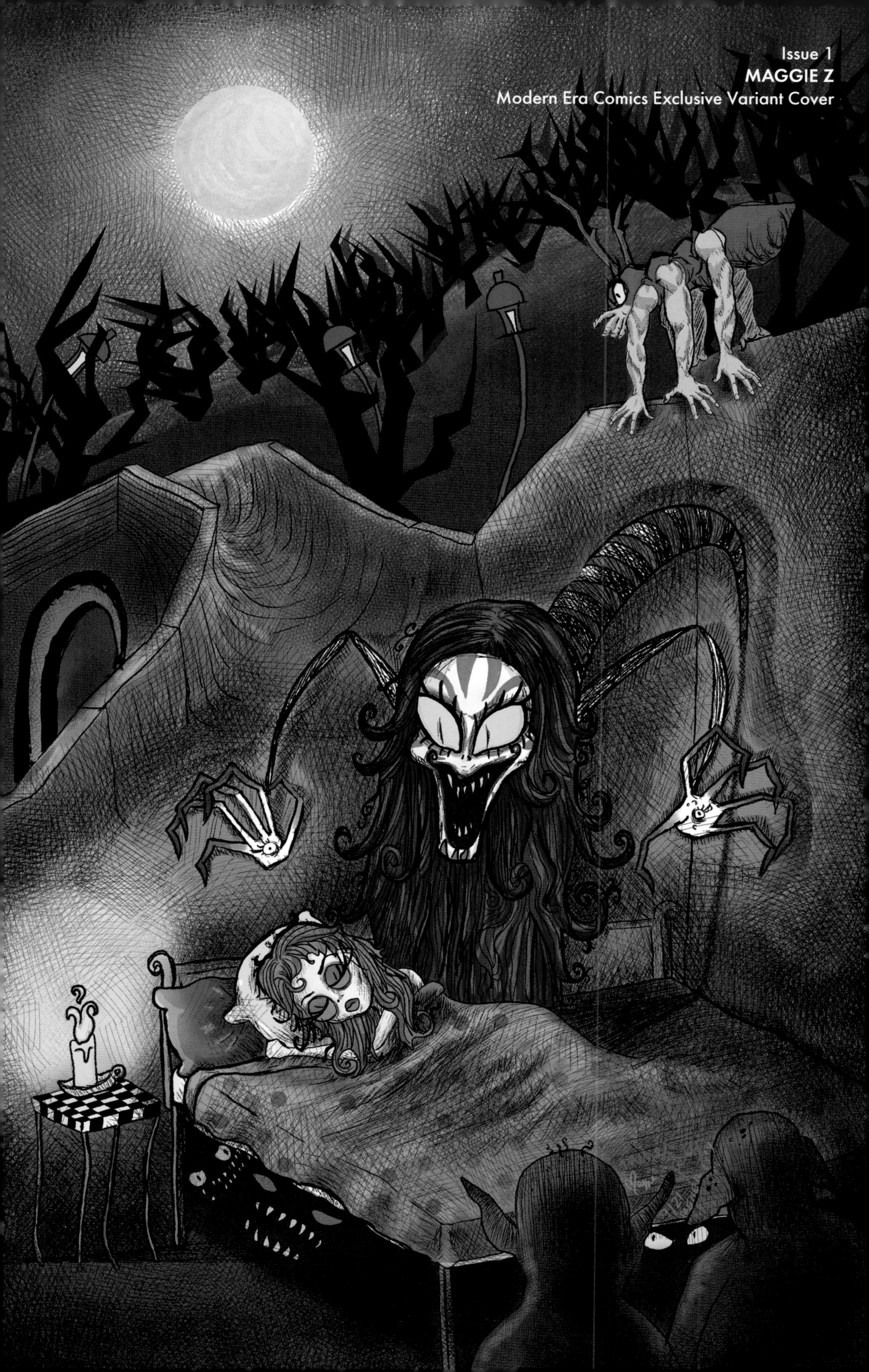
Issue 1
MAGGIE Z
Modern Era Comics Exclusive Variant Cover

Issue 1
CHINH POTTER
The Comic Book Dealer Exclusive Variant Cover

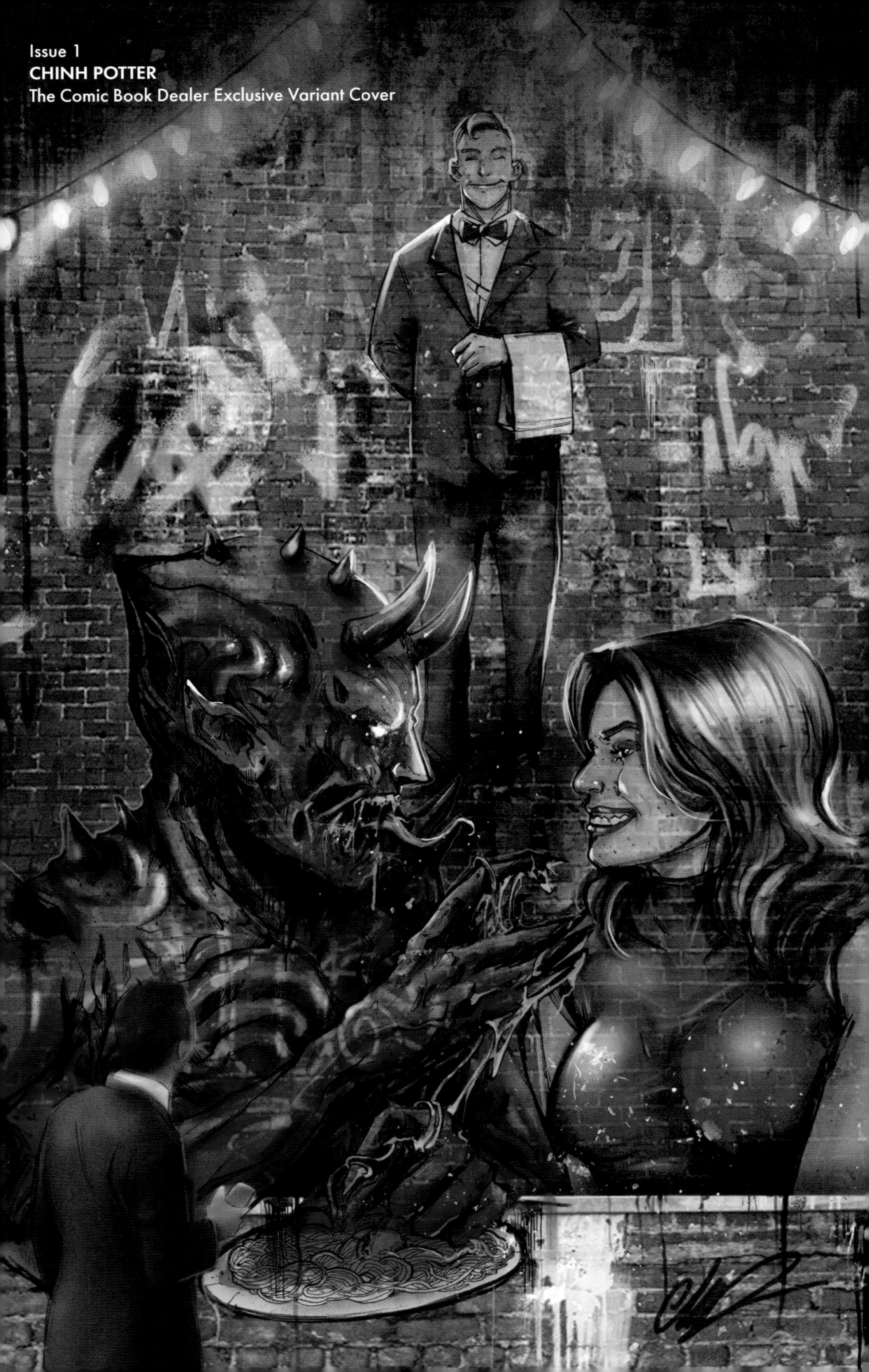

Issue 1
MARIA FRANTZ
Things From Another World Exclusive Variant Cover

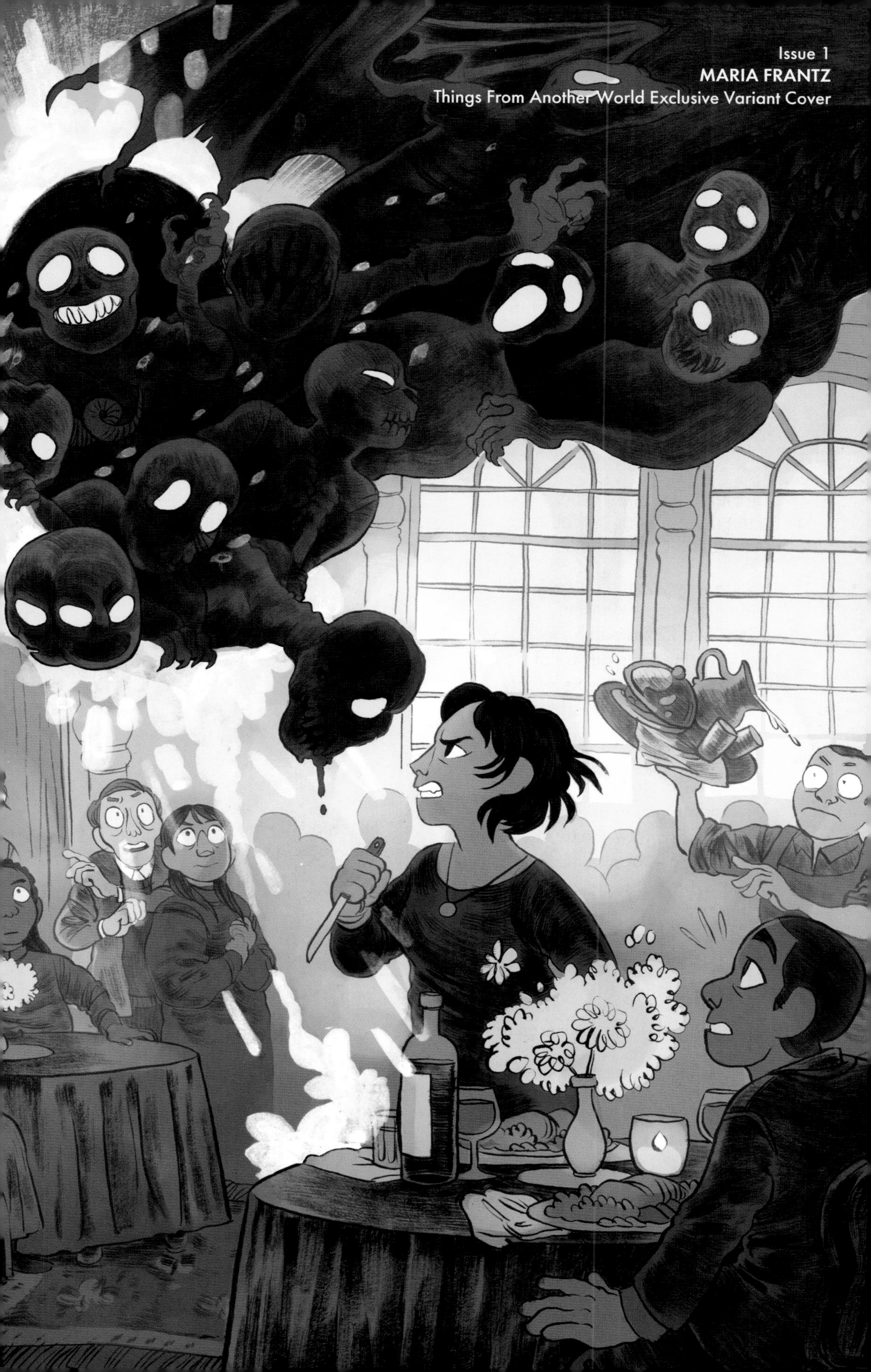

Cover yourself with

Blanket™

The mandatory nightmare suppressant.

No more sleepless days worrying about your sleepless nights.

Don't let nightmares knock on the door to **your** bedroom: cover yourself with Blanket!

Five new flavors and a new children's chewable! Mint, Ginger and Cinnamon have long been the three flavors of Blanket, but we have a new taste explosion in the world of pills! Cherry! Watermelon! Chocolate! Lemon! And Shadow! Don't forget our new children's chewable—the Raspberry Swirl! Let the fresh taste of our pills banish the sour taste of your fears!

Testimonials from real-life people who got their Blanket:

"It's not just me that sleeps better. My cat Rathbone used to hiss all night until I started taking Blanket. Now she purrs by my side!"

-Judith McCauley (F) 68 years old
Sutherland, Nebraska

"Since I started taking Blanket, I have 100% less bad dreams, and 500% more rest."

-Mapita Chacón (F) 37 years old
Vega Baja, Puerto Rico

"A little snort of whiskey and a Blanket pill each night, and I ain't got no complaints."

-Abe "Tuck" Morton (M) 52 years old
Hopkinsville, Kentucky

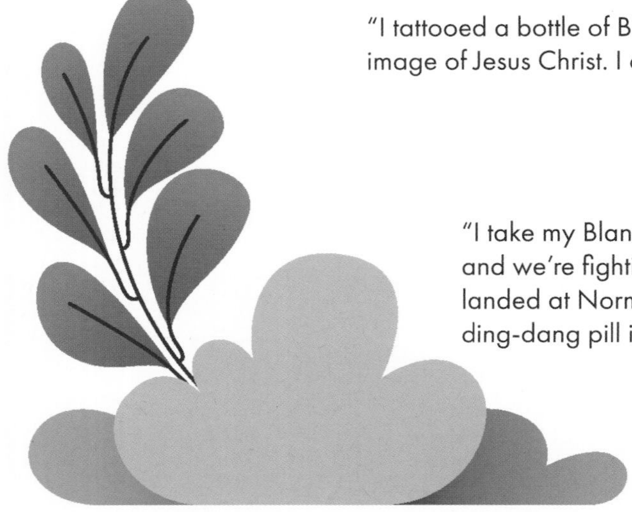

"I tattooed a bottle of Blanket pills on my back, just next to the image of Jesus Christ. I consider them both to be my saviors."

-Alejandra Jimenez (NB) 19 years old
Rio Rancho, New Mexico

"I take my Blanket pill each night because I'm an American, and we're fighting this fight together. My great-grandpa landed at Normandy and lost himself a leg: I can put a ding-dang pill in my mouth."

-Bill "Honker" Maple (M) 47 years old
Shreveport, Louisiana

Don't let nightmares take away your dreams.

We all know that the famous Klaybenheight Mixture of marijuana and amphetamines—devised by chemist Jürgen Klaybenheight—can suppress dreams, but we need our dreams to stay healthy of mind, and that's where Blanket—the superior and mandatory pill—comes in! Blanket works on the simple principle of covering your nightmares without covering your dreams! Want to dream of flying? Blanket will let you! Want to dream of kissing that special someone, swimming in the ocean, conquering other planets or winning the big game? Feel free! Blanket lets you sleep snugly in the arms of all your good dreams! But if you dream of monsters, if your dreams cause your body temperature to rise or your heartbeat to accelerate, Blanket wraps you tightly and suppresses those nightmares, so they never really begin. The 'mares can't step into our world if they never gain a foothold in your head! Feel free again, and free the world again!

Be responsible, & Blanket the world!

BLANKET: Government sanctioned & government required.

Just one Blanket pill a day. Every person. Every day. That's all it takes to save the world, if we all take our pills. But we all have to work together, and that's why it's essential to report anyone not taking their Blanket pills to the 555-2368 Nightmare Scenario Hotline. You could be eligible for up to $500.00 as a reward for helping make sure the whole world is covered with...Blanket!

Artwork by Vecteezy

BEHOLDr
FIND YOUR DREAM MATE

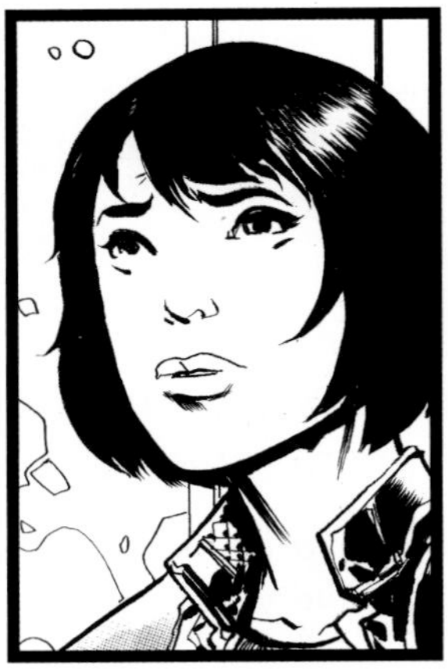

Risa Himura (37)
63 miles away

City	Los Angeles (Westside)
Age	37 years old
Height	5′ 6″
Weight	122 lbs

Eye Color	Dark Brown
Hair Color	Black
Marital Status	Widowed
Children	Machi. 12 years old
Drink	I love a whole range of cocktails! Three's my limit.
Pets	None (but I'm hoping you have one/several)

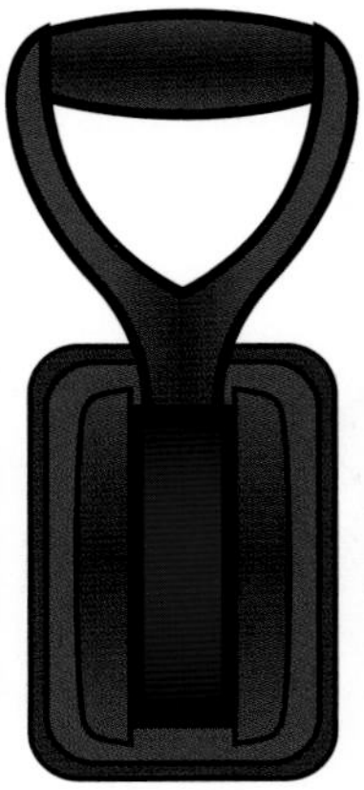

ALWAYS KNOW YOUR NIGHTMARE ALARM LOCATIONS!

Education	UTokyo, Japan: Riken (Institute of Physical and Chemical Research) in Wakō, Japan: Cognitive Studies Institute in Kitakyushu, Japan
Ocupation	Head of the Dream Research & Cognitive Studies Institute, USC.
Languages Spoken	English (fluent), Japanese (fluent, native) French and German (some)
Religion	None? (I have a shaky / scientific interest in Shinto)

Looking For	A man (probably?) who is kind, thoughtful and has a life of his own. Long term. You don't have to be smart, but please be intelligent. (yes there's a difference)
Self-Summary	Driven individual. Adores intelligence. Had my fill of rogue wannabes and just want a man (?) who understands the reasons why limits are in place. My daughter Machi is my life, so you'll have to understand and accept that. I sometimes keep weird hours. It's okay / preferable if you're a little weird, too.

Favorite Memory From Childhood	My friend Atsuko and I dressing up in costume for our combined seventh birthday party. We made our costumes (almost) by ourselves! I was Lum (a character from the Urusei Yatsura manga / anime) and Atsuko was Bulma, from *Dragonball*.
Dream Date	Conversation is key. Spark my mind and make me laugh. Whether we're at a café, a restaurant, going for a stroll through the arts district or feeding silly pigeons in a park, just...make me think. (PS: I've never been to the Huntington Library and would love to go. *hint hint hint)*
Favorite Foods	Chicken yakisoba, deep dish pizza, chocolate éclairs, onigiri, a well made mochi. I like trying new things, too.
My Weirdest Quirk	I will **always** calculate the distance between me and a flash of lightning. *(It takes thunder five seconds to travel a mile so the rough calculations are easy.)*
About Risa	Regarding my "widow" status? My husband died several years ago in a 'mare attack. I will not want to talk about this. PLEASE do not try to help me "unpack my trauma."

My Date With MONSTERS™

sketchbook
ANDY MACDONALD

**AfterShock Comics: What were your influences behind the overall look and feel of MY DAT
WITH MONSTERS?**

Andy MacDonald: I'm not sure if the influences bleed into the look and feel of the book, but I
felt like I was orbiting *Chungking Express*, *Pom Poko* and *Gilmore Girls*. I recommend watchin
all these at least once to anyone.

ASC: Do you have a favorite character? A favorite panel?

AM: I love the scene in issue four where Risa asks Hethri/Croak if he's kissing the general. It
was a nice beat of levity during all the monstercide. It was fun to try and capture the right pos
of a confused and battle-weary Risa that might have been equal parts entertained, titillated,
disgusted and proud of her friend.

"SINGLE" - Croak (B)

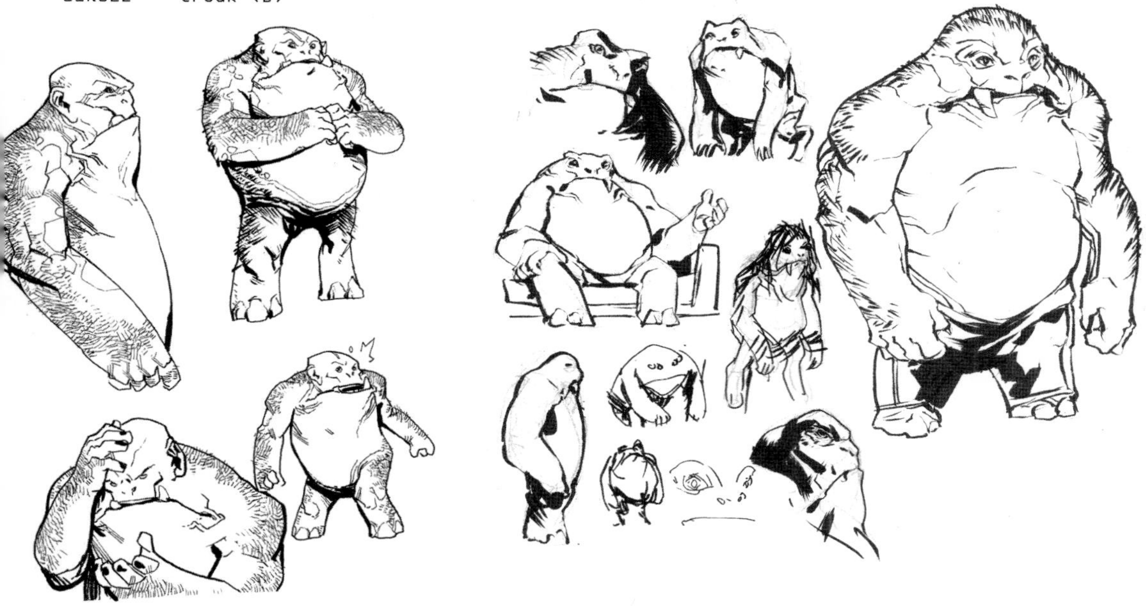

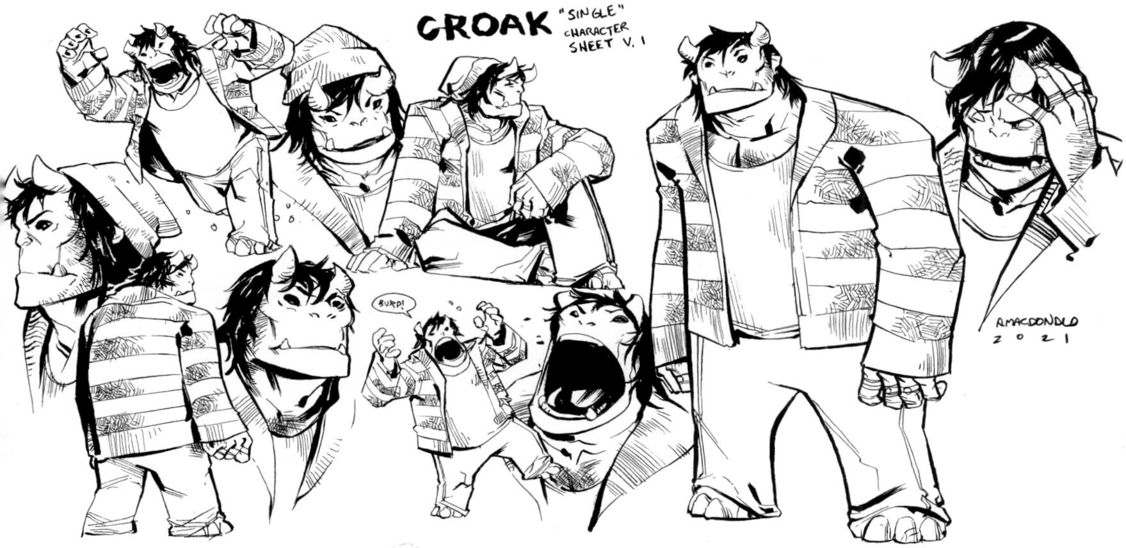
CROAK
"SINGLE" CHARACTER SHEET V.1
BURP!
RMACDONALD 2021

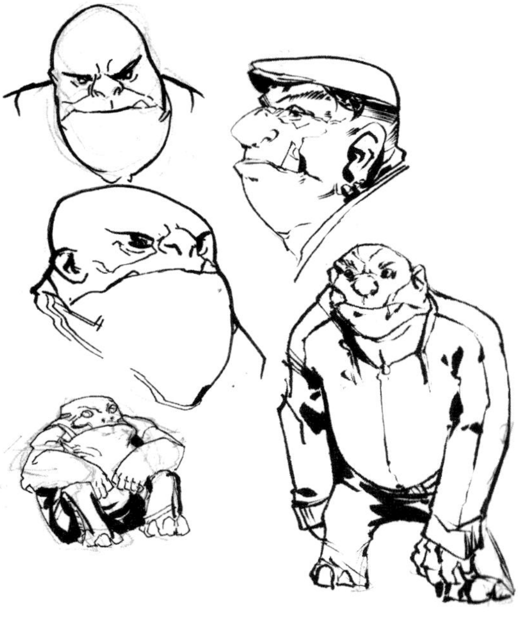

ASC: What was your favorite 'mare to draw?

AM: Definitely the Pontianak. The nightmare covered in hair with a little girl's dress on. There's so much wrapped up in that myth/monster's story that I tried to put that one in as much as possible. And...it was super fun to draw.

ASC: Any advice for artists trying to break into the industry?

AM: Make as many comics as you can. Oh, and listen. It's hard to listen with an honest ear when someone seems to be tearing your work down during a portfolio review. If you can get handle on some objectivity and listen to what people are telling you about your work, you wi improve. We can all always improve.

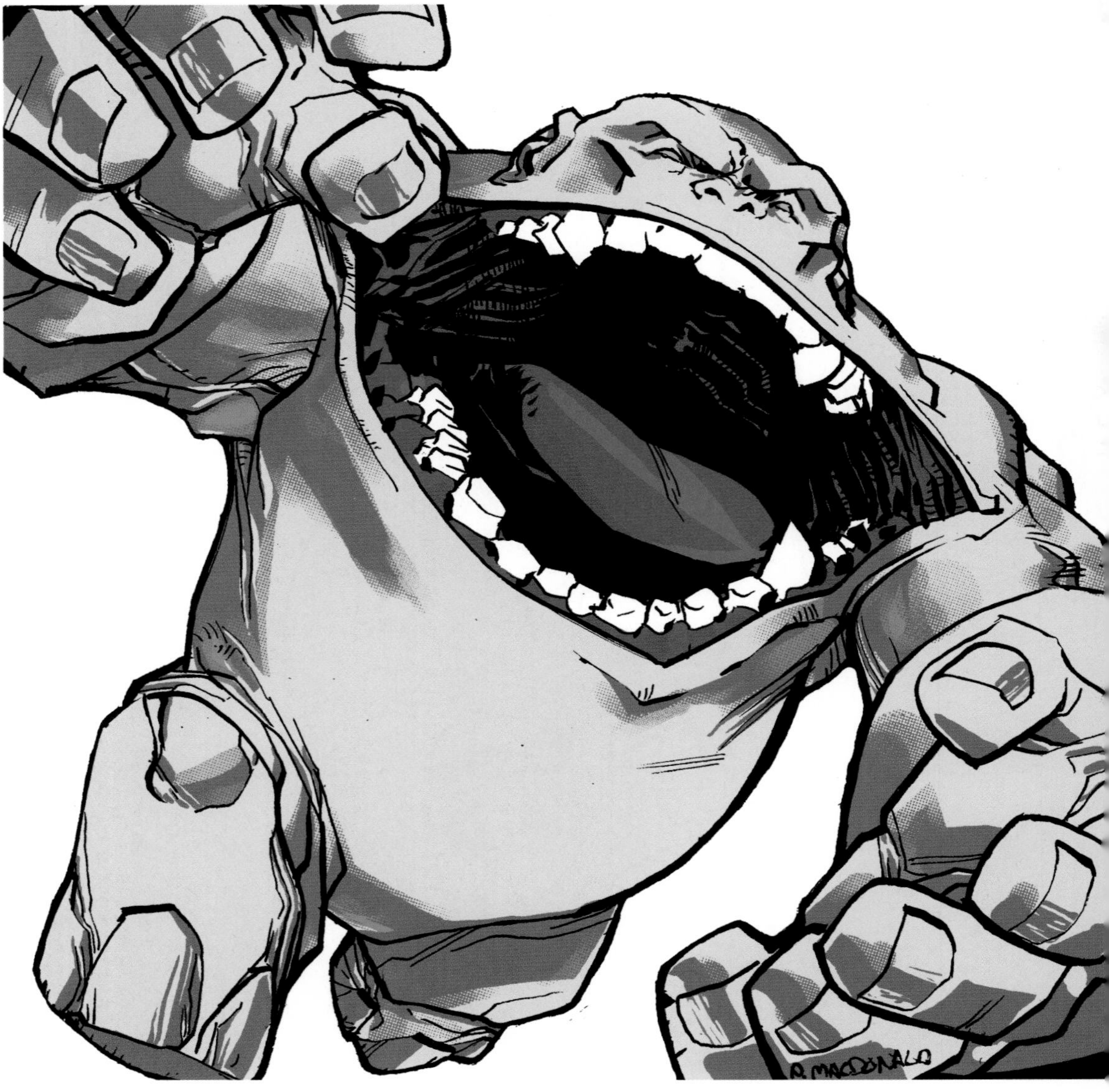
R. MACDONALD

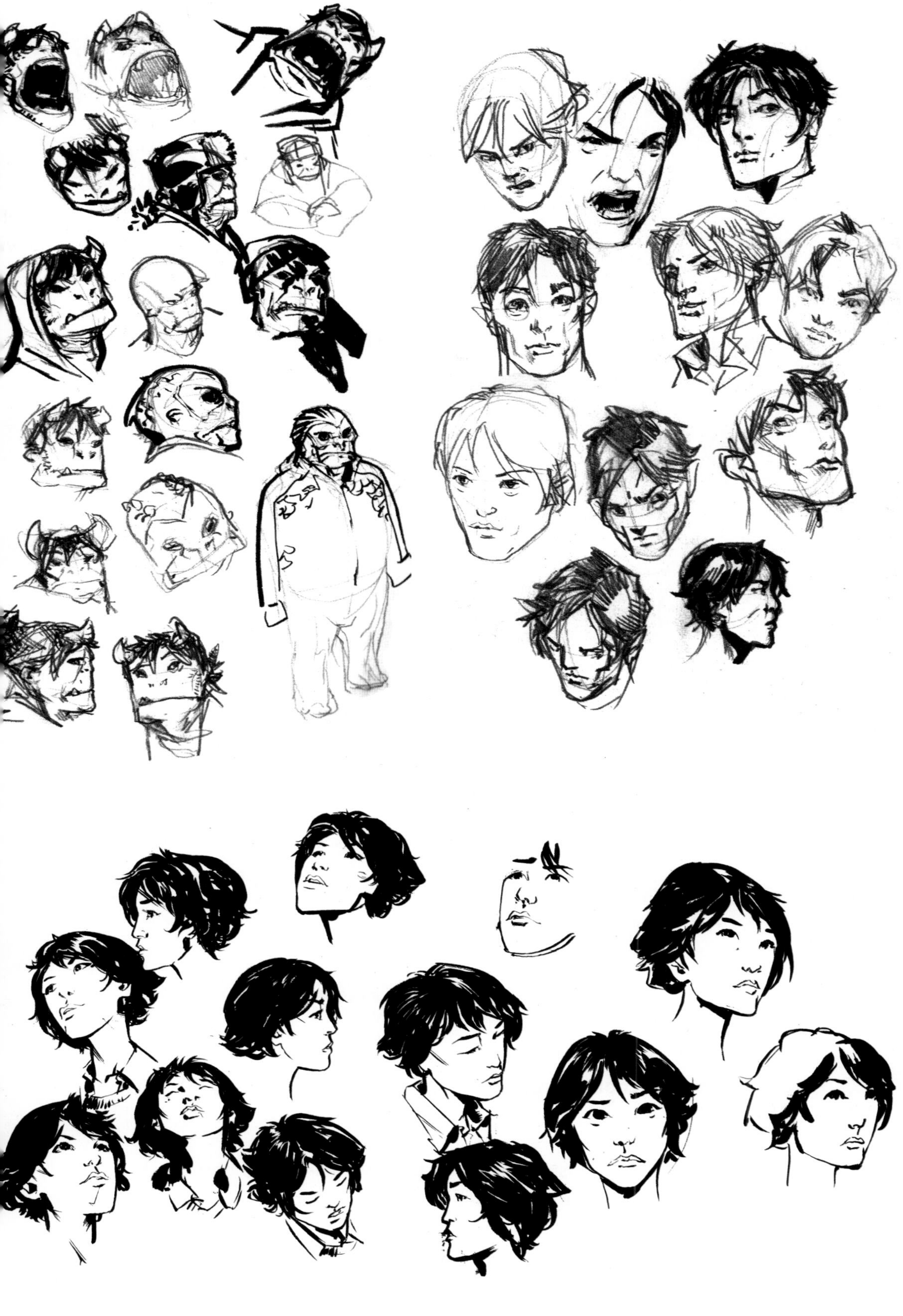

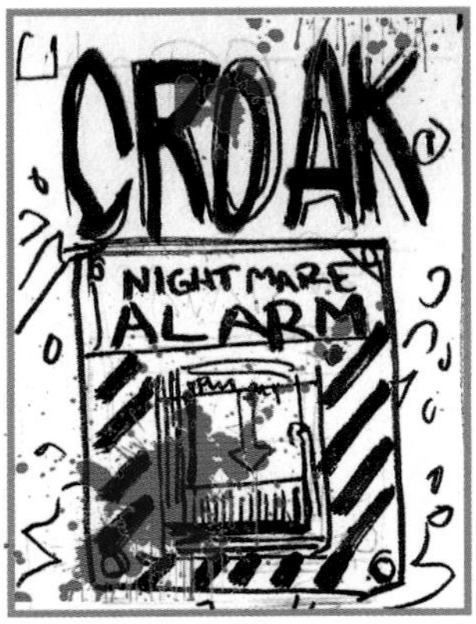
CROAK
NIGHTMARE ALARM

NIGHTMARE ALARM

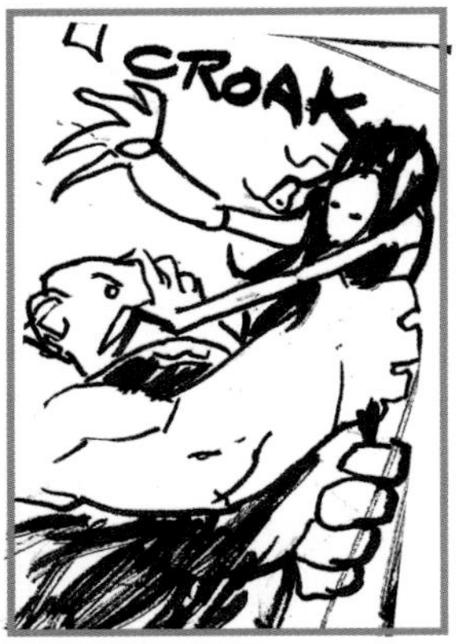
CROAK

CHUB VS. CROAK

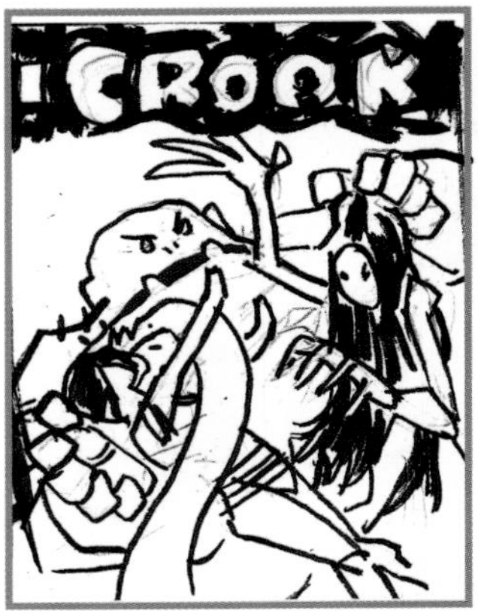

CROAK SEPARATING
CHUB FROM RISA'S HEAD

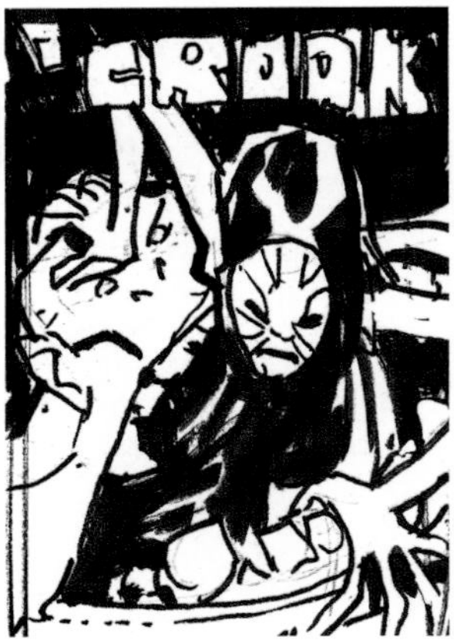

CHUB IN CROAK'S MOUTH

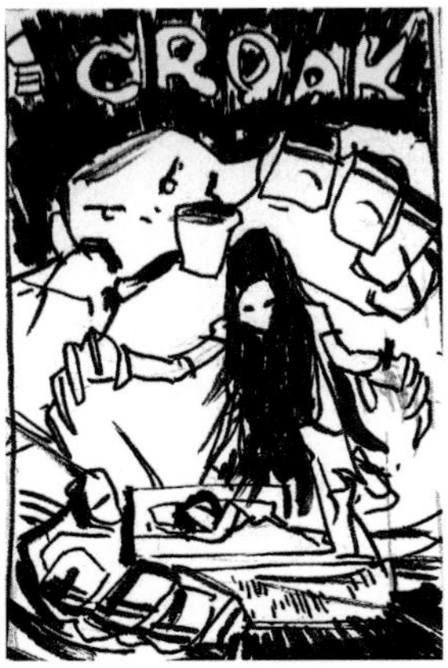

CROAK, CHUB AND
SLEEPING RISA

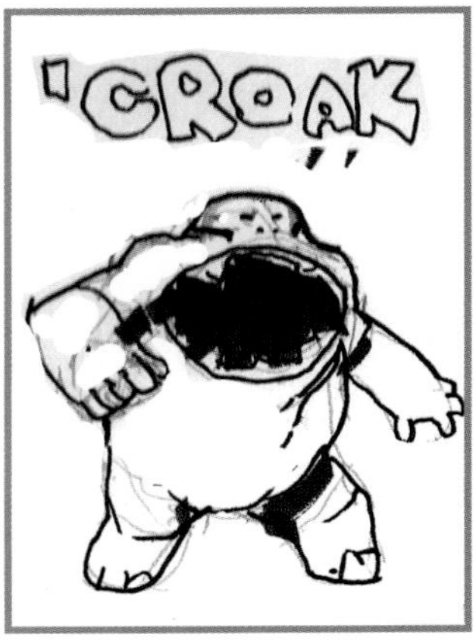
'CROAK

CROAK!

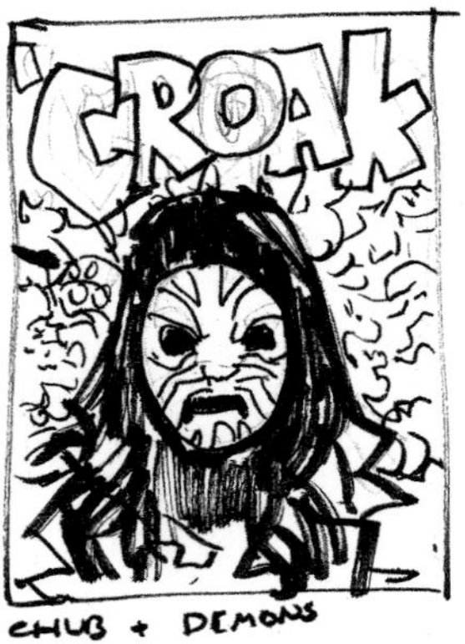
'CROAK

CHUB + DEMONS

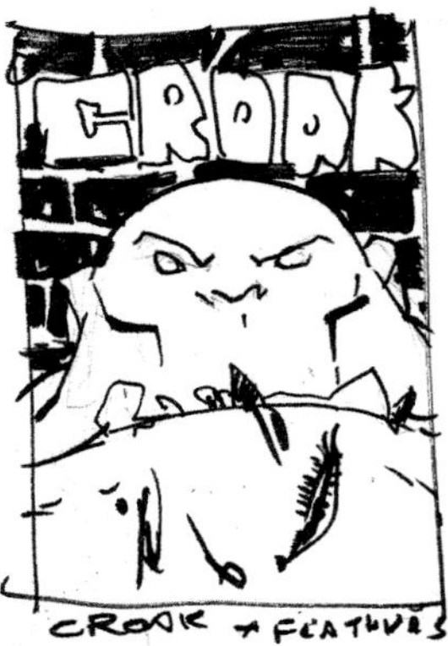

CROAK + FEATHERS

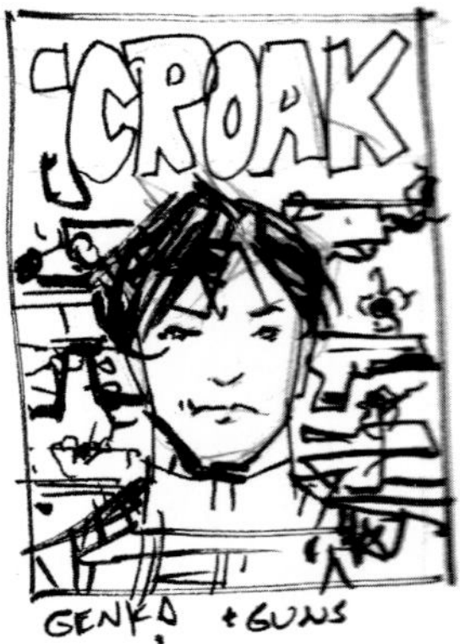
'CROAK

GENKO + GUNS

ASC: What was the most challenging aspect for you when illustrating MY DATE WITH MONSTERS?

AM: Trying to keep the romance-story vibe and not dive full-on into horror was probably the most challenging aspect illustrating MY DATE WITH MONSTERS. Luckily, there's a super-team of Paul Tobin, Teddy Leo, Christina Harrington and Mike Marts there to keep things in perspective!

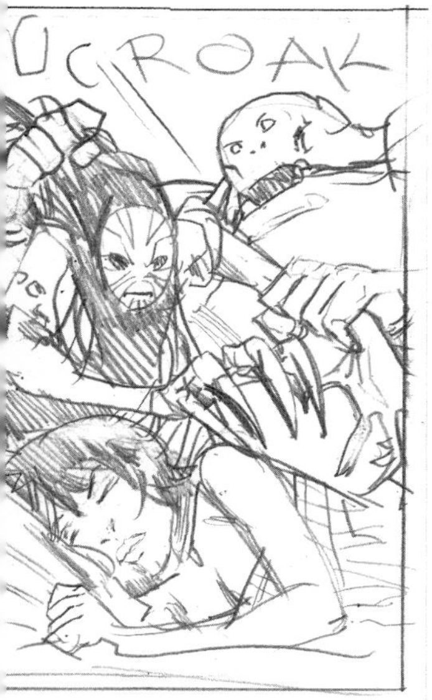
CROAK
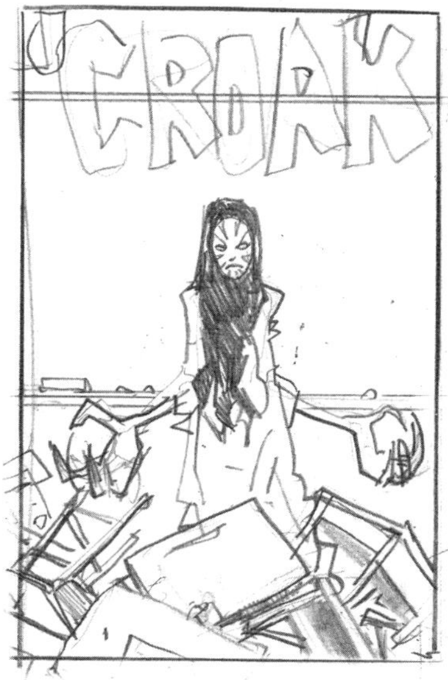
CROAK
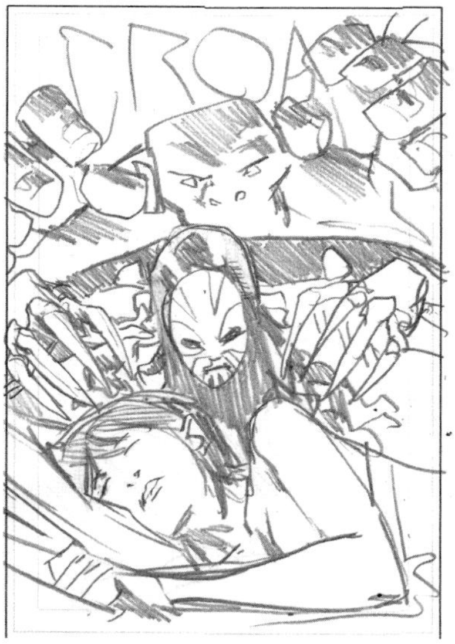
CROAK
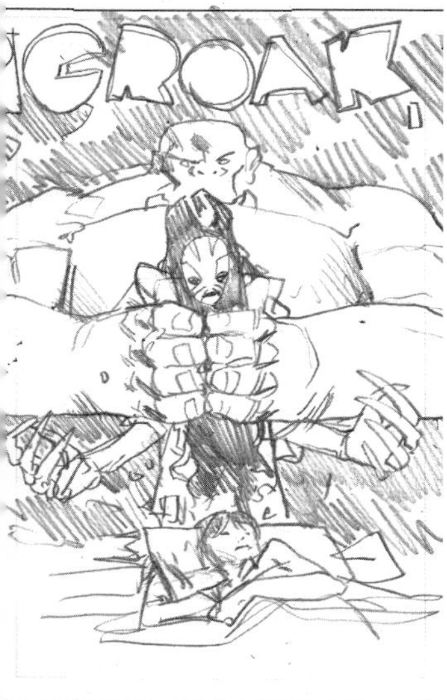
CROAK
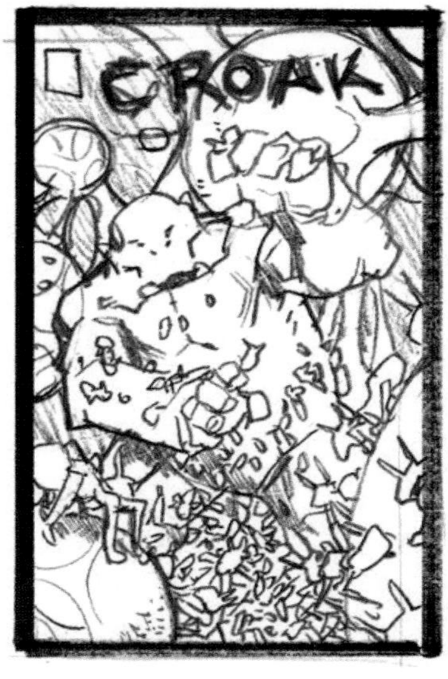
CROAK
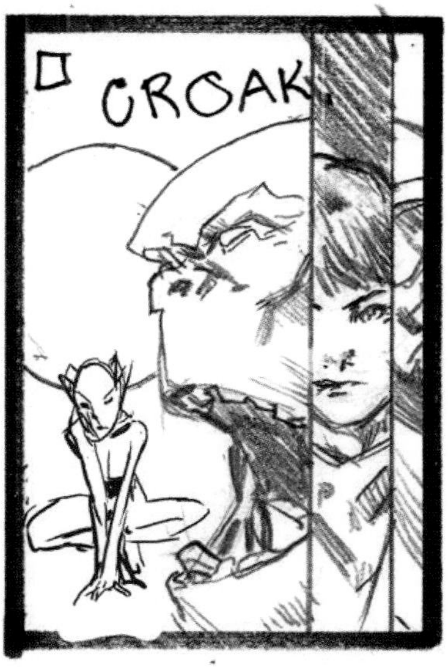
CROAK
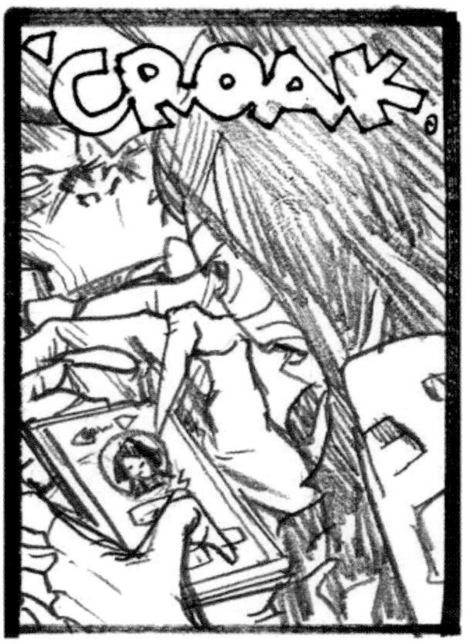
CROAK
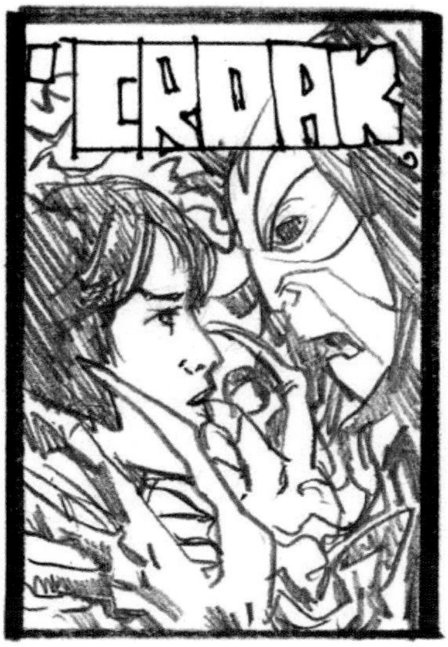
CROAK

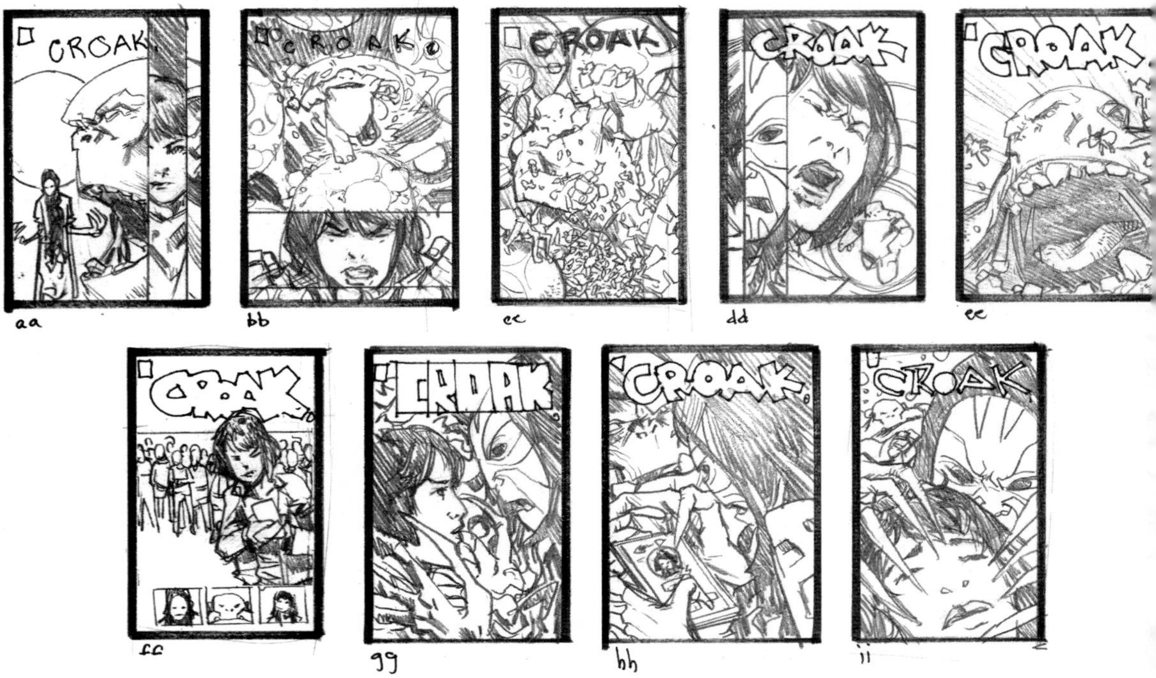
CROAK
aa
CROAK
bb
CROAK
cc
CROAK
dd
CROAK
ee
CROAK
ff
CROAK
gg
CROAK
hh
CROAK
ii

ASC: Do you have a bad first date that stands out? What happened?

AM: The first time I ever got up the courage to ask a total stranger out on a date, they agreed, and I was so stunned that I completely blanked on a plan. As a result, the meeting for coffee turned into a miles-long march around Manhattan peppered with some polite conversation a an awkward goodbye. This walking date around town did not go nearly as well as Machi an Henry's!

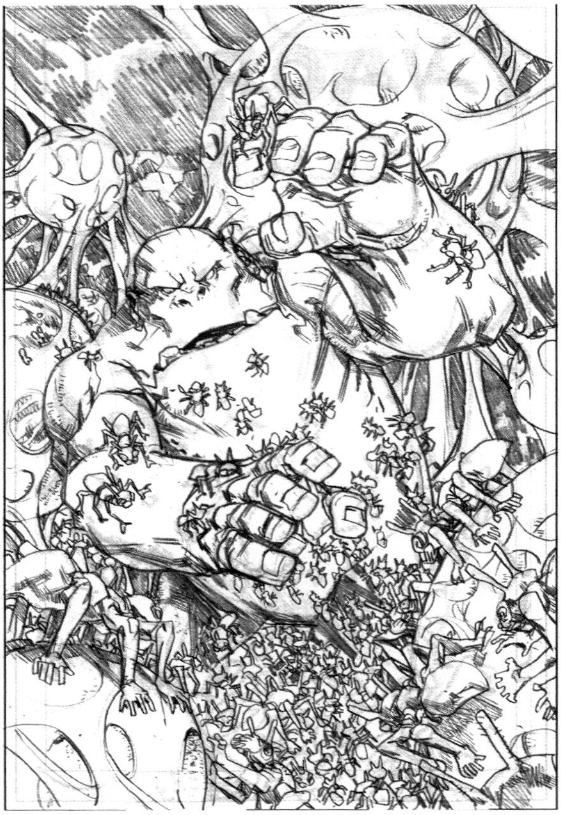

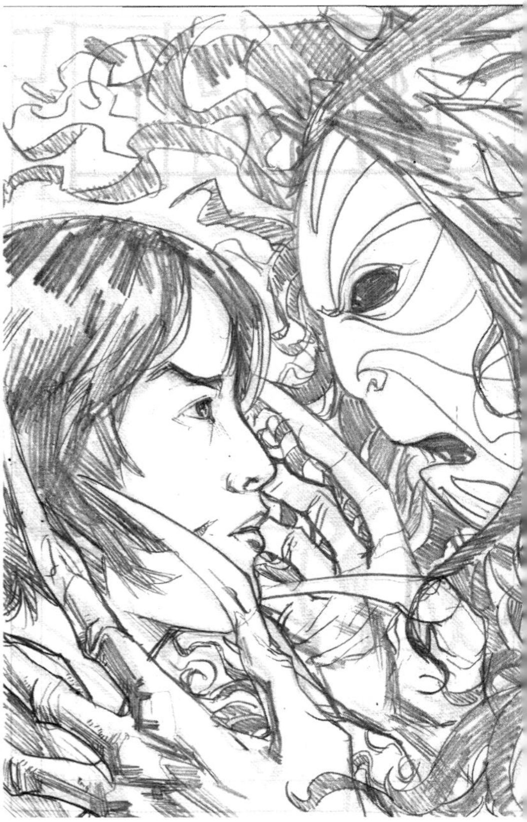

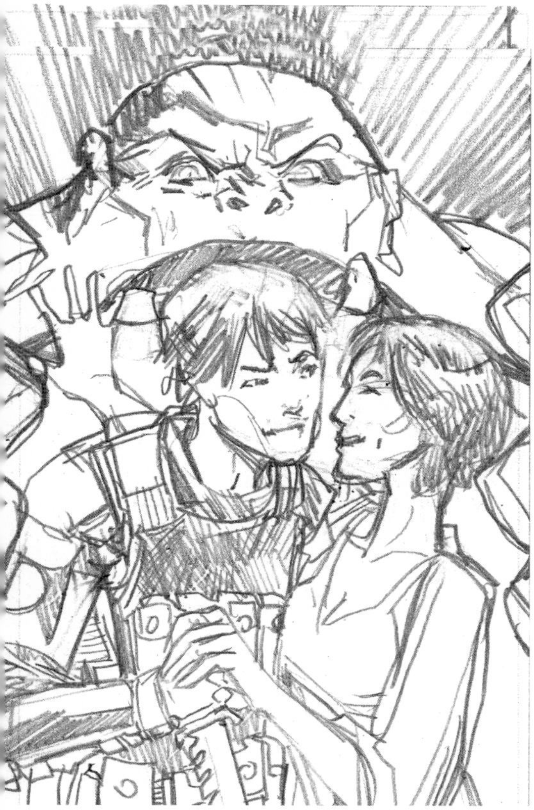

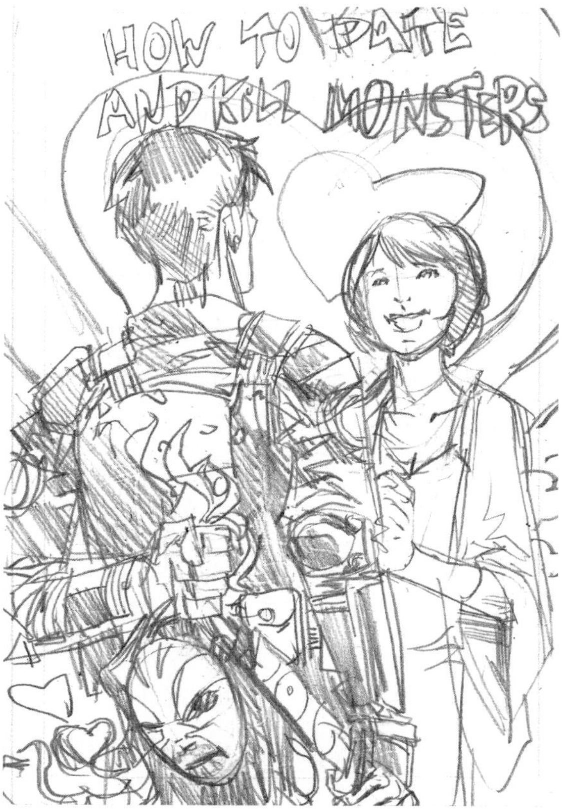
HOW TO DATE
AND KILL MONSTERS

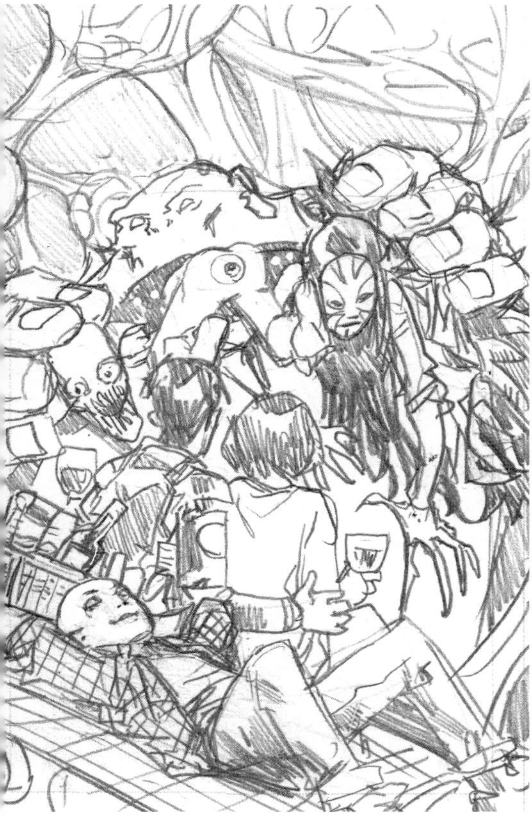

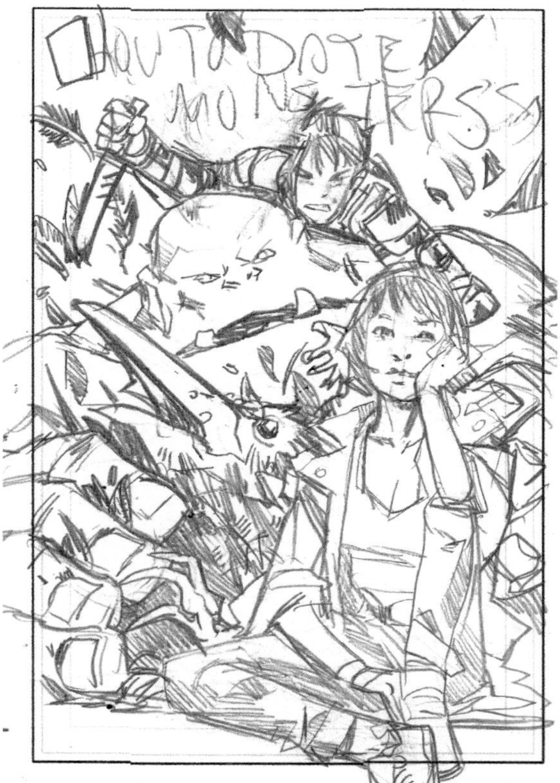

ABOUT THE CREATORS OF

My Date With MONSTERS™

PAUL TOBIN *writer*
🐦 @PaulTobin

Paul Tobin is a writer in Portland, Oregon, working in comics, novels and video games. He's written all the major Marvel and DC characters, along with media properties such as *Prometheus* and *Aliens*, as well as video game tie-ins like his critically acclaimed *Witcher* comics and his NYT best-selling *Plants vs. Zombies* graphic novels, a must-have for all school libraries. His true love is creator-owned comics such as his Eisner-nominated *Colder* horror series, the Eisner-nominated *I Was The Cat* OGN, and the multiple Eisner-award-winning *Bandette*, which he works on with his wife, illustrator Colleen Coover. In addition to *Bandette*, Paul works with Colleen on another project, co-writing their upcoming *Wrassle Castle* series of graphic novels. Paul's all-ages graphic novel, *Earth Boy*, will be released in 2021. Paul has published four novels, three in the *Genius Factor* series, along with *Prepare To Die!*, which won a starred review from Publisher's Weekly.

ANDY MacDONALD *artist*
🐦 @andymacdeez 📷 andymacdeez

Andy MacDonald...wealthy, young, handsome. A man with the brightest of futures. A man with the darkest of pasts. From Africa's deepest recesses, to the rarified peaks of Tibet, heir to his father's legacy and the world's darkest mysteries. Andy MacDonald, master of the secrets that divide man from comic book, comic book from man...

DJ CHAVIS *colorist*
🐦 @djcolorscomics

DJ Chavis didn't plan to work in comics. Fresh out of high school, he initially pursued a career in graphic design but quickly changed his discipline to sequential art. Once he discovered the wonders of coloring comic books, he was hooked. He hasn't looked back since.

TAYLOR ESPOSITO *letterer*
🐦 @TaylorEspo

Taylor Esposito is a comic book lettering professional, owner of Ghost Glyph Studios and teacher at the legendary Kubert School. A former staff letterer at DC and production artist at Marvel, he has lettered titles such as *Red Hood and The Outlaws* and *Constantine*, *Interceptor*, *Heavy*, *Finger Guns* (Vault Comics), *Exorsisters* (Image), BABYTEETH, HOT LUNCH SPECIAL, KNOCK EM DEAD (Aftershock), and *No One Left to Fight* (Dark Horse). Other publishers he has worked with include Line Webtoon (*Caster, Backchannel*) Dynamite (*Elvira, Red Sonja and Vampirella meet Betty and Veronica, Green Hornet*), and IDW (*Scarlett's Strike Force*).